THE HIDDEN FACE OF POPE FRANCIS

Paul Ariès

THE HIDDEN FACE OF POPE FRANCIS

Max Milo

Max Milo éditions, Paris, 2023
www.maxmilo.com
ISBN : 978-2-31501-145-2

From the same author

La Fin des mangeurs, Éditions Desclée de Brouwer, 1997

Les Fils de McDo, Éditions L'Harmattan, 1997

Déni d'enfance, Éditions Golias, 1997

Le retour du diable. Satanisme, exorcisme, extrême droite, *Éditions Golias, 1997*

Scientology, laboratory of the future? The Secrets of an Infernal Machine, *Éditions Golias, 1998*

Petit manuel anti-McDo à l'usage des petits et des grands, *Éditions Golias, 1999*

La Scientologie : une secte contre la République, *Éditions Golias, 1999*

José Bové, la révolte d'un paysan. Interviews with Paul Ariès and Christian Terras, *Éditions Golias, 2000*

Le Goût (with Gong Gang), Éditions Desclée de Brouwer, 2000

Animal liberation or new terrorists? *Éditions Golias, 2000*

Les Sectes à l'assaut de la santé, *Éditions Golias, 2000*

Anthroposophy : investigation on an occult power, *Éditions Golias, 2001*

Disneyland, le royaume désenchanté, *Éditions Golias, 2002*

To save the earth: should the human species disappear? *Éditions L'Harmattan, 2002*

Harcèlement au travail ou Nouveau Management, *Éditions Golias, 2002*

Your fucking brand! Éditions Golias, 2003

Démarque-toi ! Petit manuel anti-pub, *Éditions Golias, 2004*

Satanisme et Vampyrisme, *Éditions Golias, 2004*

Misère du sarkozysme. Cette droite qui n'aime pas la France, *Éditions Parangon, 2005*

Décroissance ou Barbarie, *Éditions Golias, 2005*

No conso. Manifesto for a general strike on consumption, *Éditions Golias, 2006*

Le Mésusage. Essay on hypercapitalism, *Éditions Parangon, 2007*

Learning to empty the mind (with Bernadette Costa-Prades), Éditions Milan, 2009

Disobey and grow, Les éditions écosociété, 2009

Cohn-Bendit, l'imposture, (with Florence Leray), Max Milo, 2010

La Simplicité volontaire contre le mythe de l'abondance, *La Découverte, 2010*

Le Socialisme gourmand, *La Découverte, 2012*

Lovers of the good life, Africa, Americas, Asia... what does the ecology of the poor teach us? *Éditions Golias, 2013*

Nos rêves ne tiennent pas dans les urnes, *Éditions Max Milo, 2013*

L'alimentation de la préhistoire à nos jours, *Éditions Max Milo, 2016 (forthcoming)*

For all contacts (conferences and press): paul.aries@laposte.net

Foreword
The (unsexy) underside of the Church

Every new pope represents a significant change.
But let's not expect a group of very conservative cardinals
can elect a revolutionary pope, it is impossible.
Let's just say he elected the best of the worst.

François Houtart, liberation theologian, alterglobalist.

I have always claimed my native atheism without belonging to the tribe of priest-eaters, and I can pass a cassock without croaking. So, for the last thirty years, I have willingly answered the calls of Catholics to share in ecological battles or against the extreme right. I have been for twenty years, although deeply materialist, a member of the editorial board of the Catholic review *Golias*, which accepts to cross our values; I have accepted to collaborate to the review *Relations*, published in Quebec, by the Centre justice et foi, under the responsibility of members of the Society of Jesus, notably for its special issues dedicated to the ecological crisis; I have contributed to other Catholic media such as *Les Cahiers de l'atelier* (notably for its issue on ecology and voluntary simplicity) published in partnership with Action Catholique des Enfants (ACE), Action Catholique des milieux indépendants (ACI), Action Catholique Ouvrière (ACO), Carrefour de l'Église en Rural (CER), Jeunesse Ouvrière Chrétienne (JOC), Aumônerie de l'Enseignement Public ; like *Lumière et vie*, a theological review founded by the Dominicans; like *Témoignage chrétien* or the Radios chrétiennes francophones (RCF) network; I was a long-time member of the team, mostly Catholic, of the monthly

La Décroissance (before our paths separated because I refuse to see degrowth as synonymous with austerity); I agreed to publish many works in Catholic publishing houses, in particular that of the Jesuits in Brazil (Edições Loyola). I even participated in the first two conventions of the association Christians and Peak Oil (CPP).

I have never considered the Church to be "intrinsically perverse", just to turn the words of Pope Pius XI in the 19th century against any idea of collectivism and socialism (we are far from the Stalinist monster). I have always considered that the Church was a "big family" and that it was necessary to learn to separate the wheat from the chaff when it comes to social debates. I, who like to define myself as a "growth objector in love with the good life", know how much the ecology of the poor owes to liberation theologies and to the preferential option for the poor developed in South America. Without this Christian movement, ecology today would be even worse off. I also know that just as we cannot blame communist militants for Stalin's crimes, nor the historical responsibility of party leaders, we cannot blame Catholics for pedophilia, nor for the guilty silence on these crimes, nor for the financial and political scandals that affect the Church as an institution.

I would have liked to rejoice at the election of Bishop Bergoglio as Pope, saying to myself that we were finally rid of John Paul II and Benedict XVI, who still put condoms on the Index of the Holy Office; I would have liked to rejoice that the Church was no longer systematically on the side of the powerful, as unfortunately it has been too often for the past 2,000 years; I would have liked to applaud the publication of Pope Francis' encyclical *Laudato si'* ("Praise be to you"), especially since this text has caused embarrassment to many of my (other) liberal opponents since it advocates ecology and degrowth and reexamines the world economic system[1]. But I must admit that Pope Francis does not convince me and that the French ecologist-catholic networks are not very sympathetic to me. They are no better than those who storm hospitals guaranteeing the right to abortion or those who demonstrate against "blasphemous" shows.

Finally, I would have liked to say with my friend Jean Ortiz, an excellent connoisseur of South America, that this pope, chosen as he reminds us

---

1. Jacques Garello, a liberal Catholic economist and president of the Association for Economic Freedom and Social Progress (ALEPS), Jean-Yves Naudet, an expert in the social doctrine of the Catholic Church, and Geoffroy Roux de Bézieux, the head of Phone House, Virgin Mobile and Notus Technologies, reacted in opposition to Pope Francis' remarks.

"to counteract the rise of the 'revolutions' in Latin America, to regain among the poor the ground lost by Rome, which had distanced itself from the 'peoples of God', a ground recuperated by the sects and evangelical churches of all stripes", would have suddenly found faith… revolutionary since his election to the Vatican Unfortunately, I believe that Jean Ortiz and many progressives are mistaking their dreams for reality by choosing to forget that Roman Catholic anti-capitalism has nothing in common with ours. Reactionary Bishop Bergoglio did not suddenly become a progressive pope. His sources of inspiration are more on the side of Communion and Liberation, Opus Dei, the Legionaries of Christ, than the Franciscans or the Jesuits. The Church of Pope Francis is still the one that considers, with Cardinal Giovanni Battista, prefect of the Vatican's Congregation for Bishops, that the rape (of a 9-year-old girl) is "less serious than abortion" (sic). The Church of Pope Francis is still the one that refuses to accredit Laurent Stefanini, the ambassador chosen by France to represent it at the Vatican, because he is homosexual. The Church of Pope Francis is still the one that, from financial scandal to political scandal, not to mention pedophile crimes, proves that the evil that eats away at it is structural and that it is not just a matter of lost sheep. The Church of Pope Francis is still the one that continues not to listen to its own people: 92% of Catholics are in favor of contraception, 90% are in favor of abortion, 54% say they are in favor of the right to marriage for all, 87% are in favor of the marriage of priests, 83% say they are in favor of the religious remarriage of the divorced; but the Church of Pope Francis is the one that, with the Manif pour tous, with the movement of the Vigilantes, with the Printemps français chooses to listen only to the smallest and most reactionary fringe of its flock[2].

Francis, the best of the worst

I would even like to believe, with the anti-globalization theologian François Houtart, that Pope Francis would be the "best of the worst." Unfortunately, I am not convinced of this, given his ability to hypnotize the crowds and to put to sleep those who should be vigilant, especially on the left and among atheists. It has been said that Francis would be "the pope

---

2. http://www.la-croix.com/Religion/Actualite/Selon-un-sondage-BVA-les-catholiques-francais-seraient-progressistes-2014-02-23-1110982

of the exit from the papacy": I would have preferred that he kept his red shoes and other pontifical trappings, but that he did not return to the most reactionary dogmas. Thus the former president of the Christian Democrat party, Christine Boutin, leader of all the bad fights (against abortion, the PACS, etc.), famous for having taken out a bible in the National Assembly, says she is "amazed" by the Pope's words, which call for "mercy" for homosexuals, divorcees and women who have had an abortion, and is convinced that Pope Francis will not change the reactionary positions of the Church in matters of morals. So is Christine Lagarde, the shocking head of the IMF, who, after being received in a private audience by Pope Francis, confided her admiration and claimed that they shared the same views on combating "excessive inequalities" (sic) and that "the rising tide should also carry the small boats". It is true that Francis is inventing a preferential option for the poor that bears a strange resemblance to the speeches of the lady patrons of the 19th century. This same pope also sees the devil everywhere, especially behind his adversaries. Let's be careful that he doesn't rekindle bonfires against heretics and let's be careful that his calls to a new crusade, to the *reconquista*, don't launch crowds of illuminated people to attack the Republic and secularism, under the pretext of forbidding others the right to love and to give birth as they see fit! I say it to my atheist and agnostic friends, but also to my believers: if you didn't like (too much) the Manif pour tous, that is to say the mobilization of the reactionary currents of the Church against the equality of rights in front of marriage, you may not appreciate all that is preparing behind the scenes! Francis is making eyes at you, but he is speaking in a context of the return of religion in the most questionable and dangerous forms for secularism, and this unfortunately concerns all religions, without any exception. The question is not even to probe what he has secretly in his head but in what context he speaks, by whom he is heard and with what effects. The Church has thus committed an unforgivable political fault with its homophobic and sexist gesticulations, breaking the cordon sanitaire that it had erected around the extreme right and in particular the National Front (FN). Practicing Catholics, who were already traditionally more right-wing than the rest of the population, voted less for the Le Pen family, but these same Catholics went from refusing to vote FN in two years. The first years of Francis' pontificate have resulted in a rise of the extreme right, of identity-based populism and of reaction in all countries. The Church of our children is much older than that of our parents. I am therefore writing a

---

book that goes against the grain, since 89% of French people, Catholic or not, have a good opinion of Pope Francis. And the pontiff is even more appreciated on the left than on the right[3].

The *reconquista*

The Church is always looking for its magic potion that would allow it not to evangelize but to "re-evangelize" the world of believers. The Church has tried everything: the fear of burning in hell, the prospect of paradise, the condemnation of masturbation, the war against contraception and abortion, the hatred of atheists and the fear of "reds", but nothing seems to preserve the number of believers in the rich countries of the North; on the other hand, the number of faithful is increasing faster than the demography thanks to the poor countries of the South[4]. The princes of the Church have thus chosen to use ecology as a new weapon of mass destruction against secularism and egalitarian and progressive ideas. It is not I who has chosen to put so much emphasis on ecology, but it is Francis and his entourage who have voluntarily made this tactical choice, because never in a long time has such a societal debate lent itself so much to the old nonsense that the Church gives as the absolute truth. We would be wrong not to take Francis and his flock very seriously. First of all, because the left and ecology are largely fooled by this instrumentalization of ecology against abortion, gay marriage, contraception, and the common good understood as all social rights. Secondly, because this so-called "integral" ecology is, as we shall see in the second part of this book, a way of returning to an intransigent Catholicism in the manner of the 19th century. Finally, because this Catholic integral ecology is not so much opposed to a soft ecology as to political ecology and Catholic integral humanism, in short to the Catholicism of the twentieth century which had accepted the idea of human progress. As the Catholic institute Ichtus, one of the pillars of the Manif pour tous and the Printemps français, preaches, the time has

---

3. http://www.leparisien.fr/pape-vatican/sondage-le-pape-francois-bat-tous-les-records-de-popularite-chez-les-francais-19-12-2014-4388043.php
4. In 2013, 1.253 billion Catholics were officially counted. That is an increase of 25 million baptized in the Catholic Church, 2% increase in one year. This is twice the rate of growth of the world's population, which increased by only 1%. On the other hand, Catholics have become a minority on the Old Continent, where they now represent only 39% of the population. http://fr.aleteia.org/2015/03/31/il-y-a-toujours-plus-de-catholiques-dans-le-monde/

come to close the curtain on the cult of man. Gaultier Bès de Berc, one of the gurus of integral ecology, also explains that Christian humanism was simply a response to atheistic humanism, which leads to man made God. The heresy of always.

This book is as much about Bergoglio who became Francis as it is about the Church of Pope Francis. It is not a trial of personal responsibility, but rather an account of an era: of which Church is Francis the Pope? The Church of Pope Francis is also the Church of the soldiers of God and the different movements that make it up. I will pay particular attention to the forces that carry the new ecological theses within the Church.

I am very grateful to my South American friends, especially from Argentina, but also from Quebec, Italy and France, who sent me information. I express my gratitude to the liberation theologians who no longer recognize themselves in what Rome has done with the preferential option for the poor. Without them, without them, this book would not have been possible.

Part I:
Will Francis save the Church?

Many of us believe that the Catholic Church is seriously ill, perhaps even incurable[5]. This observation is shared by Church people like the Egyptian Jesuit priest Henri Boulad, former provincial of the Jesuits in the Near East, then vice-president of Caritas International for the Middle East and North Africa, who believes that "Our Church is sick. In its current form, it will probably die, only to be reborn in another way [...]. I think that this institutional Church, this pyramid Church, must invent other forms, other ways of being present in today's world"[6], as well as theologians like Arnaud Join-Lambert who also announces in the Jesuit magazine, *Études*, the end of parishes and the advent of a "liquid Church"[7].

The Church has certainly experienced many vicissitudes throughout its two millennia. It even came close to disappearing (at least) twice: in the fourth century, in the face of the revival of pagan cults, but above all in the face of the victories of Christian Arianism[8] ; in the sixteenth century, in the face of the movements of the Reformation. The Church has always reacted in the same way, establishing new alliances with the temporal powers of the moment (political and military), even if it means abandoning the little people of believers and transforming its flock into true soldiers of God. The Church never saved itself by making a pact with the times, but by shutting itself up in its dogmas. The Catholic Counter-Reformation is

---

5. Hans Küng, *Peut-on encore sauver l'Église*, Paris, Seuil, 2012.
6. Henri Boulad, *Faith and Meaning*, Paris, Médiaspaul, 2015.
7. Arnaud Join-Lambert, "Towards a 'liquid' Church," in *Études*, February 2015, pp. 67-78. See the website of the journal *Études:* http://www.revue-etudes.com/index.php
8. Henri-Irénée Marrou, " L'arianisme comme phénomène alexandrin ", in *Comptes rendus des séances de l'Académie des Inscriptions et Belles-Lettres*, vol. 117, n° 3, 1973, p. 533-542.

the best proof of this. The Catholic Church suffers today from a multitude of crises, financial scandals, sexual scandals, political scandals, scandals of its dogmas that no longer correspond to the expectations of its own faithful, who admit that they no longer understand them and cheat on them. The Church knows that it must reform itself in order not to die. Faced with the competition of the "new religious movements" with which it maintains a curious flirtation, and also faced with a history that is accelerating and that is taking it by the throat, rendering obsolete what had made its strength. All these crises come together and reinforce each other, allowing us to speak of a true structural crisis. What links and makes sense of all these crises is fundamentally the maladjustment of the Church to its time; this Church, which for a long time was the last representative of the Middle Ages in the midst of modernity, must either look to the future or turn history upside down. The Church of Pope Francis is thus engaged in this double movement: On the one hand, "change everything so that nothing changes" according to the formula of the aristocrat Giuseppe Tomasi di Lampedusa in his novel *The Leopard*, which explains why the Church is firing on all cylinders in terms of communication and management; on the other hand, taking advantage of the collapse of revolutions and, in the religious field, of the "left-wing Catholics" and South American liberation theologians in order to revive a so-called "identitarian" Church, i.e., one that assumes its anti-modernism fully. Francis has been chosen to save the Church, but on what moral forces and what armada can he rely? Will Francis be the last pope?

A Marxist pope?

Left-wing circles believe they have found a pope in the person of Francis. Some have even wondered if this pontiff is not a Marxist. Reading the headlines is revealing: "Pope Francis defends himself of being a 'Marxist'" (*Le Monde* and *Le Figaro*), "Is Pope Francis a Marxist?" (*Le Point*), "Is the Pope a Marxist?" (France Inter), "Is Pope Francis a dangerous Marxist?" (France 24), "Pope Francis open to Marxism" (*L'Humanité*), etc. The rumor became so widespread that Rome had to deny it. No, Francis is not a Marxist, but he has known many Marxists who were "very good people," although "the Marxist ideology [is] wrong." The best response came from Oskari Juurikkala, a 2014 Novak (Catholic)

Prize-winning economist: "The pope is anything but a Marxist, [...] free-marketeers have nothing to fear from the Holy Father's speech and should even be inspired by it."

Francis can only appear as a Marxist or a communist because we no longer know what it means to be Marxist or even socialist. To be Marxist is not to note that there are rich and poor, it is to say that the wealth of some makes the poverty of others, it is to think of exploitation. To be Marxist is not simply to note that social struggles exist between employees and employers, it is to consider that this class struggle is necessary and positive because there is no possible compromise between classes. To be Marxist is not to consider that private property would be sacred and that it would constitute the basis of society, it is to differentiate between the property of personal goods and lucrative private property, in particular that of companies based on the exploitation and domination of the greatest number. To be a Marxist is not to consider that there are legitimate authorities that should be obeyed, it is to place oneself on the side of the leaderless crowds because "the emancipation of the workers must be the work of the workers themselves".

We are so used to popes and princes of the Church living in obscene luxury, in prestigious palaces and in luxury cars with drivers, that bishops who take the subway and are content with an ordinary apartment are considered saints; we are so used to the Church being on the side of the powerful that a pope who simply dares to remind us that the poor exist and that they also have the right to live is immediately considered a revolutionary and a progressive. The left that believes in Pope Francis will wake up with a hangover like it did after the Second Vatican Council. The Church had betrayed its hopes. His own, no doubt, but not those of Pope John XXIII, who was not a socialist at all, contrary to what Georges Montaron, director of *Témoignage chrétien*[9], proclaimed at the time. Pope Francis is no more or less Marxist than was John XXIII, who also spoke a lot about the poor and denounced the selfishness of the rich, but was nevertheless the heir to a hyper-traditional vision of faith. His model will remain until the end of his life Pius X, known for his anti-modernist virulence. Those who hope for a progressive revolution will unfortunately be disappointed. Francis will not be the pope of the emancipation of the poor, not because the Roman Curia would prevent him from doing so, nor because he would be very badly

---

9. Georges Montaron and Marcel Clément, *Le socialisme*, Paris, Beauchesne, 1969.

advised, as we are already hearing, but because he is not programmed for that. Horacio Verbitsky, president of the Center for Legal and Social Studies in Argentina, explained in the Argentine newspaper *Pagina 12* of March 15, 2013, that "Jorge Bergoglio is not the pope of the poor" and never will be: "Apostrophizing profiteers and preaching docility to the oppressed. In his fifteen years as Archbishop of Buenos Aires, he has done all this and more. Yet, at the same time, he has also tried to unite the opposition against the first government that has - for a long time - adopted a policy favorable to the working classes, a government that he has accused of being uptight and bellicose, because in order to do so, it has been necessary to fight with the so-called powerful mentioned in his speech. Now he will be able to continue his mission, but on a completely different scale, which does not mean that he will forget Argentina. If Eugenio Pacelli (Pius XII) received funds from U.S. intelligence to support Christian Democracy and hinder the victory of the Communists in the years following World War II, and if Karol Wojtyła (John Paul II) was the first to fight for the fall of the Berlin Wall, the Argentine pope will be able to do the same on the Latin American scale." Bergoglio will make beautiful phrases but he will defend the system. Francis is the Vatican's secret weapon for burying authentic liberation theologies and destroying South American socialism in the 21st century. This pope is Argentine because South America remains the only continent where socialism is still present with the experiences in Bolivia, Ecuador, Venezuela, Chile, Nicaragua, Dominica, Cuba, etc. This is why Bergoglio was not the candidate of the liberation theologians who, like Leonardo Boff, were hoping for the election of Sean O'Malley, a Franciscan of Irish origins, as head of the diocese of Boston.

The difficulty is that we no longer remember what the Church was like before Vatican II (which disappointed expectations) and that we have forgotten that Catholic anti-capitalism was always more to the right than to the left! Pope Francis passes for a man of the left because he criticizes the Golden Calf, but in the nineteenth century, Louis de Bonald (1754-1840), one of the fathers of counter-revolutionary thought, hostile to the French Revolution, opponent of the Declaration of the Rights of Man, defender of integral Catholicism and of the monarchy of divine right, deplored, in such harsh terms, that commerce had become "the only religion of societies" and money "the only God of men", he even added that "the duty of a government is to perfect men morally as well as physically, rather than to perfect machines". Still in the 19th century, the ultra-reactionary Pope Pius IX, in his encyclical written to denounce "the monstrous politico-religious errors of the 19th century", thundered: "Whoever does not see and feel that a society removed from the laws of religion and true justice can no longer propose any other goal than to amass and accumulate wealth"; Leo XIII, another ultra-reactionary pope, author of the encyclical *Rerum novarum*, the new cup of tea of the eco-cathos, denounced "the affluence of wealth in the hands of the few next to the indigence of the many" and the fact that "a small number of rich and opulent [...impose an almost servile yoke on the infinite multitude of proletarians".

Everyone will have understood: it is not enough to proclaim oneself anti-capitalist to be on the side of emancipation and to act against the very principle of inequality. Let's remember that the old Catholic right is coming back! We all saw it during the Manif pour tous, which was only a demonstration against equal rights for heterosexuals and homosexuals. Even an author like Jean-François Bouthors, who is not likely to be suspected of leftism, is obliged to recognize in his *Petit éloge du catholicisme français* (Éd. François Bourin, 2015) that a "Khmer Rouge" tendency exercises a curious magisterium, manipulated in the background by people who clearly pursue political objectives that must be described as reactionary. The Catholic religious intolerance that is rampant in France probably has no equivalent in other European countries.

Francis is therefore not of the left, but he knows, along with those who made him pope, that he must contain the right-wing movement of the Church, especially in the area of morals, so as not to widen the gap between the Church-institution and the real people. This is why he tries to give tokens of modernity and even multiplies signs in the direction of a Catholic left, which however no longer exists worldwide since the pontificates of John Paul II and Benedict XVI. As a result, Francis is dissatisfying his right wing without winning over his left. The Church of Pope Francis will end up losing on both counts.

A green pope?

This pope, who is not of the left, will not be the pope of ecology in the sense of the defense of popular pre- or post-capitalist ways of life. Here is a pope who, after having fought against liberation theologies, would have become an "ecologist", a "degrowthist", an "anti-capitalist", an "anti-productivist", in short, the ecologists would finally have the much hoped-for leader of a new green Church. Let's be clear: I don't blame Francis and the ecologist-cathos for not going far enough or fast enough, but for not going in the right direction[10]. The ecology of the Vatican is above all a war machine against gay marriage, the right to abortion, contraception, the relativism of values, etc. Not that the pope is insincere when he brilliantly denounces the destruction of ecosystems, but the reasons he gives are simply not acceptable to me: I don't say that it's sunny because the pope claims it's raining, but if the pope explains that it's raining because we have legalized contraception, abortion, gay marriage, because we look longingly at our own spouse, I have a duty to oppose him.

I accuse my Republican, Democrat, secularist, environmentalist, and left-wing friends of being too eager to have a Pope-as-it-is to not lose their critical thinking skills and lend the Pope much more than he himself declares. I accuse my republican, democrat, secularist, ecologist and left-wing friends of not seeing that this pope is a key piece, even more so than John Paul II and Benedict XVI, in the crusade for the "re-evangelization" of society and thus in the defeat of what we have been fighting for since Voltaire, an open and democratic society. This pope fascinates but in the way of a snake because he puts all vigilance to sleep. We are so used to the Church saying that it rains when the weather is good, in a word that it condemns all human progress in the name of its dogmas, that we relish anything that looks like a small step. A pope who would say that one can use a condom to avoid infecting one's neighbor would be a saintly layman. A pope who would simply say that having an abortion is less serious than being raped would appear as a new messiah.

A right-wing politician who would say what the Pope said would not be offered, unlike the Bishop of Rome, a card of honor for ecology. Yet what ecologist would not subscribe to the following strong words:

---

10. http://www.lavie.fr/medias/le-texte-integral-de-l-encyclique-laudato-sii-18-06-2015-64352_73.php

"Our house is burning and we look away. Nature, mutilated, overexploited, is no longer able to recover and we refuse to admit it. Humanity is suffering. It suffers from bad development, in the North as in the South, and we are indifferent. The Earth and humanity are in danger and we are all responsible for it. I believe it is time to open our eyes. On all continents, warning signals are going off. Europe is being hit by natural disasters and health crises. The American economy, often bulimic in natural resources, seems to be suffering from a crisis of confidence in its regulatory methods. Latin America is once again shaken by the financial and therefore social crisis. In Asia, the multiplication of pollution, as witnessed by the brown cloud, is spreading and threatens to poison an entire continent. Africa is plagued by conflicts, AIDS, desertification and famine. Some island countries are threatened with extinction by global warming. We cannot say that we did not know! Let us be careful that the 21st century does not become, for future generations, the century of a crime *of* humanity against life. Our collective responsibility is engaged. First responsibility of the developed countries. First by history, first by power, first by the level of their consumption. If the whole of humanity behaved like the countries of the North, we would need two additional planets to meet our needs.

These committed, iconoclastic, responsible words could pass for those of a convinced ecologist who, if he could, would change the course of our societies. This speech is, of course, that of President Chirac in Johannesburg in 2002. He has never taken any significant action on ecology. We would have applauded these words if they had been pronounced by Pope Francis. Said by Chirac, we laughed at them as we would at a good joke.

We had also found "good things" in the observations made during the Grenelle de l'environnement but we considered, with reason in view of the results obtained, that ecology was not soluble in Sarkozysm. I know that I am going to hurt some of my friends, but I also believe that *our* ecology is not soluble in the Church's thinking.

I understand that other ecologies exist, and I readily admit with the philosopher Dominique Bourg, a Catholic in good standing, who was, with Nicolas Hulot, one of President Chirac's advisors in this field, just as his ecologist ideas are today readily found within the Vatican, that "political ecology is not the natural fruit of a single family of thought, the left", but this right-wing Catholic ecology frightens me. Not on principle but because of its social and political consequences! I claim the right to be an ecologist and to defend marriage for all; I claim the right to be an ecologist and to defend contraception and abortion; I claim the right to be an ecologist and to be a sharer in all areas.

I am a growth objector, but I don't like the Catholic conception of the family, nor its defense of lucrative private property, nor the idea that there would be necessary natural inequalities, nor the submission to any capitalized Truth. My degrowth is already a disbelief in all dogmas!

Neither God, nor Caesar, nor tribune!

We will see, as we go along, that this Church takes advantage of this "ecological" encyclical to confuse the laws of life with its hypothetical natural laws (its divine laws that God revealed to the Church). It thus misses the essential point: in the face of the capitalist system which intends to submit nature to the laws of the economy (with carbon money, with patents on living things), the alternative intends on the contrary to submit the economy to the laws of living things (organic agriculture, "agroforestry", etc.). We do not need to believe in original sin and redemption for this!

We will also note that this Church takes advantage of this "ecological" encyclical to awaken the spirits of Pope Leo XIII, the author in the 19th century of the encyclical *Rerum novarum*, the father of the so-called "social" doctrine of the Church, whose pretty name should not mislead us because his project was anything but progressive. He called on the bosses to be nicer and the workers to accept their fate! It is understandable that the ecologist-cathos of the (very) hard right are rubbing their hands. Thus the pontifical knight, commander of the order of the Holy Sepulchre of Jerusalem, leader of the ecologist-cathos located on the extreme right of God, Patrice de Plunkett, maintains that the French Christian people would be behind Rome: "That the popes are radical (and integral) ecologists, it remained for a long time unthinkable for a number of Catholics in France. In their minds, ecology was a leftist fad of which they had only a vague idea, associated with firecrackers and libertinism, but which they could in no way associate with our 'values.'"

I want to believe that Christian people are not so much behind the princes of the Church as they wish to go in the direction indicated by the Pope, because even when they vote (mostly) to the right and go to Mass every Sunday, they use non-recommended means to avoid pregnancy, including before marriage, they take communion, even though they are divorced and remarried, and they even tolerate Social Security and its egalitarian ideology quite well when they take advantage of it! Ecology must not be used as a pretext to violate Catholics and push them to accept dogmas that they reject or ignore massively. We don't have the right to hide the fact that the most active ecologist-Catholic groups, especially in France after the success of the Manif pour tous, are not really left-wing and often reek of the extreme right. This is why I had launched, in 2012, with Christian Terras, the director of the religious weekly *Golias*, an appeal against the unfriendly takeover launched by this Catholic right and extreme right against ecology and degrowth[11]. I admit that we were not heard and that 2015 is worse than 2012!

That Pope Francis officially makes himself the champion of a certain degrowth should not be any more seductive, since his degrowth is that of an anti-liberal "catho right", well represented in the French media, since Vincent Cheynet (and his austere monthly *La Décroissance*) has been overtaken, in September 2015, on his right and his Catholicism, by a new ecologist-catholic review called *Limite*, launched by his own friend Bès de Berc and the very Catholic éditions du Cerf, in the wake of the mobilization against equal marriage rights and the Veilleurs movement (cf. *below*). Francis is not a "progressive" pope but a descendant of the old intransigent Catholicism of the 19th century, which also dreamed of bringing the Church closer to the people, victims of the liberal bourgeoisie, which already claimed to be anti-capitalist but confused the class struggle with corporatism. The ecology of Francis, like the social Catholicism of Leo XIII, is tributary of the Thomistic revival, with notably the reflection on the common good, the "anti-capitalist" conception of economic value, the refusal to recognize the productivity of capital, and therefore the condemnation of usury. But whereas Leo XIII read St. Thomas through the writings of the Jesuits of the journal *Civiltà Cattolica*, and in particular Fathers Taparelli d'Azeglio and Matteo Liberatore, Francis reread him through Archbishop Filippo Santoro and the very right-wing movement Communion and Liberation (of which we will speak at length). Wasn't it he who, in 2013, was charged with defining concrete choices "towards sustainable lifestyles and an economic system that encourages the full realization of the person and achieves full recognition of the rights of each person"[12]? But wasn't it also thanks to him that he became pope in the first place?

---

11. This appeal is reproduced in the appendix.
12. http://www.zenit.org/fr/articles/italie-promouvoir-des-styles-de-vie-durables

All with Francis?

This pope, who is "neither red nor green", is nevertheless very popular worldwide. Never in the 20th century has a pope been so popular, especially among those who had drifted (a little, a lot, passionately) away from the Church. The Pew Research Center, an American research center on the evolution of public opinion, notes that "with 84% of positive opinions in Europe, 78% in the United States and 72% in Latin America, Pope Francis is almost unanimously accepted on continents with a strong Christian tradition. This is obviously less the case in Africa and Asia where Christian religions are competing with other spiritual currents. The African countries tested show a certain indifference with 44% of positive opinions and 40% of no opinion. The *same is true* in Asia, where 41% of those surveyed were in favor and 45% had no opinion. The only region of the world where "Francis-mania" has not worked is the Middle East, where supporters and detractors are equally divided (25%) and where indifference prevails (41% without opinion). The pope enjoys a median average of 60 percent favorable opinions, compared to 11 percent unfavorable, in the 43 countries where people were surveyed."[13]

This "papamania" is linked to the global crisis that affects our societies and in particular to the detestable search for identity-based solutions. The success of Francis is first and foremost that of a Church that shows itself. These shock Catholics have even invented a big word to express this reality: they would be "identity Catholics" as there are identity Jews, identity Muslims, identity Buddhists... *The Cahiers libres* call on young Catholics to be identity Catholics because there would be no possible dialogue with others without a strong identity. *La Vie* (Catholic) even worries about this new tidal wave in a November 2014 article entitled "Has open Catholicism given way to bourgeois Catholicism?" "Historian Guillaume Cuchet (University of Paris-Est, Créteil Val-de-Marne) wondered about "the strange decline of open Catholicism." It seems in fact that identity Catholicism has been "since the 1960s, more 'resilient' than openness Catholicism in the face of the shock of secularization, so that the latter has ended up quite logically losing its grip on the institution, at least until recently. This is a strange decline, because one might have thought a priori that, because of its dispositions and orientations,

---

13. http://www.huffingtonpost.fr/2014/12/11/pape-francois-popularite-exceptionnelle-monde-chretien-etude-americaine_n_6309596.html

open Catholicism was better able than its identity counterpart to face the challenges of modernity and to adapt to them without disappearing in the process. The Christians of the left also question this new "fracture that is crossing Catholicism". This identity-based Catholicism is on the other hand claimed by the right-wing currents of the Church, such as Father Grosjean who, while recognizing this fracture, shows his contempt for the opposite camp: "The real divide is not between tradis and charismatics, but between those who take the turn of identified and uncomplicated Christianity and those who remain in the Church of the eighties, where it is necessary to excuse oneself for being a Christian.

I admit it: these identity Catholics scare me, as do all the political identity movements, breeding grounds for xenophobic nationalism. The Church offers to confused human beings a ready-made identity that allows them to express their fear of others without looking like an ugly xenophobe! We are rightly offended when Nadine Morano has the stupidity to speak too quickly and too loudly by claiming that France is "a white country", but we let the same or others appeal to the Judeo-Christian roots of Europe, or even to the Greco-Latin roots if not to the Indo-European ones. The unanimity that surrounds each declaration of the pope (and notably his encyclical on ecology) is only possible because we ignore that the Catholic Church intends to receive its share of the cake of the return of religion, even if it means getting into bed with certain "new religious movements" (sometimes even of a sectarian type, as we shall see) or with islamo-conservatives like the UOIF (Union of Islamic Organizations of France), which dares to establish a parallel between marriage for all and zoophilia[14]. And because we ignore that the anti-capitalism of the Church does not date from today and has nothing in common with ours and that its so-called "human" or "integral" ecology is only a way to smuggle nauseating theses against abortion, contraception, gay and civil marriage, social (social security) and sometimes political rights, freedom of thought.

Fortunately, a small village is resisting the "papamania": those Argentines, Catholic or not, who knew Bergoglio well before his election. Horacio Verbitsky, for example, has dedicated a book, *El Silencio: de Paulo VI a Bergoglio: las relaciones secretas de la Iglesia con la ESMA* [Silence: the secret relations of the Church *with ESMA*], to the links between the Church and the ESMA torture center, a book written the day after Francis' election:

---

14. http://tempsreel.nouvelobs.com/societe/20121115.OBS9549/mariage-homo-l-uoif-y-voit-un-risque-de-zoophilie.html

"Among the hundreds of emails I received, I remembered one: 'I can't believe my eyes. I am so distressed and angry that my arms are falling off. He has done it. He is the perfect person to hide moral corruption, an expert in hiding things." The message is signed by Graciela Yorio, the sister of the priest Orlando Yorio, who denounced Jorge Mario Bergoglio as the person responsible for his kidnapping and the torture he suffered for five months in 1976. Orlando died in 2000 imagining the nightmare that came true on March 13, 2013. He continues: "I am not sure that Jorge Mario Bergoglio was elected to hide the moral corruption that rendered Joseph Ratzinger impotent. What is certain, however, is that the new bishop of Rome will be an ersatz, a shoddy substitute, like the water mixed with flour that needy mothers give their children to deceive hunger." Emilio Mignone, Catholic activist, university professor and rector, vice-president of the Permanent Assembly for Human Rights in Argentina, married to Angelica Sosa - known as Chela - one of the mothers of Plaza de Mayo, cited Bergoglio in his book *Iglesia y dictadura* [Church *and* Dictatorship], as the paragon of "shepherds who gave their sheep to the enemy without defending or saving them."

Why did Bishop Bergoglio become pope?

The controversy over his equivocal attitude during the dictatorship in Argentina[15], which marked his appointment, was quickly forgotten. It is less well known that Francis missed his election against Benedict XVI, during the previous conclave, because of these same accusations. Francis has therefore taken advantage of this interlude between conclaves to refine his defense with a book that only convinces the convinced. A book (*Bergoglio's List,* 2013) by Nino Scavo, a prominent journalist in Catholic circles, even tried awkwardly to respond to the families' accusations. Bergoglio is said to have set up a parallel network to protect certain victims of the dictatorship, but which ones? on what criteria? are they primarily members of the fascist organization, the Iron Guard? It would be wrong, however, to believe that the Pope owes his election to the management of his own "biolegend" concerning his attitude under the military dicta-

---

15. "Dictature argentine : l'honneur perdu de l'Église", *Golias,* n° 149/150, May 2013; Marie-Monique Robin, *Escadrons de la mort,* Paris, La Découverte, 2008; John Dinges, *Les années Condor*, Paris, La Découverte, 2008.

---

torship. I had tried, during a television program, to open up other avenues, but the cacophony and superficiality of the media got the better of these hypotheses[16]. The evidence has since accumulated sufficiently, including from his own camp, for the hypothesis to have become a certainty: José Mario Bergoglio owes his election to his role in the defeat of liberation theology and his ability to combat what specialists call the "new socialism of the 21st century". I insist: it is not the Jesuit, who is rather cold to his order, who was elected but the bishop known for his authoritarianism and doctrinal intransigence.

This victory was sealed during a general conference of the Latin American episcopate held in 2007 and opened by Benedict XVI in the Marian shrine in Brazil[17]. This meeting is the equivalent for liberation theology of the famous Controversy of Valladolid (in 1550 and 1551) which opposed the Dominican Bartolomé de Las Casas and the theologian Juan Gines de Sepúlveda on the subject of the Indians. The bishops clashed in 2007 over the theology of the poor[18]. Bishop Bergoglio won a decisive victory with the support of a very special Vatican envoy (see *below*), reproaching, as always, liberation theology for "using a Marxist hermeneutic" and, above all, insisting on the primacy of faith in judging reality. In other words: no longer starting from the people but only from God!

Bergoglio himself presided over the commission that drafted the conclusions of the General Conference of the Latin American Episcopate in Aparecida, and he did so with the support of Filippo Santoro, an Italian who was sent to Brazil as a *fidei donum* missionary and who turned out to be a dignitary of the Communion and Liberation movement[19]. After this decisive victory against liberation theology, Santoro was recalled to Italy by Benedict XVI and appointed Archbishop in 2011. Jorge Mario Bergoglio will be made pope in 2013 in gratitude for his service. Francis has not forgotten the lesson of Aparecida, and during his trip to Rio de Janeiro, addressing the representatives of the Latin American bishops' conferences, he warned them that the "socializing reductionism" that had been defeated in Aparecida still continues to tempt the Church today. Francis takes advantage of the fact that the air of the times is no longer one of progressive revolutions to make something new out

---

16. https://www.youtube.com/watch?v=ULP6BtzFhw0
17. http://chiesa.espresso.repubblica.it/articolo/1350613?fr=y
18. http://www.alterinfos.org/spip.php?article1493
19. *Id.*

of something old, since if he takes up the condemnation of liberation theologies made by his predecessor Benedict XVI, when he was only prefect of the Congregation for the Doctrine of the Faith (ex-Inquisition founded in 1542), he cleverly distances himself from the declarations of the same Ratzinger of 1984 and 1986 by developing his own vision of an evangelical option preferential to the poor. Anticipating the demonstration, we can say that it is a matter of systematically using the "big words" emblematic of liberation theology to better water them down by emptying them of their meaning. We could say the same thing about its anti-capitalism and anti-productivism, since it is a question of diverting the criticisms coming from the social movements to rally in fine to the current of ordoliberalism. The symbol of this historical defeat of liberation theology is the divorce between the two brothers Leonardo and Clodovis Boff, two great figures of liberation theology, even if the first is much better known[20]. Clodovis, after having joined Ratzinger in 2008, just one year after Aparecida, is now close to Francis. He denounces "the error of principle on which liberation theology is based" which would be to "place the poor as the first operational principle of theology, substituting them for God and Jesus Christ". He wonders: if the poor acquire this status of "epistemological premium" what happens to faith and doctrine? The Church would become an NGO alongside other NGOs fighting for the emancipation of the poor. Clodovis Boff therefore believes that liberation theology has given all it can historically and that it should return to the truths of faith. Liberation theology would have the great defect of starting from the poor to go to the encounter with God, while Aparecida starts from Christ to go to the encounter with the poor "knowing that the Christ principle always includes the poor, while the poor principle does not necessarily include Christ". I would add that Clodovis Boff was "treated" (as they say in another field) by Filippo Santoro, the famous *fidei donum* of Rome, who, I recall, is a central figure in Communion and Liberation (cf. *below*). The supporters of liberation theology, including Leonardo Boff, have thus reacted against both the "reversal" of Clodovis and the victory of Bergoglio. Leonardo Boff writes that Aparecida "runs the risk of condemning the Church and theology to historical insignificance and pastoral sterility. He says of his brother: "This intention is like saying: 'Brother, I'm stabbing you in the heart, but don't worry, it's for your own good. I repeat: the official line

---

20. http://chiesa.espresso.repubblica.it/articolo/205773?fr=y

of the Catholic Church now consists in mimicking the words of liberation theology: thus we have a Church that has the flavor and color of a Church of the poor but that is not the Church of the poor. The Catholic Counter-Reformation had, in the 16th century, operated in this way by championing puritanism in the face of accusations from the Reformed. Moreover, the Bishop of Rome plays admirably with words by sliding insensitively from the poor (in the sense of liberation theologies), that is to say, the dominated, the exploited, to the notion of "evangelical poverty", which is, in turn, based on the seventh commandment ("the poor"), based on the seventh commandment ("You shall not steal") - a way of reminding us that the goods of the rich are sacred in the eyes of God - and on the beatitude "Blessed are the poor in spirit, for theirs is the kingdom of God" (an incentive to live in joyful sobriety, taking into account one's rank: one understands better then the role that Bishop Filippo Santoro of Communion and Liberation can fulfill concerning the definition of new ways of life). The Church of the poor according to Francis is a mixture of horse and lark, a lot of horse (of inequality willed by God) and little lark (of equality).

Pope Leo XIII was not as good a communicator as Francis, since, after recalling that the first principle of natural law according to the Church is that "men are born unequal by nature and by the will of God", he advocated resignation to the humblest, because "to possess abundant riches and other things called 'goods', or on the contrary, to be deprived of them, is of no importance for eternal felicity" (sic). Certainly, but when the Church stooped to evoke earthly felicity, it was to explain that the inequalities of nature impose different obligations, the worker must fully and faithfully provide any work to which he has committed himself by free and ethical contract (the employee's cherished freedom of contract, whereas the criterion of the contract is the bond of subordination) and the boss must give to each one what is just (a soft notion par excellence). We shall see that "justice" has nothing in common with equality. It has long been "just" that slaves obey their masters, servants and wage-earners their bosses, and women their husbands. The ways of Catholic "justice" are sometimes quite impenetrable! Saint Augustine, in *The City of God*, finds a divine origin for slavery, which, according to the Father of the Church, is the consequence of original sin or of the just war. Slavery would belong to the natural order that it would be forbidden to disturb. One even discovers on the site of the ecologist-catholic magazine *Limite* (neither left nor right, but very much to the right) a (posthumous?) eulogy of liberation theology. When the obscene recuperation is a way to kill the spirit of a current!

Francis was not made pope because he was a Jesuit (the first pope of this company founded by Ignatius of Loyola in 1539 and whose characteristic is to ask its members to make in addition to the three usual vows, poverty, chastity and obedience, This is because he symbolized a new theology of the poor, to which his theology of ecology (dare we say it) is undeniably linked, as the texts published in the context of the General Conference of the Latin American Episcopate in Aparecida prove. The new Archbishop Filippo Santoro will not contradict me, since, after having recounted that "the magisterium and the pastoral action of Pope Francis are the mature fruit of the General Conference of the Latin American Episcopate that took place in Brazil, in the Marian shrine of Aparecida, He explains what is to be understood (from now on) when the Church speaks of the "evangelical preferential option for the poor" (the introduction of the term "evangelical" naturally changes the whole meaning): "Originality is given by the irruption of the Spirit in history. This is where the prophetic force of the Latin American Church comes from, making its own the mission proclaimed by Jesus in the synagogue of Nazareth: "The Spirit of the Lord is upon me because he has anointed me. He has sent me to bring the good news to the poor" (Luke 4:18). This is where the strong affirmation of the evangelical preferential option for the poor comes from. It is simply the evangelical poverty and witness to life among the people that we see in Pope Francis' way of being and acting."

Bergoglio's hidden youth

I have often been reproached for having excused Ratzinger (Benedict XVI) for his youthful involvement in the Hitler Youth: I consider that there is indeed a right to forget and that the "in spite of ourselves" were very numerous. The Vatican had awkwardly begun by denying the facts and Father Federico Lombardi, in charge of communications, had declared: "I wish to clarify the lies written by the Israeli and international press. He [the Pope] has never been in this movement. He has never been in this youth movement ideologically linked to Nazism." The newspaper *L'Express* of May 12, 2009, however, provided some solid information: "In an interview given to the German journalist Peter Seewald in April 2005, Joseph Ratzinger said: 'As soon as I left the seminary, I was not directly in the Hitler Youth. And that was difficult because, in order to obtain a reduction in the cost of the school I needed, I had to prove that I had visited the Hitler Youth. According to a German investigation, cited by the French Catholic religious news agency I-Media, the future pope had joined the Hitler Youth, but against his will, in 1941, on his fourteenth birthday. He was classified as an "obliged member" *(Zwangs-Hitlerjunge),* different from the volunteers *(Stamm-Hitlerjunge).* It was on August 2, 1943 that he was incorporated as an auxiliary in the anti-aircraft defense."

The media have been much less curious about Francis, merely acknowledging that the young Bergoglio belonged to a Peronist youth organization. But put this way, except for the Argentines, the facts do not seem particularly disturbing. It so happens that in the course of my work on the extreme right, I had the opportunity to investigate, some years ago, this organization called the Iron Guard. Very thorough work has been published since then, including Humberto Cucchetti's book, *Serving Perón: Trajectories of the Iron Guard* (published by Presses universitaires de Rennes in 2013). Elected in 1946, Juan Perón created the Peronist Party, a movement that included the Peronist Youth, had a new constitution enacted and established a regime where political and union opposition had no place. He was impeached once in 1955, re-elected in 1973 and died in 1974. Peronism is often presented as a national-populist movement with more "brown" (fascist) than "red" (socialist) roots. The Iron Guard is not the only Peronist youth organization, but it is undeniably the one that unites its most right-wing fringe, as evidenced by its very name, which is named after a Romanian fascist organization, Legiunea Arhanghelului Mihail (Legion of the Archangel Michael, hence the term legionnaire), which launched pogroms during the Second World War, took anti-Semitic measures, proclaimed anti-social laws, and attacked left-wing militants. Unlike Nazi Germany and the Hitler Youth, membership in the Iron Guard was never compulsory. The Argentinean Iron Guard certainly renounced armed struggle, at Perón's express request, but it always defended the "revolutionary national-socialist" idea and displayed, according to Humberto Cucchetti, an eschatological political conception: popular struggles were superior to those of the vanguards and politics opposed the camp of good to that of evil.

I was surprised to discover that Massimo Introvigne (a lawyer of many bad causes of the Church, including sects and pedophilia, an ultra-conservative intellectual who we will meet again throughout this book and of whom we will draw up a rather detailed portrait later on) was also interested in Bergoglio's troubling relations with the Iron Guard. His defense was published simultaneously in *Nuova bussola*, a Catholic daily newspaper of opinion, and on the Religioscope website, in order to give it maximum resonance within the international Catholic movement.

Massimo Introvigne reduces the importance of the link with the Romanian Iron Guard: "They accepted the idea of adopting the name of an extreme right-wing European group in response to the criticism of those who considered them close to the left (which was indeed the case for many of them). However, to attribute to the Argentine Iron Guard the ideas of the Romanian Iron Guard in order to attack the Pope in this way is a high fantasy. Only the name, or almost only the name, is common to both organizations. To present the Argentine Iron Guard as a left-wing movement is a matter of negationism, unless one considers that the SA were more left-wing than the SS and Hitler than Himmler (this thesis is known to exist within certain neo-Nazi movements).

The second line of defense, contradictory to the first, is that the Iron Guard was a legitimate defense against leftist violence: Introvigne recalls "the increasingly harsh confrontation with the Montoneros, far-left Peronist militants who had turned to armed struggle; many of them came from a progressive, philomarxist Catholic background... The Jesuits linked to the philomarxist liberation theology became close to the Montoneros, while Fr. Bergoglio, who became provincial of the Society of Jesus in 1973, was hostile to liberation theology and had relations with several representatives of the Iron Guard." Introvigne is totally right on this point.

But Bergoglio's political career did not end there, since in the early 1970s he was still supporting a new structure called the Unique Organization of Generational Transfer (Organización Única del Trasvasamiento Generacional, OUTG), which resulted from the 1972 merger of the Iron Guard and the FEN (Fronte Studentesco Nazionale), another far-right organization. Introvigne does not deny this proximity and even admits that "after the coup d'état, many Peronist groups were persecuted. The leaders of the Iron Guard were protected - according to many of the texts that tell its story - by their good relations with the Navy and with Fr. Bergoglio, provincial of the Jesuits, who used the members of the Guard extensively in the process of transferring the religious to the laity of the old Universidad del Salvador (University of the Savior) in Buenos Aires, while at the same time creating a safety net for them. This way of presenting things could lead one to believe that Bergoglio opposed the military dictatorship because of his good relations with the Navy, but this would be forgetting that Admiral Emilio Massera, the Navy's commander-in-chief, was one of the three main leaders of the putsch.

Introvigne forgets to mention that Bergoglio will direct the Universidad del Salvador thanks to the OUTG and that the transfer of power from the clerics to the laity will allow, at the end of 1974, to entrust the control of it to ex-members. Massimo Introvigne forgets to mention that this university played a major role in the dictatorship, since it did not cease to work in favor of Admiral Emilio Massera, who was awarded an honorary doctorate and was the real mastermind behind the coup d'état of the three generals, which led Argentina into a long and cruel period of dictatorship successively led by Videla, Viola, Galtieri and Nicolaides. The Argentine Church was one of the most faithful supporters of the dictatorship, which from 1976 to 1983 claimed nearly 30,000 victims and cut the country to pieces. Horacio Verbitsky reports in *El Vuelo* how priests eased the conscience of airmen who threw political prisoners into the sea. The far-right activist and journalist Emmanuel Ratier (who died in August 2015), who knew Alvarez (founder of the Iron Guard) well, tells us in No. 360 of his magazine *Facts and Documents* that after the dissolution of his movement he got closer to Communion and Liberation. Massimo Introvigne acknowledges the facts and specifies that "in 1978, Alvarez met Communion and Liberation in Rome, a group with which he began to establish relations, above all through Rocco Buttiglione[21]. The latter's analyses of the Polish trade union Solidarność influenced attempts to launch political-union activities in Argentina, and subsequently a party called Solidaridad, whose impact

---

21. Rocco Buttiglione is an Italian politician, professor of political science at the University of St. Pius V in Rome. He was appointed by Barroso in 2004 as European Commissioner for Justice. A violent controversy due to his ultra-reactionary positions on homosexuals and women forced him to leave his post. Barroso wanted to re-hire him elsewhere but the European Parliament was opposed. He declares that he is excluded by the Freemasons who control the Parliament. He presents himself as center-right but is very right-wing. He will be a minister of Berlusconi, vice-president of the Chamber of Deputies. He leads the Christian Democratic Party. Buttiglione is above all the theorist of the divine foundations of the free market and globalization, adviser to John Paul II, he was the architect of the alliance between the Vatican and the American libertarians. He would still be a member of Communion and Liberation.

remained modest, especially in comparison with that of the Iron Guard and the OUTG in an earlier era, which had counted thousands of adherents and exercised real influence." Introvigne concedes that "as auxiliary bishop of Buenos Aires since 1992, Father Bergoglio initially followed these initiatives with sympathy. But relations ceased when the political insignificance of the Alvarez group became evident in an Argentina that had changed a lot, and also because of a mystical drift with increasingly singular traits. Things became more complicated for Bergoglio when Alvarez formed the Order of Mary of the Rosary of St. Nicholas, no longer recognizing Rome and creating a new liturgy, the "fideipolitical mass. Massimo Introvigne concedes that "the cult of the Virgin of San Nicolás opened the door to a rapprochement between Alvarez and Abbot Ezcurra Uriburu...". It should be noted that this priest was the founder of the nationalist movement Tacuara (characterized by its anti-communism, anti-democracy, and anti-Semitism), which was responsible for some 40 attacks. This movement claimed to be based on the doctrine of the ultraconservative Catholic priest Julio Meinvielle, who was its spiritual director, and on the thinking of the Franco-Argentine sociologist Jacques de Mahieu, a former member of the Waffen SS and long-time leader of the neo-Nazi group CEDADE (1966-1993). The evolution of *the* Order of Mary of the Rosary of St. Nicholas is of little interest to us: let us simply note that a former Peronist deputy, Segundo Ubaldo Rolón, close to the Iron Guard, was proclaimed pope under the name of Peter II and that he presents himself and his companion Maria Liliana Reyes as Emperors of the Sacred Heart!

Bergoglio's political strategy, beyond his involvement with the Iron Guard and his late differences with the OUTG, has always been to try to achieve in South America what Solidarność had succeeded in Poland: to constitute a popular (populist) alternative to the lefts. If Karol Josef Wojtyla, now John Paul II, did triumph at the end of the twentieth century in the Eastern bloc (beyond the Polish situation) and above all prevented a true socialism from succeeding Stalinism and its successors, Jorge Mario Bergoglio could well triumph over "Bolivarian socialism" at the beginning of the twenty-first century.

The Church of Francis against "21st century socialism"

Much has been said about the role of John Paul II and the Catholic Church in the collapse of the Soviet bloc and the end of "real socialism. The election of Francis is a bad blow not only against liberation theologies but also against the currents of "21st century socialism" and *buen vivir* socialism" that have been invented in South America over the last few decades and make it the only continent where socialism is still conjugated in the present, especially because of its popular roots. I am afraid that the main political contribution of Pope Francis will be to encourage the failure of socialist and ecological experiments in South America. Will Francis be the downfall of *buen vivir* socialism, ecosocialism and 21st century socialism?

The concept of *buen vivir* ("good living") socialism was developed in Ecuador by Alberto Acosta, an economist, former Minister of Energy and Mines, former president of the National Constituent Assembly, and candidate of the indianist environmentalist left in the 2013 presidential election, thinker of an anti-extractivist socialism, but also, in Uruguay, by José Mujica, known as "Pepe Mujica", former Tupamaros guerrilla, former Minister of Agriculture and Fisheries, President of the Republic of Uruguay (2010-2015). I had the pleasure of publishing texts by these two fellow fighters in the bimonthly magazine *Le Sarkophage* and then the monthly *Les Zindigné(e)s*. Pepe Mujica explains, for example, that "one should not waste one's life accumulating. It is the need to accumulate that distorts the intelligence of intelligent people. This civilization is a deception, it makes us believe that we can continue to accumulate without ceasing and this is not true, and it makes us believe that everyone will be able to consume as much as they want, and this is not true either. Here we come close to the thought of Leonardo Boff who explains that the meeting between liberation theology and political ecology is obvious because "the same logic of the dominant system of accumulation and social organization that leads to the exploitation of workers also leads to the plundering of entire nations and ultimately to the degradation of nature"[22].

The concept of "21st century socialism" was proposed by the Chilean sociologist and political scientist Tomás Moulian in his book *El socialismo del siglo xxi. La quinta vía* [Socialism in the 21st Century: The Fifth Way].

---

22. Paul Ariès, *Amoureux du bien vivre, Afrique, Amériques, Asie, que nous apprend l'écologie des pauvres*, Villeurbanne, Golias, 2013.

Tomás Moulian studied at the Pontifical Catholic University of Chile and later at the Catholic University of Leuven (Belgium). For a long time, he directed the Institute of Sociology at the Catholic University of Chile and then the Paulo Freire Institute of Social Education (a popular education movement). At first a member of the Christian Democratic Youth, he became involved in the MAPU (a left-wing workers' and peasants' organization) in the Chile of Allende's Popular Unity and then actively participated in the resistance against Pinochet's dictatorship. After the return to democracy, he became a fellow traveler of the Chilean Communist Party and was proposed for a time as a candidate of the United Left in the 2004 presidential elections. In 1999, Tomás Moulian wrote his book *El consumo me consume* [Consumption consumes me] in which he denounced the consumer society but also the Catholic tradition of austerity. Starting from Max Weber's analysis that establishes a link between religious asceticism and the emergence of capitalism, he rejects the puritanical critique of desire (that of right-wing degrowth) and advocates an internal critique of desire (that which we carry out in the name of an emancipating "more to enjoy"). The Venezuelan president Hugo Chávez will popularize the concept of "socialism of the 21st century" which seeks its references on the side of the Latin American critical thought of the 20th century with the Peruvian José Carlos Mariátegui, the Cuban Fidel Castro, the Nicaraguan Augusto César Sandino, the Salvadorian Agustín Farabundo Martí... President Chávez explains on the occasion of the World Social Forum of Porto Alegre, in 2002: "We must claim socialism as a thesis, a project, a path, but a new type of socialism, a humanistic socialism that puts people first and not machines. "

Argentina is of course the first country where the election of Bergoglio as pope has had the indirect consequence of removing the "left" from power. Vatican Radio congratulated itself the day after the defeat of the Peronist candidate: "End of an era for Argentina after the election of Mauricio Macri". This victory of Mauricio Macri is that of the conservative and liberal right and the most reactionary fractions of the Catholic Church against Daniel Scioli, candidate of the left-wing coalition in power in Argentina since 2003. Mauricio Macri is like Argentina's Berlusconi: the son of a wealthy family, he made a name for himself as the president of a major soccer club, trained at Argentina's Catholic University, founded his own party and became the mayor of Buenos Aires, a federal entity in its own right in 2007. His main advisor is Ecuadorian Jaime Duran Barba, a consultant to large firms and a right-wing presidential candidate in Ecuador. Argentina's population is 75 per cent Catholic, despite increasing competition from North American evangelical sects. Despite its power, the church has never managed to oppose certain social reforms implemented since the military dictatorship: same-sex marriage, the right of trans-sexuals to undergo surgery, etc. The big financial oligarchies, especially the employers grouped in the Argentine Business Association, and the media lobbies had expressed their preference for "Macrism" with the support of part of the Church. This victory for the right is also the consequence of the mobilizations against the adoption of the law legalizing "marriage for all", since the Church mobilized more than 50,000 demonstrators on the eve of the vote in Parliament, calling the law "diabolical" and contrary to the family and the natural order. The left, which wanted this law, had placed it under the auspices of the French Revolution and started the great parliamentary debate on July 14. The divorce between Bergoglio and the left, however, did not begin with this law. Bergoglio criticized most of the Kirchner couple's decisions long before 2010. President Néstor Kirchner (2003-2007), who died in 2010, already referred to Bergoglio as the "spiritual leader of the political opposition" and criticized him, as a former resistance fighter, for his role and that of the Church under the military dictatorship. He also accused him of making the Church "behave like a political party" and of being in systematic opposition to any socially emancipatory project. The disagreements go back to at least 2003 and led the president of the Republic to refuse to participate in the *Te Deum* organized every year to commemorate the first autonomous Argentine government. Bergoglio never hesitated to add fuel to the fire, making his spokesman declare during the 2005 crisis that there was no relationship between the Church and the government. The conflict did not end with the election in 2007 of Cristina Fernández Kirchner (wife of Néstor Kirchner who was seriously ill at the time). In March 2008, for example, Bergoglio opposed resolution 125, which taxed exports of soybeans, sunflowers, corn and wheat, thus supporting the opposition of the employers' unions in these four major sectors. It should be remembered that more than 90% of Argentina's soybeans are transgenic. The Church also opposed the nationalization of pension funds, which was tantamount to re-establishing a pay-as-you-go system that benefited the poor. Bergoglio intervened in a particularly forceful way in 2010 during the debate on equal marriage rights, publishing a letter on July 9 in which he declared that "there is also the envy of the devil, through whom sin entered the world, who cleverly aims to destroy the image of God: man and woman are mandated to grow, multiply and subdue the Earth", adding that "the father of lies seeks to sow confusion and deceive the children of God". What a way to literally demonize one's opponents! After Bergoglio's election, however, President Cristina Fernández Kirchner made a gesture of appeasement by issuing a lengthy statement: "In my name and in the name of the Argentine government, representing the people of our country, I wish to greet and express my congratulations on being elected as the new Roman pontiff of the Universal Church..." The Argentine Church will react by calling for an "ethical revolution" and to form new elites "in the truth" and capable of appreciating the constant exercise of social values... Cristina Fernández Kirchner, not being constitutionally able to run for a third term, will therefore support Daniel Scioli, candidate of the center-left... Macri is elected with 52.11% of the vote and the support of conservative Catholics. Francis had made it known through his journalist friend Alicia Barrios that he wanted "a government that looks the poor in the eye, with an economy led by good men and not by the savage forces of the market. The Pope's representative in Argentina, the Apostolic Nuncio of Paraguay, Archbishop Eliseo Agriotte will come to greet President Macri on behalf of the Pope. Argentine priest Guillermo Karcher, a member of the Holy See team, also met with members of the new government and offered Francis' congratulations and blessings to the new team in power. It has been written that Bergoglio had a bad relationship with Mauricio Macri. What the pope criticized him for was not being right-wing, but for not being right-wing enough by not appealing a decision in favour of gay marriage. Bergoglio said at the time that Macri was "gravely failing in his duty". The right-wing candidate has learned his lesson and was keen to disavow his spokesman, who claimed the right of people to marriage and abortion... He expressed his "deep respect and admiration for Pope Francis" adding "I am in favour of life" and recalling that he had vetoed, as mayor of Buenos Aires, an autonomous federal entity, the Supreme Court ruling on March 13, 2012, recognizing abortion in cases of rape. Relations remained so tense that Cristina Fernández Kirchner refused to attend the inauguration ceremony of the new president. As soon as he took office, the new president announced his intention to reduce the number of public jobs that would be created to "accommodate friends and family members. He also announced his desire to reorient Argentine diplomacy by ending Mercosur, the South American customs union, hostile to the United States, inviting on the very evening of his election to overthrow the Venezuelan government and inviting Lilian Tintori, wife of Leopoldo López, son of one of the most powerful families in Venezuela, leader of the opposition, sentenced to 13 years in prison for organizing the 2014 riots that killed 43 people. In addition, President Macri's decision to devalue Argentina's currency by 30 percent has thrown tens of thousands of protesters into the streets.

I have never idealized Hugo Chávez's Venezuela and its authoritarian regime and the productivist nature of its oil rent-based socialism/state capitalism, but the defeat of the left in the December 6, 2015 legislative elections is a bad thing for Venezuela and the region. The victory of the alliance of the right and social democrats/liberals known as the "Table of Democratic Unity" against the socialist candidates of President Nicolás Maduro, successor to Chávez who died in 2013, is not only a consequence of the economic crisis and the oligarchy's stranglehold on the media but also of the Catholic Church's commitment against the Bolivarian revolutions. The defeat of the Venezuelan socialist party candidates was welcomed by Manuel Valls in a letter to Jesus Torrealba, leader of the Table of Democratic Unity, ex-teacher, ex-member of the communist party, which he left in 1974, when he was only 16. Since then, he has become an extremely popular radio producer, banking on the aspiration of the *barrios* (inhabitants of the working class neighborhoods) to belong to the new middle classes. Relations between the chavist left and the Church of Rome, which have never been good, have deteriorated over time. The Catholic Church even accused President Chávez of supporting a dissident Catholic Church, the Reformed Catholic Church, which was officially recognized by the government in 2008. The defeat of chavism was prepared for a long time by the oligarchies, with the active support of the United States and the Church, as part of a real strategy of tension that created a climate of permanent coup d'état, which even gave rise to a few attempts. The year 2015, which will lead to the electoral defeat of the left, sees the Church becoming more and more openly involved against it. The operation was launched in January by Archbishop Óscar Andrés Rodríguez Maradiaga, Archbishop of Honduras, but above all secretary of the C9 (that small group of nine cardinals charged by Pope Francis with advising him on internal reforms in the Church). He proclaimed the end of chavism because of the shortages (the Church even mentioned the shortage of mass wine and hosts) while the government denounced the economic manipulations. A few weeks later, it was the turn of the Venezuelan Episcopal Conference to take up this criticism of "21st century socialism" presented as totalitarianism. It called on the population to reject "the decision of the national government and other organs of public power to impose a political-economic system of a Marxist or communist socialist type. The Archbishop of Cumana, Diego Padrón, explained to the voters that "the socialism of the 21st century" "contains many elements of Marxist-Leninist socialism that does not work. Nor does it work in Cuba. The government will accuse certain fractions of the Church of supporting coup attempts including the one of February 12, 2015. Young officers of the Bolivarian National Armed Forces aborted a new coup attempt involving high-ranking military officers and civilians linked to the far-right organization Primero Justicia with the support of the CIA. Venezuela has been facing a real "low intensity war" since the April 2002 coup d'état, which led to the arrest and detention of President Chávez for 47 hours. President Nicolás Maduro then sought a historic compromise with the Church by receiving Archbishop Padrón and Archbishop Parolin, the Vatican Secretary of State, at the palace and offering as a token of goodwill the re-examination of the situation of Ivan Simonovis - a former Caracas security officer - who was sentenced to 30 years in prison for his participation in the coup against Chávez in 2002. The opposition, however, denounced this as manipulation. Ivan Simonovis was finally placed under "house arrest" for "medical reasons" as of September 2015, but the violence persisted. The regime's attempt to use the Church to dialogue with the opposition and counter the violence that is developing on both sides fails. The Archbishop of Caracas, Jorge Urosa Savino, calls for closeness to God to reject violence and denounces the "moral crisis, a crisis of values, attitudes, motivations and conduct in the country" (sic). In early September 2015, this archbishop, president of the Venezuelan bishops' conference, member of the Pontifical Council for Justice and Peace, member of the Pontifical Commission for Latin America, a non-member but reputedly close to Opus Dei, took advantage of the hijacking of the Lord's Prayer into a prayer for Chávez by a delegate of the Venezuelan Socialist Party to further raise the pressure a few months before the legislative elections: "Our Chávez who is in heaven, on earth, in the seas and in us [...] do not lead us to the temptation of capitalism, but deliver us from the evil of oligarchy [...]" The bishops' conference officially protests and speaks of the sin of idolatry and blasphemy: "Symbols, prayers, and religious elements must be respected"; "No one is allowed to change the Lord's prayer or any other Christian prayer. " The controversy became so great that President Maduro himself felt compelled to defend the Venezuelan Socialist Party delegate and spoke of "a new Inquisition at work to massacre this humble woman" (sic). The Church did contribute to the Venezuelan left losing the legislative elections.

Why is Bergoglio called Francis?

Pope Francis is a good marketing product because since Benedict XVI the Catholic Church has entered the era of modern management. Francis continues and accentuates what was started by his predecessor. Two vital areas, communication and finance, are now partly outsourced to large international capitalist groups, the same ones that advise economic firms and develop the global strategies that Francis denounces!

Benedict XVI appointed Greg Burke, a prominent American journalist from Fox News, as *senior communications adviser* to the director of the Press Office. Burke is now the head of communications for the Secretariat of State, which is headed by the Vatican's number two. The head of the Vatican bank, Ernst von Freyberg, was also joined by two specialists in communications and finance, Max Hollenberg and Markus Wieser of Communications & Network Consulting. Francis has reinforced this movement by calling on the largest consulting groups such as KPMG, McKinsey, Ernst & Young, Promonotory Financial Group, etc.

Pope Francis of course explained in his first address to the press that he decided to call himself Francis as a tribute to St. Francis of Assisi. This name was suggested to him, at the time of his election, by the Brazilian Archbishop Claudio Hummes, who would have whispered to him "Don't forget the poor! Created Cardinal in 2001 by John Paul II, elevated in 2006 to the position of Prefect of the Congregation for the Clergy by Benedict XVI, and also a member of the Congregation for the Doctrine of the Faith, Hummes is a man of apparatus and orthodoxy who governs the 408,000 Catholic priests. Bishop Claudio Hummes is one of those priests who, although rather open-minded in their youth (hence his friendship with former Brazilian President Lula), have become increasingly reactionary. In the year 2000, he sadly made himself known by harshly sanctioning one of his priests, *Padre* Valeriano Paitoni, for having admitted that AIDS patients could use a condom[23]. It will be remembered that, in violation of protocol, this archbishop was at the side of the new pope during his appearance on the balcony of St. Peter's Palace. Archbishop Hummes, although a Franciscan, is above all a defender of the charismatic movement, which he believes is the postmodern response to modernity. Hummes is also known as a proponent of an evangelical preferential option for the poor that would no longer pit rich and poor, bosses and employees, but would work for goodwill among all God's children.

Bergoglio, as a good communicator, chose Francis as his name for pope, at the very moment when the Church is caught in repeated financial scandals with accusations of corruption, hidden financing, money laundering, arrests, suicides, document theft, Vatileaks, etc. The triggering event for Benedict XVI's resignation was the 2012 disclosure of secret documents by his own butler Paolo Gabriele (arrested on May 23, 2012 and imprisoned in the Vatican, sentenced to 18 months in prison with a suspended sentence, then pardoned by Pope Benedict XVI two months after his conviction). The objective was to push the Pope to resign in order to protect him from a future scandal, given the malfeasance and fratricidal wars, as evidenced by the confidential report given to the Pope on the very morning of his resignation, a report he had commissioned and for which he had given responsibility to Msgr. Julián Herranz Casado, an important member of Opus Dei since 1949. I am afraid that when the report was released, the shadow of a "gay lobby" within the Roman Curia was raised to better conceal the financial affairs, thus giving the international media a bone to pick.

Since then, Rome has carefully prepared its defense by hiring international advisors specializing in global financial capitalism and appointing Ettore Gotti Tedeschi, very close to Opus Dei, an international banker, to head the Institute for Religious Works (IOR - the Vatican bank) with the mission of reforming it to allow it to be on the list of banks that respect the anti-money laundering standards developed by the OECD. Gotti Tedeschi had participated in the preparation of the encyclical *Caritas in veritate* published by the Pope in July 2012 and which called for more transparent rules for the global financial system... It is known, thanks to the stolen and published documents, that Gotti Tedeschi, head of the IOR from 2009 to 2012, already wanted, against the wishes of other leaders, to accelerate the financial transparency of the Church. The Holy See's accounts are

---

23. http://golias-news.fr/article1109.html

in fact a labyrinth of corruption and money laundering whose known origins go back to the late 1980s, when Italian justice requested the arrest of the North American archbishop, Paul Marcinkus, long-time president of the Vatican bank. Marcinkus was a curious character, an interpreter for John XXIII, a bodyguard for Paul VI, and for a long time the third most important person in the Vatican before becoming the head of the IOR, where he became a specialist in tax havens and a friend of mafia networks. John Paul II used the argument of territorial sovereignty to oppose his extradition and avoid prison for services rendered to Rome, such as the secret financing of the Polish trade union Solidarność which he supported. Archbishop Marcinkus ended his days playing golf quietly in Arizona and leaving behind him 3.5 billion dollars in losses and dark corpses, such as Roberto Calvi, president of the Ambrosiano bank, partner of the IOR, found hanged on June 18, 1982 under the Blackfriars Bridge in London, or Michele Sindona, another Italian criminal banker, appointed financial advisor to the Vatican by John Paul II, member of the P2 lodge, who dies in prison while drinking a cyanide coffee. The venerable of the P2 lodge, Licio Gelli, member of the Knights of Malta, close to Silvio Berlusconi who belonged to his lodge, is suspected of having been involved in all the major Italian affairs of the post-war period. Gelli first took refuge in Argentina, where the P2 lodge had worked during the time of General Alejandro Agustin Lanusse (1918-1996) - as in other American countries - in the so-called "Gianoglio" operation, to facilitate the return of Perón. Admiral Massera, a member of the P2 lodge, was a great friend of Bergoglio. The former leader of the P2 lodge died in Arezzo, where he was under house arrest, on December 15, 2015, at the age of 96. Some authors, among them British journalist David Yallop, even hypothesized that Archbishop Marcinkus would have played a role in the surprising death of John Paul [1], after 33 days of pontificate, due to disputes over how to manage the finances of the Catholic Church.

But Ettore Gotti Tedeschi was to remain in office for just under three years. He was forced to resign by a vote of no confidence by all the bank's directors, just two days after the arrest of the pope's butler, while Italian justice was looking into a suspicious transfer (which was blocked) of 30 million dollars between the Vatican bank and Crédit Artigiano, and Gotti Tedeschi said he feared for his life and had made written arrangements in case of an accidental death... A statement will explain (a rarity in the Vatican) that the governance of the IOR had "deteriorated" between 2009 and 2012, under Gotti Tedeschi's presidency. There were even rumors that he was suffering from serious psychiatric problems. Since then, justice has recognized his innocence regarding the suspected money laundering and is now focusing on those who had gotten him removed from the IOR leadership, such as Paolo Cipriani, the IOR's director general, and his number two, Massimo Tulli, who had to resign in July 2013. Gotti Tedeschi explained himself in April 2014 in the Spanish Catholic magazine *Vida nueva*: "What I feel is bitterness, because it was the magistracy that brought to light the truth about what happened, while inside the Church, on the contrary, seems to prevail until now the position of the one who wanted to put me on the sidelines."

The German Ernst von Freyberg, a brilliant economist and renowned financier, married to a French woman and belonging to the highest aristocracy, member of the Sovereign Military Order of Malta, was then chosen by Benedict XVI in February 2013 to head the IOR and try to prevent new scandals. But, bad luck, we learn that part of his fortune comes from the fact that he is president of the Blohm & Voss shipyards in Hamburg, which manufacture luxury yachts but also... warships. He will commit himself not to deliver the latter.

Under his leadership, the Vatican bank has begun negotiating with Italy to lift (soon?) banking secrecy, in the manner of Switzerland and Liechtenstein. Francis simultaneously set up the C8 (the Council of Eight Cardinals, which became the de facto C9 in 2014 with the addition of Archbishop Parolin, Vatican Secretary of State) under the authority of Honduran Cardinal Óscar Andrès Rodríguez Maradiaga[24].

A new coup in July 2014: Ernst von Freyberg was replaced (at the initiative of C9?) by the Frenchman Jean-Baptiste de Franssu, another great aristocrat, a specialist in asset management. His mission will be to make the Vatican bank a true commercial bank capable of competing with the largest financial institutions by relying on asset management but also on "ethical" investment funds. Jean-Baptiste de Franssu was appointed on the advice of the Spaniard Vallejo Balda, the Prefecture's number two for economic affairs and a member of Opus Dei. This French financier is of course no stranger to the Church, since he participates in many Vatican commissions and actively supports the World Alliance of Youth, which is responsible for defending the Catholic conception of the family and sexuality within the major institutions (notably the UN).

---

24. See *above* "The Church of Francis against "21st Century Socialism"".

But a new scandal erupts again in November 2015 with a new case of leaks and the publication of compromising documents. This affair led to the immediate arrest of two characters, the sulphurous Francesca Immacolata Chaouqui, an eccentric consultant used to modernize the image of the Vatican bank, and above all Monsignor Lucio Ángel Vallejo Balda, the Opus Dei man behind the appointment of the new head of the Vatican bank... Francesca Immacolata Chaouqui would soon be released because of her close collaboration with the Vatican gendarmerie. Accused by Mgr Vallejo Balda of being responsible for the leaks, she in turn accuses the Spanish prelate of having recorded Pope Francis without his knowledge... These two presumed innocents (at the time of writing) were part of the famous Commission on the organization of economic and administrative structures (COSEA), charged by the Vatican with making proposals to ensure full financial transparency of the IOR! Two books, *Avarice* by Emiliano Fittipaldi, a journalist with the weekly *L'Espresso*, and *Via crucis* [Way of the Cross] by Gianluigi Nuzzi, of the Mediaset television group owned by the Berlusconi family, report that the donations received by the Holy See for the poorest were partly diverted to satisfy the luxury tastes of prelates. According to Emiliano Fittipaldi, 400 million euros were diverted from the "denier of St. Peter" for the needs of the Curia. The author takes as an example some 200,000 euros diverted from a foundation dependent on the Catholic hospital Bambino Gesù ("Child Jesus") to finance the renovation of the apartment of Cardinal Tarcisio Bertone, former number two of the Vatican. The 700-square-meter luxury apartment is far less modest than the 70-square-meter apartment that Pope Francis occupies at St. Martha's residence.

Didn't the conservative bishops, who elected Bergoglio knowing his taste for the apparent signs of frugality, and himself choosing to call himself Francis, rely on what sociologists call "magical thinking" which always consists in believing that "saying is doing"[25]? As if having a pope named Francis in reference to St. Francis of Assisi, the very image of material poverty, were enough to make a Church that is immensely rich a Church that is poor for the poor, as if this communication operation were enough to make people forget not only the repeated financial scandals but also the fact that this extreme wealth is due to agreements with Mussolini but also to relations with certain fascist states such as the misnamed "Independent State of Croatia" during the Second World War. Class action

---

25. John Langshaw Austin, *Quand dire, c'est faire*, Paris, " Points Essais ", Seuil, 1991.

suits were filed in 1999 in the United States by Holocaust survivors against the Vatican bank (protected by its status as a sovereign state) and also against the Franciscan Order of Friars Minor[26].

Our society, which loves legends, wants to believe the good Pope Francis when he says that he wants "a poor Church for the poor" or when he reminds us that "Peter does not have a bank account" (sic). Bishop Bergoglio could not ignore the work of the great Italian historian Giacomo Todeschini, professor at the University of Trieste, a great specialist in the economic role of the Franciscans[27]. Francis of Assisi and those close to him, like Thomas of Celano, were not a priori opponents of wealth, they even wanted economic actors to make their private wealth bear fruit through the production and circulation of goods, because what they were fighting against was hoarded wealth, that of the landowner and the aristocrat... In other words, St. Francis of Assisi is a father of capitalism, not of anticapitalism. According to St. Francis of Assisi, each person must find his or her place in society according to his or her ability to circulate wealth, to produce value. Professor Todeschini goes even further by noting that this Franciscan religiosity (that of the followers of evangelical poverty in the Vatican sauce) has provided a large part of the vocabulary of the Western capitalist economy. The Franciscan vocabulary would thus have created the capitalist economy... thus the exploitation of the wage earners, thus the impoverishment of the greatest number.

Giacomo Todeschini explains how austere degrowth, that of the Catholic right, is of great interest to the reactionary Church of Francis: "Beyond the irenic epinal image of Francis of Assisi as a kindly madman talking to birds and wolves, the sources reveal to us above all the history of a movement approved by a theocratic papacy (that of Innocent III and Gregory IX) establishing, as a criterion for defining Christian perfection, voluntary poverty, that is, the imitation of Christ as God capable, in his infinite power, of stooping to human mortality. Voluntary poverty thus appears, from the Middle Ages, as the conscious and sublime manifestation of a power, the power to renounce legitimately possessed wealth. Far from being a challenge to institutions, this choice of poverty affirms the

---

26. According to *Les Echos*: "No one really knows the real extent of the real estate patrimony linked to the Holy See, which would represent 20 to 22% of the total real estate assets in Italy.

27. Giacomo Todeschini, *Franciscan Wealth. De la pauvreté volontaire à la société de marché*, translated from the Italian by Nathalie Gailius and Roberto Nigro, Lagrasse (Aude), "Verdier Poche", Verdier, 2008.

will of perfect Christians to model themselves on the example of Christ by imitating the most paradoxical but at the same time the most imposing manifestation of divine power, the renunciation of the external, visible, material signs of this power. Both doctrinally and politically, voluntary poverty thus appears as the revelation of a rare and exclusive capacity for self-denial, reserved for an elite of inspired people illuminated directly by the divine spirit."

This austere degrowth is only a cover for evangelical poverty. One can be convinced of this by observing what this Church does to liberation theology and the preferential option for the poor.

What preferential option for the poor?

On September 11, 2013, Pope Francis received the 85-year-old Peruvian priest Gustavo Gutiérrez, considered one of the fathers of liberation theologies, since the publication in 1971 of his book *Theology of Liberation*. The meeting was cleverly staged by Rome, which paradoxically expected a kind of blessing of Pope Francis by Gutiérrez.

This return to grace of liberation theologies is celebrated by the networks of the Catholic right, including the journal *Limite*, but also by the Socio-political Observatory of the diocese of Fréjus-Toulon (famous for its dedemonization of the National Front). This meeting is the result of a long work of the Roman Curia to disarm liberation theologies and make them harmless: it is more accurate to speak of hijacking than recuperation, because it is a question of moving from a preferential option for the poor, aiming to eradicate poverty by suppressing the enrichment of a minority at the expense of the others, to an evangelical preferential option for poverty which does not (yet) dare to say its name, but which, under the guise of ecology and degrowth, advocates austerity for the poor while justifying, in God's plan, the existence of the rich.

Rome will show its teeth as long as these theologies represent a danger: John Paul II will affirm as early as 1973 that this "conception of Christ as a political man, a revolutionary, as the subversive of Nazareth, does not correspond to the catechesis of the Church. Ratzinger, then prefect of the Congregation for the Doctrine of the Faith, confirmed this condemnation without any ambiguity. He silenced more than a hundred theologians close to the people, including his ex-friend Leonardo Boff, who was condemned to "penitential silence" in 1984. The latter finally gave up the priesthood in 1992 in order to get married. Things began to move with the retreat of the revolutionary currents, to the point that Gutiérrez (who was never sanctioned) would be rehabilitated in 2004 by a letter from the same Ratzinger who "thanks the Most High for the satisfactory conclusion of this path of clarification and deepening. This return to normality was confirmed by the publication in 2004 of a book co-authored by Gustavo Gutiérrez and Archbishop Gerhard Ludwig Müller, the latter having become the head of the Congregation for the Doctrine of the Faith (formerly the Inquisition). The princes of the Church have thus pulled off a very nice coup by seizing on concepts thought to shake up the capitalist world and to challenge their authority. This bad move against liberation theologies had been prepared by Ratzinger who developed, as early as 1984 and then in 1986, what could be an acceptable liberation theology because it was cooked in the Vatican sauce. We must therefore oppose the theologies of liberation as conceived by the left-wing currents of the Church to the same theologies revisited by its right-wing currents.

John Paul II, less sympathetic to left-wing circles than Francis, also wrote that "the Church is deeply committed to this cause [of the worker], because she considers it her mission, her service, a test of her fidelity to Christ, so as to be truly the Church of the poor. And the poor appear in many ways; they appear in different places and at different times; they appear in many cases as a result of the violation of the dignity of human work" (*Laborem Exercens*).

Ratzinger's Instruction, *Libertatis Nuntius* (1984), against liberation theology said nothing different than Francis' text, but, other times other morals, while it was understood in its time as a declaration of war against liberation theologies, Francis' sweet words are received as a declaration of love. I invite the reader to read carefully this excerpt from Ratzinger's Instruction, and he will discover that the first "liberation" is that from original sin. Those who are fortunate enough not to have been born guilty of this dogma can undoubtedly act more effectively for the other liberations: "Liberation is first and foremost liberation from the radical bondage of sin. Its goal, and its end, is the freedom of the children of God, the gift of grace. It calls, as a logical consequence, for the liberation of multiple servitudes of a cultural, economic, social and political nature, all of which derive ultimately from sin, and which constitute so many obstacles preventing people from living in accordance with their dignity.

To discern clearly what is fundamental and what belongs to the consequences is thus an indispensable condition for a theological reflection on liberation. Indeed, in view of the urgency of the problems, some are tempted to place the emphasis unilaterally on liberation from earthly and temporal bondages, so that liberation from sin seems to be relegated to second place, and thus no longer has the primary importance that it has. The presentation of the problems they propose is thus confused and ambiguous. Others, with the intention of acquiring a more exact knowledge of the causes of the servitudes they wish to eliminate, make use, without sufficient critical precaution, of instruments of thought which it is difficult, if not impossible, to purify from an ideological inspiration incompatible with the Christian faith and with the ethical demands which flow from it."

The liberation theologians responded through the voice of Enrique Dussel: "The question is not to be able to eat something freely, but the question is to have something to eat", and they added that the popular Church, as understood by the Church since Vatican I, with Catholic Action in particular, is only a collaboration with the apostolate of the hierarchy, In other words, it is a way of maintaining the dependence of all lay movements on the "clerical class", whereas it would be necessary to put an end to the dualism between first and second class Christians and to eliminate the distinction between clergy and laity. In other words, never a Church conceived in the medieval mode, never this most centralized institution in the world, will be able to carry a theology of liberation, nor a theology of ecology. Ecologists have said enough that we need to invent another way of doing politics not to also want another way of doing religion! This is why liberation theology insisted so much on basic ecclesiastical communities, the only way to put an end to an intrinsically inegalitarian Church and allow it to carry a message of equality[28].

These same liberation theologians explain that the problem is not to demonstrate that God exists but that God is with the poor, in their struggles for liberation and, in particular, in the ecology of the poor; They add that popular pastoral work is not built from the outside but from the inside, that it does not go from the top to the bottom but from the bottom to the top, that evangelization (if we must keep the word) does not consist fundamentally in confronting atheism but idolatry (sic), that it is therefore appropriate to refuse the war of religions, sectarianism and proselytism.

---

28. Quoted in François Houtart *et al*, *Ruptures sociales et religion*, Paris, L'Harmattan/ Centre Tricontinental, 1994.

The Catholic Church cannot, for apparently dogmatic reasons, but in fact because it has always defended the powerful, even within itself, call into question the very structure of the (sinful?) inegalitarian system, it can only imagine making inequalities more bearable.

At a time when ecologist-Catholics are rediscovering the social doctrine of the Church, do we need to remind them that Pope Leo XIII, even before any social reform, preached submission to the people in the name of patience in the face of their bad fate: "The first principle to be put forward is that man must be patient with his condition; it is impossible for everyone in civil society to be raised to the same level [...] because it is she (nature) who has arranged among men differences as multiple as they are profound." The Church, however, does not dare to go to the end of its thesis, maintaining that since it has always been so, it will also always be so, so it has promised, for two millennia, an improvement and preached patience. The Church of today, like the Church of yesterday, invites, in reality, to accept the inequality of conditions and suffering and to reconcile the rich and the poor.

We will see, along the way, that the same dogmas which, in the name of the Christian faith, oppose the emphasis on "earthly servitudes" are also those which will prevent the planet from being saved.

The preferential option for the poor, seen from the left

Liberation theologies develop three revolutionary ideas.

As Gustavo Gutiérrez argues, "Liberation theology tells the poor that the situation they are living in is not God's will. It thus takes the opposite view from the usual theses advocating patience and submission. It even says that poverty is only the consequence of economic exploitation, so if there are impoverished people it is because there are enriched people. No compromise is therefore possible, and it is on this point that liberation theologians have been accused of making a pact with the Marxist devil. Liberation theologies also advance the notion of a "structure of sin": neither capitalism nor capitalists can be moralized.

The second major idea was to participate actively in the popular struggles, especially against the military dictatorships supported by the United States. The North American government considered that liberation theologies constituted a threat to its interests and called in the famous Rockefeller report (1969) and then in the Santa Fe documents (written between 1980 and 1986 by the CIA) for the development of sects ("new religious movements") to compete with a Church that was too insubordinate to the powerful[29].

The third major idea was the impossibility of developing a preferential option for the poor without at the same time changing the Church, without developing grassroots communities and questioning the distinction between clergy and laity. Liberation theologies are multiple because they depend on the historical contexts in which they are born: alongside a South American liberation theology, there are African and Asian liberation theologies, and we can even speak of women's liberation theologies when the Gospel becomes a source of commitment for the emancipation of women. All these liberation theologies, seen from the left, affirm that poverty is always an evil, that it destroys families and the human person, in short that the Church must fight against what generates poverty, capitalism and "maldevelopment" and must become a Church of the poor. The poverty that liberation theologians speak of is therefore first and foremost, and sometimes even exclusively, real poverty, material poverty... The voluntary poverty of those who choose to live like the poor cannot be justified by the idea that poverty is good in itself but by solidarity with the poor. Gutiérrez uses an image to make himself better understood: Jesus takes upon himself the sins not because he loves them, but because he loves sinners.

The preferential option for the poor, seen from the right

The preferential option for the poor in the Vatican style says something quite different. It is no longer a question of eliminating social inequalities, since Rome reminds us that they are natural and therefore inevitable because they are expressly willed by God, but of reminding us that no one, poor or rich, is outside the love of God. It then says that, even more than material and economic poverty, the Church must fight against cultural and especially evangelical poverty.

Father Pierre Coulange, theologian and economist, is a regular on the platforms of the Association pour la Fondation de Service politique (AFSP), which also publishes the journal *Liberté politique*, the Association

---

29. Paul Ariès, *Le retour du diable*, Villeurbanne, Golias, 1997; "Les sectes et le rapport Rockefeller at http://www.alterinfos.org/archives/DIAL-479.pdf; https://www.monde-diplomatique.fr/cahier/ameriquelatine/eglise

of Catholic Economists (AEC) and Ichtus. This member of the Notre-Dame de Vie Theological Institute has been much in demand lately because he is a good specialist in this new "preferential option for the poor in Pope Francis' exhortation" since he is the author of a thesis published under the title *God, friend of the poor: a study on the connivance between the Most High and the little ones*. Pierre Coulange readily acknowledges that the concept needs to be clarified. He wants to distinguish between what Francis takes from tradition and what he brings. The Pope takes from tradition the idea that "God loves the poor, and since we are in the image of God, we too must love the poor" (sic). Pierre Coulange insists, moreover, on the fact that poverty according to Francis must be understood in a broad way and not only from a material point of view: the concern for the poor is first of all the concern for their souls, thus their evangelization! Pierre Coulange also explains that this preferential option for the poor does not mean choosing the poor against the rich. For this notion is neither excluding nor even based on factual observations. Pierre Coulange then develops what would be new in Francis. The Pope would break with the condemnation of avarice and the avaricious, in short, it would no longer be a question (only?) of condemning those who let the poor starve. In this way, Francis would put an end to the moralizing discourse of the pre-19th century and even to that of a certain conception of the Church's social doctrine, for he would make poverty a "theological category" and no longer a sociological one. The preferential option for the poor would therefore have nothing in common with the point of view of the NGOs, because it would be a discourse on God... As a consequence, Francis would command us to move from humanitarianism to charity, because if humanitarianism reminds us that there is something human in every man, charity reminds us of the presence of God in every poor person. Pierre Coulange wants to prove that Francis maintains that the word solidarity is worn out, because it should aim at more than the relief of material misery, since it would be a question of reaching "the contemplative dimension of love" (sic). Good charity would therefore not consist in doing good but in loving God, through the poor. Pierre Coulange defends himself, of course, by refusing to see in this attitude of contemplation only cynicism, but he reminds us that for Francis it is not a question of proceeding to another distribution of goods and wealth, because "we desire more", "our dream goes further" (sic). The Catholic of the 21st century is still invited to love the poor as another Christ (for this reason it is better that there are enough poor people left), but what is new is that the Church recognizes that these poor people have an active role in salvation, they are exemplary, "because by their sufferings they know the suffering Christ". Father Coulange finally presents us with a first-class burial of liberation theologies.

The preferential option for the poor with Opus Dei

The dilemma is simple: can one believe in the preferential option for the poor when the Legionaries of Christ, Communion and Liberation, and Opus Dei are leading the way? One of the main conductors of this music is Martin Schlag, Vicar General of Opus Dei in Austria, Papal Chaplain in 2012, consultant to the Pontifical Council for Justice and Peace, professor of moral and social theology at the Pontifical University of the Holy Cross, and a great defender of this new preferential option for the poor. Martin Schlag explains in his sermons to members of Opus Dei that Francis' words on the preferential option for the poor resonate deeply with the writings of St. Josemaría Escrivá de Balaguer (founder of Opus Dei). "It can be said that the founder of Opus Dei lived and learned to live a 'preferential, but not exclusive, option for the poor'"[30]. Schlag readily acknowledges that Josemaría Escrivá de Balaguer did not speak openly of this notion, since during his lifetime it had a different content because of the Marxist heresies. The new liberation theology would, of course, have nothing in common with the one that had led the churches of America to engage in struggles alongside the peoples.

The preferential option for the poor proposed by Opus Dei has two sides: first, it is to organize the integration of the poor into the market economy (capitalism), because this would be the only way to prevent revolutions and to deconstruct the welfare state (i.e., the social state). The integration of the poor countries into the capitalist economy is however the accentuation of the inequality of the terms of trade, it is the reinforcement of extractivism in the service of the big firms, it is the destruction of the local economies and the subsistence agriculture! The integration of the popular circles within the capitalist economy is the break-up of the other pre- or post-capitalist ways of living, of the other ways of thinking and dreaming, it is the end of any autochthony of the people of little, it is the homogeneity of the capitalist ways of life!

---

30. http://www.fr.josemariaescriva.info/article/saint-josemaria-et-son-amour-des-pauvres-

I would like to draw the reader's attention to the second aspect of the preferential option for the poor according to Opus Dei. The Vicar General of Opus Dei explains that "one cannot speak of love for the poor in the spirit of Saint Josemaría without mentioning the virtue of poverty (Holy Poverty with capitals). The Church even has a word to justify this need to keep the poor poor poor: "Christocentrism". Martin Schlag justifies this Christocentrism by explaining that "the source of these two virtues, love of the poor and poverty, is the same. It is the Christian's desire to imitate Christ our Lord in order to become one with Jesus, our model. He even specifies: "When we speak of 'love of the poor' we speak of it in the socio-economic sense, referring to those people in our society who suffer from lack of material means and not to those people who strive to live individually in detachment." And: "If we are close to Christ, if we follow in his footsteps, we must love poverty, detachment from earthly goods, privations with all our heart" (J. Escrivá, *Forge*, 997). He then quotes the founder of Opus Dei to help us understand what true charity should be: "Christian charity is not limited to helping those who need financial resources. It aims above all to respect and understand each individual as such, in his or her intrinsic dignity as a human being and as a child of the Creator" (J. Escrivá, *When Christ Passes By*, 72). Schlag concludes on this point: "These words are the opposite of a reduction of love to the poor and needy, a political program of class struggle as was the case in the programs of radicalized liberation theology."

For Opus Dei, it is not a question of fighting poverty by fighting capitalism, but of living evangelical poverty! Martin Schlag sums up this new option with a series of questions: "To what extent is it necessary to do without everything in order to live an 'evangelical' poverty and thus identify with Christ? And to what extent is the Christian obliged to give alms to the poor? Must he give only his superfluous? Or should he also give his necessities? And what is necessary? The essence of the answer lies in its conclusion: the preferential option for the poor does not exclude love for the rich because it is a secret: "A secret - A secret, to be shouted from the rooftops: these world crises are crises of saints. God wants a handful of men "his own" in every human activity. - And then *pax Christi in regno Christi* ('the peace of Christ in the kingdom of Christ')" (J. Escrivá, *Camino* [Way], 301).

From the preferential option for the poor to the privileged love of the rich

The Neocatechumenal Way is part of the new battalions of the Church with which Francis, like Benedict XVI or John Paul II before him, hopes to "re-evangelize" the planet. I explained in *The Return of the Devil* (*op. cit.*) how this type of movement imitates the forms of religiosity of the "new religious movements" and sometimes even of the sects in order to develop a reactionary psycho-religiosity on the political level. The neo-catechumenal path, like the whole charismatic movement, in fact recycles in the Church the theology of prosperity that was first born within the Pentecostal movements. Jesus came to preach to the poor so that they could become rich. The faithful are promised prosperity, health and freedom from demonic influences, hence the importance of the laying on of hands. The central thesis of prosperity theology is that social ills are a divine punishment reserved for unbelievers and that they can only be overcome by conversion (*born again, as* President G.W. Bush claimed to be) and not, of course, by struggles or social laws. The most famous theorists of this trend are Kenneth Copeland, a very controversial televangelist and author of *The Laws of Prosperity* (1974), and the Brazilian theologian Edir Macedo Bezerran, the richest man in Brazil according to *Forbes* magazine, founder of the Universal Church of the Kingdom of God. These theses have gradually infiltrated the Catholic Church, first in its economic circles and in Michael Novak's entourage (see *below*), and then more widely, forcing Francis to remind people that salvation does not lie in a theory of prosperity. Even Filippo Santoro, then bishop of Petrópolis (Rio de Janeiro state), a member of Communion and Liberation, was forced to declare that "the rise of the sects represents a serious failure for liberation theology: the poor, on whom it counted for revolutionary change, have chosen capitalist redemption, preferring to embrace the theology of prosperity.

The Neocatechumenal Way, a charismatic movement recognized by John Paul II, present in more than 6,000 parishes in more than 120 countries, often denounced for its sectarian aberrations, including by Rome, also advocates a kind of theology of prosperity. The words of Thierry Bizot, a program producer, grandson of Jean-Jacques Bizot, deputy governor of the Bank of France, nephew of Jacques de Larosière, governor of the Bank of France, lover of Francis ("I only know people who love the pope"), and member of the Neocatechumenal Way, show how the preferential option for the poor can sometimes lead to the affirmation that the rich are more in need of God's love: "I am often asked if my encounter with Jesus has changed my relationship with money. Around this question always hovers the famous sentence of Jesus about the rich, for whom it would be more difficult to enter the kingdom of heaven than for a camel to pass through the eye of a needle [...]. When I reread this parable of the rich young man, I cannot see any condemnation. On the contrary, it is said that Jesus, and this is rare enough to underline, loves this young man right away. Moreover, when the young man asks what more he can do, Jesus gives him a magnificent gift: he offers him to come with him, in his own circle, in his VIP square one might say [...]. Jesus looks at him sadly as he leaves and notices something very simple, one could say something that is based on common sense: it is more difficult for the one who is rich in this life, rich in goods, material or immaterial, to give up everything, than for the one who has nothing to lose. The rich man therefore needs Jesus' love more than the poor man"[31].

Francis a reforming pope?

Francis is undoubtedly a reforming pope, and it is even certain that he will face resistance from a large section of the Roman Curia. It is true that Bergoglio was made pope by the bishops and not by the Curia, but to imagine that the latter could be opposed to the conclave is a shortcut. Some people, however, speak of a good pope being prevented by an evil Curia. We heard this argument before at the time of Vatican II when it became clear that the hopes of left-wing Catholics would be largely dashed. No one can deny the impact of the centralism of the Curia within the Church, but this image of the good king poorly advised or poorly served by those close to him serves above all to mask the influence of the networks that make and unmake the (strategies of) popes, such as Opus Dei, Communion and Liberation, and the Knights of Columbus. Francis appears in the eyes of those who made him pope in 2013 and also of those who support him within the Curia (because they are undoubtedly in the majority to be favorable to him) as the pope of the last chance to

---

31. http://bizot.blog.croire.com/2012/05/12/riche-et-pauvre/

try to save the Catholic Church. To save the Church not so much from its adversaries as from itself, because the Roman institution is today out of breath, if not seriously ill. The Church certainly suffers from financial, political and sexual scandals, but it suffers above all, like all institutions, from its inability to question itself. This sociological law is even truer for this institution, because of its centralism and the weight of its past that sticks to it.

Paradoxically, what made the Church strong in the 20th century - being a medieval monarchist institution in the midst of modernity - can become a weakness when history accelerates too quickly for it. Hence the temptations of the Church to cling to the past, to miss the good old days, and the temptations of another part of the Church to jump over the wall, imagining that being postmodern would be a way of reconnecting with pre-modernity, by overlooking the three cursed events that were, in its eyes, the philosophy of the Enlightenment, the French Revolution and the Russian Revolution. The Bolshevik parenthesis seems to be closed in the eyes of many princes of the Church with the collapse of the Soviet bloc, but also with the reversal of the essence of liberation theologies.

The parenthesis opened with the French Revolution could also be in the process of being closed with the victory of the third world conservative revolution: the first one having seen, in the aftermath of 1789, all the reactionary forces (including the Catholic Church) rise up in reaction to the philosophy of the Enlightenment, in Portugal with miguelism, in Spain with isabellism, in France with all the counter-revolutionary currents; the second conservative revolution has its roots in the wave of conservative revolutions that hit Europe between the wars (in Italy, Germany, Spain, Portugal, and the Vichy France that a certain Church held dear); the third conservative revolution was born in the aftermath of the Second World War around the book by Russell Kirk (1918-1994), *The Conservative Mind: From Burke to* Eliot, in which the American Catholic political scientist intended to give new foundations to neoconservatism in order to break with the nostalgia of the Old Regime, which was already considered far too Franco-European... This theme would be taken up by Friedrich August von Hayek in his famous article "Why am I not a conservative? "This third conservative revolution will triumph with Pinochet, Reagan, Thatcher, Sarkozy, etc.

The Church of Francis translates into the Catholic field the victory of this third conservative revolution which forces it to be less "conservative" in certain areas (such as communication style). Francis wants to reform many things in order to save the Church and its power and even to try to regain certain positions in society. We would be wrong to imagine that this strategy opposes two clear-cut camps, in the sense that not only do the boundaries remain fluid according to the issues, but also in the sense that each prelate is himself divided, divided... One does not change so easily a 2,000-year-old institution, especially when it risks calling into question certain consequent material advantages. Francis is thus taking up the fight of Benedict XVI and John Paul II to put order in the Church's accounts and to submit them to the principles of accounting and management that the smallest association under the 1901 law practices. The management of the Vatican is a real mismanagement with uncontrolled expenses, with a total absence of forecasting, with the absence of estimates, etc. Francis thus affirmed before COSEA in July 2013: "It can be said, without exaggeration, that a large part of the expenses are out of control [...]. The number of employees has increased too much. This situation is wasting a lot of money [...]. We must go further in clarifying the origin of expenses and the forms of payment. We need to have a protocol from quotation to payment. One of the managers told me: "When people come to present us with an invoice, we have to pay". Well no, we don't pay. If work has been done without an estimate, without authorization, we don't pay...". The Pope even insists on "details", recommending to ask for three estimates for the same project and above all to read the fine print, "the paragraphs, that's what they say, I think?", before making decisions[32]. That Francis wants to engage in an accounting reform of this nature is certainly noteworthy, but that does not make him in any way a "revolutionary" pope!

Francis also attacks some of the ostentatious signs of wealth of the princes of the Church, and in particular the size of their apartments: "Bishop de Paolis, cardinal and prefect emeritus of the APSA, has 445 square meters, a slum similar to that of the cardinal and prefect emeritus of the Congregation for Institutes of Consecrated Life and Societies of Apostolic Life, Archbishop Franc Rodé, or that of the very traditionalist Archbishop Burke (417 m2). A little more than the 356 square meters of Cardinal Kurt Koch, President of the Pontifical Council for Promoting Christian Unity, and a little less than the 500 square meters of Cardinal

---

32. Gino Hoel, "La guerre de la Curie contre le pape François," in *Golias-Hebdo*, No. 407, week of November 12-18, 2015.

Ouellet, Prefect of the Congregation for Bishops.... These needy cardinals usually pay symbolic annual rents: 29 euros per year, in the heart of Rome."[33] My friends at the catholic magazine *Golias* are pleased with Francis' choice to live in a modest 70 m2 apartment, but that in no way makes him a "revolutionary" pope, nor even a "progressive" pope in the 20th century sense!

Francis also intends to profoundly overhaul the structures of the Curia and their functioning, which is, at times, rather... surprising. The commission created for this purpose in July 2013 and called "commission on the economic and administrative structures of the Holy See" was dissolved six months later while Francis had taken the wise precaution of appointing only lay people to it, with the exception of Bishop Balda, secretary since 2001 of this prefecture of Economic Affairs (who was arrested in November 2015 by the Vatican gendarmerie in the context of the second Vatileaks affair). Reforming the structures of the Vatican does not, however, make Francis a sympathetic pope, but a more effective one, knowing in particular how to learn from the management advice that the Church buys at a very high price from the main capitalist management consulting groups (see *below*). Francis is not reforming the Church to make it a poor Church at the service of the poor, he is reforming the Church to enable it to get through the current bad patch and to put it in a position to win its share of the market for the return of religion.

Francis' close guard: a quarteron of *monsignori*

The Pope does not seem to be in a hurry to reform the Curia for the simple reason that he has set up a small parallel Curia that is totally submissive and faithful to him, composed essentially of Argentine and Maltese religious... which naturally makes the Italians, who are usually the recipients of these posts, uncomfortable, as well as certain prelates. For example, the Cardinal Archbishop of New York, Timothy Dolan, does not hide his disappointment: "We wanted a pope with good management and leadership skills, and so far we haven't seen much."

This parallel Curia is composed of about ten men. The Maltese Alfred Xvereb, former second secretary to Benedict XVI, and Fabian Pedacchio

---

33. *Id. at ibid.*

Leaniz, a creature of Archbishop Giovanni Battista, are just two examples. These shadowy men carry out Francis' orders, but Francis has his own advisors or "go-to" men he knows he can count on: Cardinals Oscár Maradiaga, Lorenzo Baldisseri, Claudio Hummes and Archbishop Filippo Santoro, who work alongside Cardinal Pietro Parolin.

Archbishop Pietro Parolin has been Francis' official right-hand man since he appointed him Vatican Secretary of State. Trained at the school for nuncios (ambassadors) of the Church (Pontifical Ecclesiastical Academy), he is a man of the shadows, specializing in the most sensitive issues such as the Gulf War, the Nuclear Non-Proliferation Treaty, North Korea, the Middle East, etc. His dispatch to Venezuela by Benedict XVI in 2009 as apostolic nuncio has been interpreted as a relegation, even a sanction. This assumption underestimates the threat that the Vatican sees in the renewal of 21st century socialism in South American countries: the Church wants to defend its interests and prevent a revival of liberation theologies based on the ongoing Bolivarian revolutions. On this occasion, Benedict XVI elevated him to the dignity of archbishop. Pietro Parolin adopted as his motto "Who can separate us from the love of Christ"... by which he meant not the socialism of President Chávez! Venezuela wanted to renegotiate the existing concordat with the Vatican and denounced the interference of the Church hierarchy in the country's affairs, including by welcoming a protest leader, a student refugee at the embassy. President Chávez, never stingy with a good word, he who usually calls *monsignori* "cavemen" and "troglodytes", declared in welcoming him: "You have to perform an exorcism in the Vatican office in Caracas." Pietro Parolin will make a series of compromises with the authorities. The negotiations (still) in progress are not only about Venezuela but about all the countries involved in the Bolivarian Alliance, which groups together the socialist countries of Latin America. Francis called Pietro Parolin to his side in August 2013 and made him a cardinal in February 2014. He is responsible for carrying the Pope's word including when he says at a ceremony honoring the founder of Opus Dei: "He [the Pope] hopes that the precious example of the priestly life of St. Josemaría, precursor of the Second Vatican Council when it proposed the universal call to holiness, will awaken in all the faithful of the great family of Opus Dei a certainty," including when he judged that the Irish vote in favor of same-sex marriage would be a "defeat for humanity," justifying these unacceptable words by admitting that they were those of the Pope himself (sic).

Monsignor Lorenzo Baldisseri was much less known to the general public until the day of the pope's election. Francis' first gesture was to remove his own parma-red skullcap and place it on the head of the man who was then serving as secretary of the conclave, thus making the archbishop a cardinal or, in his own words, "You are a cardinal by halves," since the official act of appointment was still missing. This "half-cardinal" appears strangely on the balcony at the side of the Pope, still ostensibly wearing the skullcap handed down by Francis. This "half-cardinal" will also impose his presence during a hushed meeting organized the day after the election for the cardinals in title... Specialists recall that far from being a tradition, there is only one other case in history, when John XXIII, just elected, gave his own skullcap to Alberto di Jorio, who was also the secretary of the conclave that had just designated him.

Monsignor Lorenzo Baldisseri is in fact a man of the cloth who first made his career in Vatican diplomacy, then was appointed by Benedict XVI as secretary of the Congregation for Bishops, meaning that he had the central responsibility for preparing the appointment of bishops. Francis has also since entrusted him with the responsibility for the difficult synod on the family in October 2015. Lorenzo Baldisseri was also one of the prelates present (he was then there as apostolic nuncio, i.e. Vatican ambassador) during the famous meeting in Aparecida... This Monsignor was always the man of the difficult missions of the Church; thus, it is he who will be in charge of re-establishing the tarnished prestige of the Church in Haiti, where the episcopal hierarchy took position against the popular demands, whereas the people of the Church recognized themselves in the theories of liberation and created basic communities. The history of the Haitian Church allows us to understand what is at stake under the notion of the popular Church. The Haitian Episcopal Conference of August 29, 1987, openly warned against the notion of the popular Church, which was dear to Father Aristide, not yet president of the Republic, but a fervent follower of liberation theologies: "The Church is not born of the people, if the word 'people' is given a purely political content, by reducing it to certain strata of the population to the exclusion of certain groups that are considered not to belong to the people. This necessarily introduces into the Church the class struggle, the acceptance of violence and a certain political radicalization. The bishops even added that "the popular Church opposed to the Church presided over by its legitimate pastors [...] is a 'deviation' to be combated." The consequences were tragic: not only did the bishops deepen the gap between the Church hierarchy and the people, but they also designated Father Aristide, spokesman for the popular Church, as a prime target. Several attempts to attack him and other "red" priests failed, including the burning of the Church of St. John Bosco during a ceremony organized by Aristide, which left 12 dead and dozens injured... As soon as he was elected president of the center-left Republic, Father Aristide suffered an attempted coup d'état organized by the former leader of the "tontons macoutes" with the complicity of the archbishop of Port-au-Prince, Mgr Ligondé, uncle of the ex-wife of the dictator Duvalier[34]. Half a million demonstrators from the working class neighborhoods prevented the success of the putsch. The angry people then turned against the Church: the cathedral and the headquarters of the Episcopal Conference were set on fire while Bishop Ligondé was forced into hiding. The mob ransacked the residence of the Apostolic Nuncio and humiliated him by publicly undressing him. The crowd reproached Bishop Ligondé for having, in his sermon of January 1st, 1991, legitimized a priori the coup d'état that was to come. An old story? Not so sure! Bishop Ligondé died on April 8, 2013. The religious ceremony took place in the presence of the Apostolic Nuncio Bernardito Auza. In his homily, Bishop Guire Poulard, praised the former archbishop of Port-au-Prince who, he said, was an outstanding humanist and philanthropist...!

Monsignor Óscar Andrés Rodríguez Maradiaga is the first minister of Francis. His biography has the same shadows as the Pope's, and his positions, which seem to be very sympathetic, become darker upon examination. Maradiaga has already been twice *papabili* ("pope in waiting") despite his young age, and he could well succeed Francis. Among other things, the pope has asked him to head the C9, the group of nine cardinals charged with advising the pope on reforming the Curia, and to preside, in October 2015, over the last council on the family. Óscar Maradiaga has been denounced for his attitude towards a military coup, in this case the one of June 28, 2009 in Honduras, which he publicly supported despite the dozens of deaths, thousands of arrests, the use of torture and the closure of protesting media, such as Radio Progreso run by Jesuit fathers, which earned him the nickname *Cardenal Golpista* ("cardinal putschist") painted in large black letters on the walls of religious establishments. Maradiaga also played a major role

---

34. Paul Ariès, *La Scientologie, laboratoire du futur ? Les secrets d'une machine infernale*, Villeurbanne, Golias, 1997.

in the surrender of liberation theology in 2007, as he helped Bergoglio and Santoro draft the final document. However, Óscar Maradiaga is known as a convinced anti-capitalist, a resolute opponent of liberalism, proposing, for example, to partially cancel the debts of 18 poor countries. Óscar Maradiaga is considered to be a friend of the poor, to the point that he is presented as a continuation of liberation theologies, although he was one of their main destroyers. He does not hide his reactionary character in matters of morals, going so far as to maintain that "the use of condoms does not prevent the transmission of AIDS at all". Bishop Maradiaga was to be awarded an honorary doctorate from the Catholic University of Paris in 2009, the same day as the very Catholic Michel Camdessus, former head of the IMF, who is responsible for globalized capitalism. An international mobilization allowed to suspend this disastrous project. Thus, those who defeated liberation theology are now presenting themselves as the heirs of the movement, in order to better occupy the field and prevent, in effect, any new revolutionary heresy. Bishop Maradiaga is still the head of Caritas International.

Archbishop Filippo Santoro is an Italian archbishop, a true champion of liberation theology at the Aparecida Convention, an important member of Communion and Liberation, which he led in South America, and was appointed Metropolitan Archbishop of Taranto by Benedict XVI. He was appointed metropolitan archbishop of Taranto by Benedict XVI. We remember that it was he who was charged by Francis to define new ways of life in accordance with his new theology of poverty and ecology. I will speak more about his movement Communion and Liberation later.

We have already mentioned Monsignor Claudio Hummes, the one who indirectly breathed the name of Francis into the future pope, prefect of the Congregation for the Clergy, who governs the 408,000 Catholic priests. This prince of the Church never ceases to affirm that "the Church no longer functions" and that "it needs a reform of its structures". Close to the poor, since he had created a street ministry for the homeless, he fights the (political) theologies of the revolution and relies on the charismatic renewal to fight the evangelists using the same means as they do.

Pope Francis is therefore as reactionary as his predecessors in the area of morality (marriage, contraception, abortion) and it is not by chance that it is under his pontificate that Christian crowds, particularly in France, have marched against equal rights and the questioning of sexist clichés. Pope Francis can, however, take advantage of the zeitgeist to move on to other retrograde themes, something his predecessors could not afford given a much less favorable ideological balance of power. The Church is an old lady who has often known how to choose the right men at the right time, taking into account the different circumstances and potentialities.

The Pope's networks

Despite the dogma of papal infallibility, which proclaims that the bishop of Rome cannot err when he speaks *ex cathedra* on matters of faith or morals, and despite the power of the Curia, the management of the Church is a collective affair in which numerous movements, obediences and orders participate. Not in the sense that the Vatican is governed by democracy, but by intrigues, twists and turns, power struggles, and alliance games that are made and unmade according to situations and opportunities that are often very earthly. These large battalions of the Church that are now in the ascendancy are no longer those of past centuries, including the 20th century, with Catholic Action. What are the networks on which Francis can rely to govern the Church?

Pope Francis and Communion and Liberation

Benedict XVI was known for his ideological closeness to the ultra-conservative movement Communion and Liberation (Comunione e Liberazione), founded in 1954 by Don Luigi Giussani (1922-2005) in order to reconcile faith, economic and social commitment and politics. Ratzinger presided at the funeral of the founder of Communion and Liberation, who should soon be canonized (the process is underway).

Pope Francis is also very close to Communion and Liberation, so much so that the *National Catholic Reporter* spoke of "one of Pope Francis' allegiances" that may well tell us something about the future of the Church. Not only did Bishop Bergoglio speak regularly at the big meeting in Rimini, but he also promoted Luigi Giussani's book. The *ciellini* (members of Communion and Liberation) have long been the most resolute opponents of the Jesuits and in particular of the Jesuit cardinal of Milan, Carlo Maria Martini (1927-2012), who considered that the Church was "two hundred years behind" and whom the progressive currents wanted to see elected pope.

Communion and Liberation is, like the other new big battalions of the Catholic Church, an ultraconservative and very authoritarian organization. Communion and Liberation thus proceeded to idealize the Middle Ages as a blessed period of profound unity between faith and life. Luigi Giussani maintained that medieval man was the ideal human being. Communion and Liberation rejects the philosophy of the Enlightenment and condemns modernism and the attitude of openness to the world, but without showing anti-intellectualism, which has allowed it to be present in the academic world. Communion and Liberation organizes every year the great meeting of Rimini which gathers about 700,000 people and which has received (four times) Cardinal Ratzinger, who became Pope Benedict XVI, John Paul II, the Argentinean bishop Bergoglio, who became Pope Francis, but also Silvio Berlusconi, Mario Monti, Tony Blair, Lech Walesa... And, on an infinitely more modest level, myself, curiously invited to give a conference against "McDonaldisation" and junk food (without knowing what I was getting into).

The Church of Rome knows it can count on this movement, as in 1974, when the Vatican entrusted it with the fight against the law establishing divorce in Italy, while the other currents, notably the dioceses, were reluctant. Communion and Liberation then published a curious eight-page document, "About Divorce", with a circulation of nearly one million copies, which described divorce as a "bourgeois reform" (sic), a prose that was symptomatic of its desire to blur the boundaries and not be seen as a conservative movement.

Communion and Liberation will always know how to turn its vocabulary, its forms of action, its know-how in terms of agitprop against the left. The movement openly claims this mimicry by explaining that it is indeed borrowing the structures of the left but bringing another soul. Communion and Liberation is a religious, political and financial force. The Communion and Liberation movement is often accused of being a "Church within the Church" (*Chiesa netta Chiesa*) because of its strategy of conquering power to the detriment of the other movements of Catholic Action and the parishes. It has half a dozen bishops and a great many institutions. This lay organization has become the most important in Italy, with about 120,000 members, 90,000 of whom are in the peninsula alone.

Communion and Liberation is also sometimes derisively referred to as "Communion and Billing" because of its considerable economic power, estimated at about 5% of Italian GDP, with a network of 34,000 commercial and industrial companies and more than 1,000 organizations in the non-profit sector.

Communion and Liberation is, along with Opus Dei, the Church's main instrument of intervention in the political field, but whereas Opus Dei aims to convince the powerful, Communion and Liberation seeks to create a large popular party. Communion and Liberation was therefore designed above all to engage in politics, from Christian Democracy to Forza Italia through various movements. Thus Mario Mauro, elected on the lists of Berlusconi's Forza Italia, vice-president of the European Parliament (2004-2009), Minister of Defense in the Letta government under the Civic Choice movement, which he left in 2013 to found The People for Italy is a prominent member of Communion and Liberation. He had even been a serious candidate for the presidency of the European Parliament elected in 2009 despite (thanks to?) his strong positions against the "Christianophobia" of Europe. Communion and Liberation is now suffering from the explosion of Berlusconi's party and the scandals involving some of its leaders. For example, the megalomaniac Roberto Fornigoni, who built the tallest tower in Italy to house his offices when he was president of Lombardy (between 1995 and 2012), was forced to resign because he was accused of fraud and misappropriation of public funds. He was immediately rehired as president of the parliamentary committee on agriculture, before being indicted again in another financial scandal, this time involving the Maugeri Foundation. The bad tongues estimate the gifts from which he would have benefited at nine million euros and the embezzlement of funds at 70 million euros.

Communion and Liberation is therefore obliged to be more discreet and to choose as successor to Fr. Luigi Giussani a Spaniard, Fr Julián Carrón. Communion and Liberation was not officially among the organizers of the great Manifesto for All that mobilized a million people in Rome to defend the "traditional family", but curiously, among the organizers was Senator Roberto Fornigoni of Area Popolare (self-identified as a center-right movement)! Pope Francis also refrained from participating directly in this (spontaneous?) demonstration, but took advantage of the rally to denounce "the ideological colonizations that poison the family".

Pope Francis will do nothing, however, against the Communion and Liberation octopus, despite the political and financial scandals that are accumulating, because of its religious, economic and political, but also ideological weight. Communion and Liberation is an essential laboratory of ideas for Francis, even if this influence is not claimed or even systematic. That is why Pope Francis met on March 7, 2015, in St. Peter's Square, with more than 80,000 members of the movement on the occasion of the sixtieth anniversary of its birth and the tenth anniversary of the death of its founder. Communion and Liberation is thus all the more comfortable with Pope Francis' condemnations of "savage capitalism", as one can be certain that it is this movement that has passed on to him the codes of this critique rather than liberation theologies. Communion and Liberation denounced international capitalism, financial capitalism and the "power" that manipulates it, long before Francis did. Communion and Liberation accused Christian Democracy for a long time of having allowed "neo-capitalism" to develop to the detriment of Christianity: "Capitalism finds its origin in the bracketing of the living fact which is the Church as the body of Christ.

Communion and Liberation today provides other essential notions that are immediately taken up by Pope Francis and the eco- Cathos. Thus Roberto Fontolan, director of the International Center of Communion and Liberation (at the international congress on the mission of ecclesial movements and new communities in the formation and dissemination of faith, organized on May 16, 2013 at the Pontifical University Regina Apostolorum, in Rome), explains that "the current crisis, in fact, even before being a religious crisis is an anthropological crisis." Communion and Liberation also intends to impose, especially on Europe, the question of "Christianophobia".

Pope Francis and the Legionaries of Christ

Sexual pervert, pedophile, psychopath, morphine addict, bribe taker, forger, plagiarist, identity thief, liar, manipulator, schemer, swindler, thief, criminal, incest offender, these are some of the charges against Marcial Maciel (1920-2008), founder of one of the most powerful congregations in the Catholic Church today: The Legionaries of Christ, with whom I had to battle at length when I was working on the issue of cults and mental manipulation[35].

This far-right organization has long been protected by the Church of Rome, notably by Popes John Paul II and Benedict XVI. Its founder was

---

35. Paul Ariès, *La Scientologie, laboratoire du futur ? Les secrets d'une machine infernale*, Villeurbanne, Golias, 1997.

exonerated after investigations conducted in his defense; arrested by the police for possession of drugs, he was released at the request of the Church. It was not until 48 years after the first accusations that the Church was forced to recognize the infamy of one of its dignitaries and agreed to withdraw his pastoral prerogatives on May 19, 2006! This all-powerful leader will be sentenced to a suspension *a divinis*.

For decades, the Legion of Christ accused all those who spoke the truth (and often their sufferings) of being slanderers, of being Satan's minions, in short, it rallied around its leader who enjoyed a senseless cult. Since then, the Vatican has been obliged to recognize that Marcial Maciel was not the only pedophile criminal in this all-powerful organization. The question of the dissolution of this movement was therefore openly asked, but the Vatican chose to keep this armed arm of the *reconquista*. The movement was simply put temporarily under the tutelage of a special papal emissary, Cardinal Velasio de Paolis, but these repeated scandals did not prevent Pope Francis from solemnly greeting "the community of the Legionaries of Christ and its new priests" at the end of 2014: 35 new Legionary of Christ priests were even ordained! The Pope's delegate made a mind-blowing speech on this occasion, reversing victims and perpetrators: "You have suffered much. You have suffered the shame of being accused, looked upon with suspicion, exposed to public opinion, also within the Church. You have known how to accept this suffering [...] for love of the Church and the Legion." The crimes of Marcial Maciel and some others are not only personal faults but the consequences of a way of operating and undoubtedly also of a certain ideology. This very special treatment of the case has provoked the anger of many victims of pedophile crimes. One of them, the Frenchman Xavier Léger, interviewed by AFP, declared: "This mea culpa forbids the members to go into the details [of the crimes]. It tells them: from now on you have no right to seek the truth [...]. What has happened for a month and a half is a grooming. The facade has been redone. This chapter was the ratification of a process orchestrated upstream" in the Vatican, to save a powerful congregation, "an irreformable sect", from possible dissolution, he insists. I understand the anger of these victims when I learn that Pope Francis has appointed Father Fernando Vérgez Alzaga, a well-known Legionary of Christ, as secretary general of the Vatican governorate (government) and elevated him to the dignity of bishop. Rome does not intend to do without this movement, despite its very heavy liabilities.

The Legion controls the Zenit press agency, which is responsible for Vatican communications in six languages, and manages 12 universities. The most important of these is Francisco de Vitoria in the suburbs of Madrid, not to mention the prestigious Regina Apostolorum University in Rome, which is responsible for the training of exorcists, of whom Francis is very fond today. The Legionaries of Christ are considered by Rome as the spearhead of the Catholic Church against the "new religious movements". In a way, it is a matter of copying for the benefit of the Church what works well elsewhere. Here we find Massimo Introvigne, the great defender of the sects, who for a long time refuted the accusations of pedophilia against Marcial Maciel, who today explains that it was a plot against the Church. This central figure of the *reconquista* teaches in the universities of the Legionaries of Christ and Opus Dei and is the general delegate of the Catholic Alliance (Alleanza Cattolica), an extreme right-wing political party that advocates, of course, the social doctrine of the Church and, no doubt, will soon be a champion of ecology. This busy business card has not prevented him (or at least allowed him) from being the official representative of the Organization for Security and Cooperation in Europe (OSCE), in charge of the fight against "racism, xenophobia and discrimination", especially discrimination "against Christians and members of other religions".

The Legionaries of Christ, true champions of anti-communism and anti-socialism, are ready to support all the operations of Pope Francis that go in the direction of an ever more intransigent Catholicism. Eduardo Robles Gil, the new Superior General of the Congregation, has just announced that the Legion will resume its role in evangelization missions, especially in schools. These Legionaries of Christ are not Jesuits and they have their own interpretation of ecology and the preferential option for the poor.

Pope Francis and Opus Dei

Progressive Catholics and atheists who hoped that Pope Francis would at least distance himself from Opus Dei will be very disappointed[36]. The prelate of Opus Dei, Bishop Javier Echevarría, recalls that the Pope has always been able to work with the faithful of Opus Dei, and that he took

______

36. Christian Terras, *Opus Dei, Enquête au cœur d'un pouvoir occulte*, Villeurbanne, Golias, 2006.

advantage of a trip to Rome when he was still Archbishop of Buenos Aires to pay his respects for forty-five minutes at the tomb of the sinister Josemaría Escrivá de Balaguer. Francis' appointment was "received with deep joy" by Opus Dei. However, this is not the first time that the left has taken some people close to Opus Dei for wild ducks, as it did when Bishop Oscar Romero was murdered because the crime called into question his analysis. The newspaper *L'Humanité* of February 6, 2015, headlined, thirty-five years after the tragedy, "Archbishop Romero martyr of the poor" in order to justify its blissful admiration for Pope Francis, while Opus Dei rightly claimed Archbishop Romero. The Archbishop of San Salvador was murdered on March 24, 1980, by CIA-funded "death squads," but he was not a liberation theologian and friend of the poor, but an ultraconservative. On the day he was murdered, he was attending a retreat organized by Opus Dei. The Church expressly beatified Archbishop Oscar Romero, extending the traditional qualification of martyrdom to Christians who died "for the sake of the faith" (*in odium fidei*) and not for political reasons. Opus Dei needed this beatification of one of its own to better legitimize its own preferential option for the poor. The same Church has refrained from beatifying other priests who were murdered in South America or elsewhere when they defended revolutionary ideas.

Opus Dei welcomed the Church's desire to regain political control, especially with the organization of demonstrations against equal marriage rights or against abortion.

Opus Dei remains an essential actor in the mobilization of society in the field of morality (abortion, marriage for all) but also in that of ecology. It does not hesitate to put its structures at the service of these struggles and to circulate the methods of agitprop with the aim of creating a sort of international religious activist movement, of which France offers a good example.

Ludovine de La Rochère, true leader of the Manif pour tous, former press officer of the French Bishops' Conference, communications officer of the Jérôme-Lejeune Foundation, daughter of Baron Armand Mégret d'Étigny de Sérilly, niece by marriage of Bertrand Dutheil de La Rochère, vice-president of the Rassemblement Bleu Marine, was solemnly received by Pope Francis, on June 12, 2014, in the house of Saint Martha in Rome, where she had been invited to participate in his private mass. I do not know, of course, what they may have exchanged, but Ludovine de La Rochère is in all the wrong moves... She is the one who represents this reactionary

Church at the congress of the UOIF (Union of Islamic Organizations of France) in order to organize a front of conservative religions at war against the destruction of the "traditional family", and she is also the one who is present at the convention organized in Spain by the Association of Catholic Propagandists in which members of Opus Dei, the Legionaries of Christ and Communion and Liberation are present. Ludovine de La Rochère shared the podium with Isabel Tocino, a former minister in the Aznar government, head of a large investment bank and member of Opus Dei. According to the latter, abortion is the "contraceptive method of the young" and "the cause of the atrocious demographic crash". The president of the Manif pour tous explains docently: "They say that there are several types of families and that it's wonderful, but it's completely false!"[37]

Ludovine de La Rochère also intervened on behalf of the ultra-conservative Catholic association *Hazte Oír* (Make yourself heard). This association is close to the extreme right-wing circles in North America. It also maintains relations with the Mexican Yunke, an extreme right-wing secret organization founded in the 1950s which campaigns for "the defense of the Catholic religion and the fight against the forces of Satan".

Opus Dei also puts its power at the service of the new encyclical *Laudato si'*. The current Prelate of Opus Dei explains that the spirituality of Opus Dei's work is "one of the most effective keys to understanding the scope of this beautiful encyclical *Laudato si'* and, above all, to responding to the challenges - optimistic, but resolutely realistic - that it presents. Opus Dei students from more than 200 universities around the world met at the 47th edition of their UNIV Forum to work on the topic of "Ecology of the Person and the Environment," and solemnly pledged to the Pope to spread his ideas in this new religious front. They were received in general audience by the Holy Father. Opus Dei also claims to be close to the theology of poverty, and even to have some ownership of the notion of the periphery used by Francis. Finally, Opus Dei declares that it is fully in agreement with the Holy Father's fight for women: "This is not a new subject, because the very development of the Church has always been deeply supported by women. In Opus Dei, women have always been considered to have a central role to play in the life of the Church.

Pope Francis is not breaking with the tradition of his predecessors. In 1982, the Catholic Church granted Opus Dei the status of a personal

---

37. Ethnologists have established that there are multiple conceptions of the family. We know that the African family is not ours.

prelature. This means that its jurisdiction does not extend to a territory (as with a bishopric) but to individuals. The diocese of Opus Dei is attached directly to the Pope. Its prestige is also due to the beatification (1992) and canonization (2002) of Josemaría Escrivá de Balaguer by John Paul II. Opus Dei's credo is the reconciliation of the Church with capitalism, a capitalism that is certainly moralized, but what capitalist does not support the same thesis and fight unbridled capitalism in the name of the general interest? Opus Dei has always been on the side of the powerful, including dictatorships, for example under Franco (in Spain) and Pinochet (in Chile), in the name, of course, of its "love of the poor" and its "spirituality of work" (sic). As Opus Dei leader Rafael Alvira says, "the entrepreneur is the aristocrat of modern times, with the obligations and constraints of any aristocracy"; you almost sound like a member of the Tradition Family Property (TFP). The great victory of Opus Dei in this area is undoubtedly the encyclical *Centesimus Annus*, in which John Paul II signed the Church's commitment to the market economy... and which Francis has not questioned!

The liberal (but not Catholic) Guy Sorman, despite having taught at the Pontifical Catholic University in Chile, defends Opus Dei and its gospel of wealth tooth and nail. He explains (not without reason) that "the enemies of the Work are also enemies of capitalism. He develops his thesis: "The defenders of capitalism would hope for a towering, ethical and not just technical legitimization of the free economy. Opus Dei will certainly not change the world, but it can change the Church, and that's not so bad [...]." Guy Sorman is just wrong when he believes that in the 21st century he can still oppose the supposedly anti-capitalist Jesuits to the pro-capitalist Opus Dei: "Are we to conclude that eventually the anti-capitalist Jesuits will be replaced by the pro-capitalist Opus Dei?" The "Jesuit" Pope Francis is certainly reviving the old Christian anti-capitalism but in the name of a productive and moralized capitalism. In short, either the religiously uneducated left is wrong about Francis or the political expert Opus Dei is right about the new pope.

Pope Francis and the Knights of Columbus

Since his election, Pope Francis has received at least four times Carl Anderson, the patron of The Knights of Columbus, an ultraconservative organization founded in 1882 in the United States by Father Michael

J. McGivney, the son of Irish immigrants, whose canonization is already well underway under U.S. Archbishop Daniel A. Cronin.

Carl Anderson, received in Rome on June 25, 2014, on the occasion of the Italian translation of a book dedicated to the glory of Father McGivney, stated in an address to the apostolic nuncios that "Father McGivney embodied what Cardinal Bergoglio has already mentioned, that is, a priest who rolled up the sleeves of his cassock in order to be at the service of his people.... Father McGivney's vision prepared the Knights of Columbus to fully accept the role of the laity in the life of the Church as proposed by Vatican Council II. [...]. Today, the world is focused on the example of Pope Francis who has provided a powerful personal witness of charity and love for his neighbor."

That the Church needs to make saints for itself would not be so bad if the Knights of Columbus, which was already the armed wing of American conservative Catholics, was not becoming one of the main political-financial powers of the Church of Francis!

Carl Anderson, although already a member of this partly secretive order, held various positions in the U.S. presidency between 1983 and 1987: special assistant to the president, director of communications, and religious advisor to President Reagan. John Paul II did much to promote him within the Church by appointing him to key positions in its governmental apparatus: member of the Pontifical Council for the Family, member of the Pontifical Council for Justice and Peace, member of the Pontifical Council for Social Communications, special advisor to the Committee for the Respect of Life, etc. His successor, Benedict XVI, appointed him to the direction of the IOR (the Vatican bank)[38]. He became supreme head of the Knights of Columbus in 2000, after having been its deputy secretary general for a long time. Today, he is close to Francis, who appreciates his positions and his financial generosity (see *below*).

Carl Anderson is therefore a central figure in the Church of Francis. He has nevertheless raised many controversies both for his remarks (comparing the law on abortion to the law on racial segregation in the United States) and for his salary as philanthropic CEO of 500,000 dollars per year! Carl Anderson also made ambiguous remarks during the earthquake that struck Haiti in 2010. While he intends to distance himself from the thesis of certain evangelists, he nevertheless draws a parallel with the Lisbon

---

38. It was he who obtained the departure of his former president (in what some Vatican experts considered to be a fratricidal war between Opus Dei and the Knights of Columbus).

disaster of 1755 and its religious implications: "The tragedy in Haiti will have a long-term psychological impact comparable to the Lisbon earthquake of 1755. That earthquake was followed by a tsunami and a fire that destroyed almost the entire city and killed nearly a million people. The Lisbon disaster changed the thinking of many of the great intellectuals of the eighteenth century, including Voltaire [and] Kant [...]. The earthquake took place during the feast of All Saints in a predominantly Catholic country, so that many Christians in Europe have begun to question their faith in God. In the coming days, perhaps we will see something similar. So Haiti today is a test of our faith in God and our commitment to our fellow human beings."[39]

Carl Anderson is the only layman who regularly attends the world synods of bishops as an auditor (especially on questions of morality). The Catholic City presents the Knights of Columbus as an alternative to Freemasonry and thus as a weapon against "value relativism". This organization, which counts several bishops among its semi-clandestine ritual initiates, also includes many American leaders, among them Jeb Bush, candidate in the 2016 Republican presidential primaries (before throwing in the towel in February 2016), brother of G.W. Bush and son of G.H.W. Bush, former presidents of the United States.

Carl Anderson, moreover, received the cross of officer in the National Order of Merit on October 16, 2015 from the President of the Polish Republic, Andrzej Duda (a member of the conservative Kaczyński brothers' party), who is often portrayed as intellectually close to Opus Dei. The Knights established in Poland since 2006 have 4,000 members there. Polish Bishop Janusz Stepnowski, a member of the Knights of Columbus, a member of the Congregation for Bishops, has just been elevated to the rank of honorary prelate of His Holiness... Is it a coincidence that he has been very involved in the handling of the "South America" issue?

This order is established in 12 countries and mainly in the United States, Canada, Mexico, Poland, the Philippines and Cuba, but also, since 2015, in France. The "Colombians" were largely in the driver's seat during Francis' visit to Cuba, where Cardinal Jaime Lucas Ortega y Alamino of Havana is a longtime friend of the Knights of Columbus.

This order has 15,000 structures with 1.8 million members, all of whom are men and only "practicing Christians" and "in union with the Holy

---

39.http://www.zenit.org/fr/articles/l-aspect-spirituel-de-la-souffrance-de-haiti-par-carl-anderson

See", committed to the defense of the true Catholic faith, the Christian family, private property, the fatherland... I would gladly add the Vatican's finances to its power!

In the eyes of the Vatican, the Knights of Columbus are the symbol of the "new preferential option for the poor" because they have known, for a century, how to relieve working-class families with parish benefit societies and now with insurance systems (sic). The order thus translates the will of the theorists of the "third world conservative revolution" to substitute social aid systems (such as Social Security) with solutions borrowed from the world of finance and insurance. Everyone would become the owner and therefore responsible for his or her financial portfolio (retirement plans, life insurance) in accordance with God's plan, which would guarantee the centrality of the person, the family and property. The poorest would benefit from charitable "good works", in the good tradition of the Church of the patronesses and the big bosses. The enemy of all time remains the common goods in the sense of solidarity. It is not only because Obama's public health bill obliged mutual insurance companies to reimburse contraception that the "Colombians" were also involved in the fight initiated by the Church: admitting a French-style Social Security would be diabolical in itself! The order markets a very complete portfolio of financial products. In 2014, it sold $8.2 billion worth of life insurance... It now manages a portfolio of more than $100 billion (it is easy to understand how Francis intends to make the Vatican bank one of the largest financial institutions in the capitalist world!). The order is now playing in the big league... It was awarded the "World's Most Ethical Company" prize by the Ethisphere Institute in 2014 and 2015, along with other firms such as Elbit Systems of America and Rockwell Collins (companies in the military sector), Levi Strauss and Co, Ford, US Bank, Chemical Compagny, Kellogg's, Microsoft, L'Oréal, Xerox, Pepsi Cola, etc. The Order of the Knights of Columbus is therefore a leader in business ethics, in short, a laboratory of so-called "moralized" or ethical capitalism.

The Knights of Columbus order is also a Vatican money pump. Francis received the supreme knight on December 12, 2014, the latter presented him with a check for $1.6 million for the "personal works of the pope" and a $400,000 contribution for the Christians of the East. The order is said to have donated 1.5 billion to the Vatican in ten years.

The order of the Knights of Columbus not only legitimized the conquest of the Americas by Christopher Columbus, but also intended to remind

Protestants that the discoverer of America was an ardent Catholic. This organization is therefore also an essential patriotic force and this dimension is said to be at the heart of the initiation to the fourth rank (or degree) which constitutes the summit of the initiatory journey. The "Colombians" are very present in the American armed forces and especially in most of the military bases established abroad. Already at the end of the Second World War, President Roosevelt declared that the American army would not be what it is without the constant support of this half charitable, half patriotic/nationalist Catholic organization.

The Order of the Knights of Columbus is naturally involved in all fights, especially against abortion rights and homosexuals. Pope Francis therefore sent a message of support to the Knights of Columbus on the occasion of the last convention of the Knights of Columbus, through the intermediary of Secretary of State Pietro Parolin. He praised the efforts of the "Colombians" to oppose those who want to confine religion to the private sphere and defend the role of the Church in the public square. In other words, according to Pope Francis, the Knights of Columbus would be the very prototype of the activist Church he wants. They would be among the best defenders of religious freedom and the common good as the Church naturally understands it.

Massimo Introvigne, the protector of the Church

Massimo Introvigne, a graduate of the Pontifical Gregorian University, a lawyer, and a teacher at the Regina Apostolorum Atheneum belonging to the Legionaries of Christ, is an ultraconservative Catholic who should logically, according to the media's analysis grid, hate the pope for his supposed Marxism, for his "progressive" sympathies, and for his companionship with the left. However, Massimo Introvigne published a book in Italy, *Il segreto di Papa Francesco* [The Secret *of Pope Francis]*, just a few months after the election of Francis, which will soon be translated into French.

Faced with sectarian aberrations

Massimo Introvigne, with whom I crossed swords for a long time when I worked alongside the anti-cult associations CCMM (Centre contre les manipulations mentales), UNADFI (Union nationale des associations de défense des familles et de l'individu victimes de sectes) and the Mission interministérielle de lutte contre les sectes (MILS), is one of the main players in the troubled relations between the religious world and the extreme right. A member of the Res Publica foundation launched in 1999 by Silvio Berlusconi, he is above all the general delegate of the Catholic Alliance (Alleanza cattolica), an ultraconservative religious association founded by Giovanni Cantoni, a leader of the Italian far right, a journalist who has long worked for the *official* Vatican *newspaper* and also for the Movimento sociale italiano - Destra nazionale, (Italian Social Movement - National Right) created after the banning of the National Fascist party at the end of the Second World War. Giovanni Cantoni directs the very important Institute for Social Doctrine and Social Information (IDIS) as well as Massimo Introvigne directs the Center for the Study of New Religions (CESNUR), two organizations that the Catholic Alliance promotes on its sites and whose influence has become considerable. Giovanni Cantoni claims to be close to Plinio Correa de Oliveira, founder of the extreme right-wing society Tradition Family Property (identified as a sect by the French government), whose values the Catholic Alliance defends, however[40], and to Gomez Davila (1919-1994), a Colombian Catholic philosopher who proclaims himself hostile to the concept of sovereignty of the people, which he presents as responsible for the destruction of society; for Davila, Vatican II would be a dangerous adaptation of the Church to the decadent modernity Alleanza Cattolica naturally emphasizes the social doctrine of the Church, that is, its desire to build a society according to God's plan.

Massimo Introvigne is best known in France for his systematic defense of movements identified as cults, such as Scientology. He is considered the main opponent of the anti-cult fight.

Francis and the "gay lobby"

It is less known that Massimo Introvigne has also become the great specialist in the defense of the Catholic Church against accusations of pedophilia, going so far as to publish a detestable book on pedophile priests (*Preti pedofili*, soon to be translated into French). He even defended Marcial Maciel, guru of the Legionaries of Christ, before his

---

40. http://Benoît-et-moi.fr/2010-I/0455009cf20864101/0455009d3a0bca311.html

movement and the Vatican were forced to acknowledge the crimes committed. All this would not be so serious if Massimo Introvigne did not have a very good press in the Catholic media. Thus, *La Croix*: "Without denying the tragic seriousness of pedophile acts committed by priests and religious, the director of the Center for the Study of New Religions (Turin) dismantles the arguments used to amplify this phenomenon in the media. The figures: in the United States from 1950 to 2002, 4,392 American priests (out of approximately 109,000) were accused of having relations with minors and a little more than a hundred (or 0.9%) were convicted in civil courts. This percentage is lower than that of other categories of professionals in contact with young people. The author denounces the role of insurance companies, which pay a large part of the compensation, and of lawyers, who receive a large part of the money. In short, for the Italian sociologist, this crisis of pedophile priests looks very much like a "secularizing propaganda directed against Benedict XVI."

Massimo Introvigne, in a text entitled "The UN declares war on the Church", denounces the report of the UN Commission for the Rights of the Child. He strongly attacks the president of the Commission, the Peruvian Susana Villarán, mayor of Lima but also convinced catholic: "In permanent controversy with the bishops of her country, in particular with the cardinal archbishop of Lima, Mgr Juan Luis Cipriani, for his unbridled activism in favor of the homosexual "marriage", of the ideology of the kind and of the abortion. A regular marcher at Gay Pride, Villarán has distinguished herself by attacking the Church on abortion and homosexuality and has symbolically "married" (same-sex "marriage" in Peru does not exist at this time) same-sex pairs, including her party mate and close collaborator Susel Paredes and her "fiancée" Carolina. Provocatively, the ceremonies took place in the Park of Love in Lima, Peru, where traditionally the bride and groom are photographed under the famous statue *The Kiss*, by sculptor Victor Delfin."

While sympathizing with the victims of pedophile crimes, Massimo Introvigne deploys the defense system that has since become the one in Rome. He explains that the accusations against the Church are a case of "moral panic", that is, a "social hyperconstruction". He does not yet dare to say a rumor, but the idea is similar. There would be no specificity of the Church in this field, and the Church would be less affected than other institutions or professional environments working with children. The problem, when it exists, would not be that of the celibacy of priests but first of all of homosexuality: 80% of pedophiles would be homosexuals and this figure would rise to 90% in the Church. The Church would have suffered from too much tolerance (sic) towards homosexuality in its seminaries, especially in the 1970s, when the great majority of priests found guilty were ordained. The major responsibility would thus fall on the ideas of sexual liberation and May 68. The Church's accusers are not so much trying to protect children as to defend the RU 486 pill (abortion), euthanasia, the recognition of homosexual unions... The Pope, by defending the family, would be the number one enemy of these very powerful lobbies: "These more or less Masonic lobbies underline the sinister power of technocracy evoked by Benedict XVI in the encyclical *Caritas in veritate*, and the denunciation by John Paul II himself in the "Message for the World Day of Peace" in 1985, about "hidden designs" - alongside others "openly propagated" - aimed at subjugating all peoples to regimes in which God does not count. In truth, this is an hour of darkness, which reminds us of the prophecy of a great Catholic thinker of the nineteenth century, Emiliano Avogadro della Motta (1798-1865), according to which the ruins caused by secular ideologies would be succeeded by an authentic "demonolatry" which would manifest itself in particular in the attack on the family and on the true concept of marriage."[41]

Rome has heard Introvigne, since from now on priest candidates with deep-seated homosexual tendencies cannot be ordained[42]. We have here a new proof that the Church that speaks of "gay lobby" is indeed an ultra-reactionary Church. It is ultra-reactionary first of all because it establishes a link between homosexuality and pedophile crime, and also because by making pedophilia a consequence not of its own functioning (celibacy, among others) but of sexual liberation, it transfers the responsibility for pedophile crime to the rest of society, and in particular to the progressives. The Church forgets, in the process, that the main blame is not for having sheltered pedophile priests but for having protected them, for having put pressure on the victims' families. We must therefore take very seriously the latest declarations of the Pope who, while receiving a homosexual couple during his trip to the United States, while declaring "if a person is gay, who am I to judge him?

To speak of a "gay lobby" within the Curia, in relation to pedophilia cases or financial scandals, is to make the crimes committed in the

---

41. http://Benoît-et-moi.fr/2010-I/0455009cf20864101/0455009d3a0bca311.html
42. http://www.croire.com/Definitions/Mots-de-la-foi/Vocation/Homosexualite-et-vocation

Church a matter that does not concern the Church, it is even to pose the Church as a victim but also as a solution. Pope Benedict XVI convened a commission of three cardinals: Julián Herranz, Josef Tomko and Salvatore De Giorgi to discover the origin of the leaks concerning the financial scandals. The three cardinals reportedly told the pope about the existence of a very influential "gay lobby". Homosexual meeting places frequented by clerics were mentioned. Reference is made to prelates being blackmailed for not respecting their vow of chastity (sic). Francis continued in the same direction when he declared in July 2013 that there was indeed a "gay lobby" within the Vatican. A fraction of the Church, not only the one made up of homosexual priests, has well understood how Rome and especially Francis are (re)building a war machine against homosexuals, both to clear the Church of accusations of protecting pedophiles, but also as a counter-fire to all the repeated financial scandals, while pocketing the benefit of appearing more suitable than others, more honest than all those who pact with modernity.

This is why the Polish priest Krzysztof Charamsa, *a* theologian at the Congregation for the Doctrine of the Faith, reputed to be close to Ratzerian conservatism, chose, on the eve of the October 2015 synod on the family, to loudly reveal his homosexuality and his relationship with a Catalan man, thereby risking condemnation by the Church and isolation. The media chose to retain only part of his testimony: "The Church is behind the knowledge that humanity has reached [...]. I hope that the synod will face the question of the gay faithful and their families. If I chose to speak now, it is because I was afraid that it would not be the case. The issue had disappeared from all official statements." The priest Krzysztof Charamsa has indeed castigated the "institutional homophobia" of the Church, even mentioning a majority of homophobic homosexuals. An analysis confirmed during a program broadcast on France Culture on September 8, 2015 during which another priest returned to his own experience: he explained that he had confessed his homosexuality to the director of the seminary of Nancy, who accepted him with good graces. He then discovered an ecclesial milieu that was largely "homosexualized": according to him, half of the seminarians, professors, priests and bishops spent their time "looking at" and he had relationships with several of them, including a well-known bishop. This same milieu considers that having relations between men (religious or not) would not constitute a transgression of the principle of chastity (sic).

I'd like to end with the 2011 case between the Vatican and Irish Prime Minister Enda Kenny, a member of the center-right Catholic party Fine Gael, after the publication of the Cloyne Report on child abuse in the diocese of Bishop John Magee, who served as personal secretary to three popes (Paul VI (1897-1978), John Paul ¹ (1912-1978) and John Paul II (1920-2005)). Speaking in Parliament, the prime minister said, "The rape and torture of children was downplayed or 'managed' in order to uphold the primacy of the institution, its power, strength and reputation." The Vatican, of course, did not react, but... Massimo Introvigne immediately went up to the net: while acknowledging that the majority of deputies and 72% of the population would be in favor of severing diplomatic relations with the Vatican, he explained that, in these pedophilia cases, the essential would be elsewhere: "The most serious aspect of the story is a bill that, if approved, would force priests to report information of abuse of minors, even learned in confession: if they did not do so, they would risk five years in prison. On this last proposal, first of all, we must be very clear. This is a very serious and unprecedented violation of religious freedom. Not even the worst of the anticlerical governments of the nineteenth and twentieth centuries in France have ever dared to attack the secrecy of confession." The defense system is particularly devious because it calls for blocking behind the Church in the name of religious freedom. Introvigne forgets one thing: if the Irish church had followed its own rules in this matter, as set out in the 1996 *Framework for a church response*, the victims would not have numbered in the dozens. But the Vatican went over the heads of the Irish bishops' conference in a confidential letter from the apostolic nuncio to the Irish bishops a year after they adopted the *Framework*. In the letter, the Vatican noted that the Congregation for the Clergy, then headed by Cardinal Darío Castrillón Hoyos, had distanced itself from the Irish recommendations and said that the obligation to report sexual abuse to the Irish authorities was subject to "strong moral as well as canonical reservations. He recommended that bishops adhere strictly to the procedures of canon law. The Colombian-born cardinal, then head of the Pontifical Commission Ecclesia Dei, was in charge of relations with traditionalist communities. He considered that the faithful of the Society of Saint Pius X were not themselves schismatic. He considered that if he had been aware of the negationist remarks of Bishop Williamson ("I believe that there were no gas chambers"), he would not have asked for his retraction before the lifting of the excommunication. The cardinal is also listed on the Opus Dei website, where he testifies to the sanctity of its founder.

When the Church plays the victim...

The consequences of this hardening were not long in coming. The Church of Francis chooses to look like a victim in the face of modernity. This posture goes far beyond the massacre of Christians in the East and the repression of religious minorities (for example in China or in Putin's Russia), which, far from calling for the strengthening of the religious, shows the topicality of defending and extending the sphere of secularism within the public sphere. French Cardinal Jean-Louis Tauran, president of the Pontifical Council for Interreligious Dialogue, spoke at the last meeting for friendship between peoples in Rimini, organized each year by Communion and Liberation, to explain that 200 million Christians in the world are at risk of persecution. Of course, he called for the defense of "religious freedom according to the meaning given by Massimo Introvigne and his CESNUR" (see *above*). A 2015 report by the international foundation Aid to the Church in Need establishes that Christianity is threatened with extinction in entire regions of the world.

Things become problematic when the Church, claiming to be a minority in France and as such threatened and repressed, calls on its most fundamentalist followers to stick together. The diva of the Manif pour tous, in offering a T-shirt to the Pope, did she not go so far as to declare that those who wore this symbol would end up in prison! The princes of the Church take advantage of this to call heretics those who sometimes dare to call it intolerant and obscurantist.

The Church needs to feel isolated, unloved, in order to turn its faithful into new soldier-monks ready to do battle with diabolical adversaries. This syndrome of the entrenched camp appears systematically in the theses developed by the Vatican because it allows it to launch its troops into battle, hence the insistence on sacrifice, on accepting to be martyrs of the faith. We are thus witnessing the prolegomena of a return to holy war. A document of January 16, 2015 of the International Theological Commission maintains that it is not the monotheistic religions that are violent, but the dictatorship of relativism that would claim to drive faith out of the public sphere! A certain Church therefore responds to the obligation of Muslims to pray in the street, for lack of sufficient mosques, with street prayers, including with loudspeakers, even though it has a large number of churches. This document also says that Islamist terrorism would only be a dialectical consequence of secularism because it implies the repression of religion in the private sphere. One often hears that the Church would be a sect that would have succeeded. This thesis is absurd: the Church is a sect that has failed because it has been forced to open up to the world, it has been forced to renounce its omnipotence.

... to justify his aggressiveness

The beginning of Francis' pontificate will go down in history as the one that saw tens of millions of the faithful take to the streets, occupy the public space, not to join in the struggles of other citizens, but to reclaim the political terrain through provocation. Here the Church mobilizes against equal marriage rights, elsewhere against the legalization of contraception, and still elsewhere against the right to abortion. This militant Catholicism is a belligerent and identity-based Catholicism. The Manif pour tous, the attacks on secularism and the ecological question are only bridgeheads in a global strategy of *reconquista*. It is not by chance that on this occasion the most intransigent, fundamentalist and fundamentalist currents are surfacing! The muses of the Manif pour tous - like, as we shall see, the activists of ecology in the Vatican sauce - have quite a religious and even political background.

This return to politics is reminiscent of the "politics first" of Action Française, whose current members are investing in the new fronts (notably ecology). Pope Pius XI had, of course, condemned Action Française on December 29, 1926, putting its daily newspaper and numerous books on the Index, and even forbidding its members to receive the sacraments, but his successor, Pius XII, lifted the ban in 1936, as part of his priority fight against communism. Rome reproached Action Française for subordinating religion to politics, because of its "integral nationalism" (Charles Maurras). Francis is not of this vein, since he calls for the subordination of politics to religion, in the name of an intransigent, "integralist" conception of Catholicism. He draws on the experience of Opus Dei, but above all on that of the Communion and Liberation movement (see *above*).

The Church would thus be the sole bearer of solutions to the current systemic crisis, because it would be the bearer of truth (divine and natural) in the face of lies. This new political practice of the Church is based on a text desired by Cardinal Ratzinger and approved by John Paul II in November 2002. This doctrinal note, entitled "Questions on the involvement and behavior of Catholics in political life", is well worth reading. The time is no longer for founding Catholic parties because of the extreme weakness of the Church in society, but it is also no longer for participating in social movements at the risk of diluting Catholic dogma. Catholics are thus invited to participate in politics again, but no longer on an equal footing with other citizens and defending common values, because the "relativism of values" would henceforth prohibit taking the risk of "confusing consciences with risky compromises" (sic). This new strategy is the opposite of that of the workers' priests who fought alongside the workers and their unions on the basis of social demands alone. This doctrinal note from the Vatican also maintains that cultural relativism and ethical pluralism are in themselves favourable "to decadence" (sic); that ethical pluralism (freedom of choice of values) is not a condition of democracy; that citizens do not have to claim the freedom of their moral choices, nor a greater autonomy in this domain; that legislators do not have to forget the principles of natural ethics; that the conceptions of man, of the common good, of the State must be submitted to the judgment of this moral norm (which only the Church can of course define); that political freedom does not have to be based on the relativistic idea that all conceptions of the good of man have the same truth and the same value; that democracy is only possible insofar as it is based on a just conception of the person (which only the Church holds); that secularism must be understood as an autonomy of the civil and political sphere from the religious and ecclesiastical sphere, but not from the moral sphere (as defined by the Church); that Christians are free to join the parties of their choice, but that these movements must defend the revealed truth held by the Church, etc.

Francis even formalized this return of the Church to politics on April 30, 2015, when he received members of the Italian Christian Life Communities and those of the Italian Student Missionary League, dependent on the Jesuits. Things are clear: Christians have the duty to engage in politics, but they should no longer do so by founding a Catholic party (given the secularization), but by getting involved in social and political movements, but by putting forward their faith and the dogma of the Church. In other words, it is no longer a question of being present at the side of those who suffer and struggle, as progressive Christians and liberation theologians have always done, but of carrying the Church's dogma within these movements. This new crusade, to which Francis calls, is therefore at the crossroads between a policy conceived in the manner of Communion and Liberation and the Manif pour tous type of mobilizations that the Church has exported to many countries in order to reaffirm the presence of God in the street. Francis reminds us that Paul VI maintained that being involved in politics is the highest form of charity, which is why it is necessary to accept to get one's hands dirty and Christians involved in politics must be considered as martyrs, because they accept "the daily martyrdom of imperfection" (sic). Does getting one's hands dirty for these Christians mean accepting to make a pact with the extreme right? Pope Francis is playing a very dangerous game because this new way of doing politics (which was the way of the 19th century) will awaken the old demons of the Church and the conflicts between religion and secularism, Republicans and anti-Republicans.

This conception of political life is anti-republican and must be fought. No one intends to force Catholics to have abortions or to develop a rich sexuality, but let them not pretend to govern our own lives! True democracy is always to postulate the competence of the incompetent, it is therefore to refuse any idea of capitalized Truth, of dogma brought from outside. The Church considers that true democracy would be to leave open the way to apply one's own values and not to define them together. No, true democracy is always to put the truth to the vote!

Why is Pope Francis reading the novel *The Master of the Earth*?

Catholics, the main target of the current anti-religious polemic, are also, according to the Vatican, the only ones who can resist decadence. For months now, Pope Francis has been referring to the futuristic novel *Lord of the World,* published in 1907 in London by Robert-Hugh Benson, a young Anglican clergyman who was ordained by his own father, the Archbishop of Canterbury, but converted to Roman Catholicism in 1903 (otherwise Francis would probably not be talking about it). Francis explains that this novel of anticipation allows us to understand, better than his own speeches, the "ideological colonization" from which humanity is suffering today. The novel depicts the struggle of good against evil, of God against the devil, of the Church against the socialists and Freemasons in a context of apocalypse. It shows a Catholic Church resisting the diabolical works of technical progress, Godless humanitarianism, the commodification of man, the abolition of borders, the idolatry of power and the victory of secularism, the idea of a world government, etc.: in short, what Francis is talking about. In short, what Francis is talking about. The hero of the book is, of course, a Catholic priest: "[Percy] saw before him, offering himself to his choice, the two cities of Saint Augustine. One was that of a world born of itself, self-organizing and self-sufficient, a world interpreted by socialist, materialistic, hedonistic forces [...]. And as for the other world, Percy saw it unfold before his eyes, speaking to him of a Creator, a Creation, a divine goal, a redemption, a transcendent and eternal reality, from which everything had sprung and to which everything led. One of these two men was the vicar of God, and the other an impostor, the enemy of God..."

The Church likes to present itself as persecuted and prey to violence. This apocalyptic and eschatological vision is always fraught with danger when the apocalypse is confused, yesterday as today, with the antichrist. Didn't Father Benson, author of Francis' fetish novel, confide in 1905: "The antichrist is beginning to obsess me", in the manner of Pope Francis rediscovering the devil, a real person, in the Vatican cellars. This way of doing politics is particularly dangerous when it no longer opposes values, conceptions of society, but good and evil.

Unfortunately, we have a series of recent illustrations of this with the reminder that the Church does not have to dialogue on an equal footing with other movements and with the recent affair of Bishop Luc Ravel, bishop of the French armies since 2009. This bishop, who intends to speak as a soldier of the Christian combat, published a text under the title "The complicated war" in the February 2014 issue of the *Monthly Bulletin of the military chaplaincy*, in which, seeking who the real enemy is, he explains what good is the fight against the "manifest evil" (Islamist terrorism) if we support the "devious evil", this "ideology of self-righteousness" that makes abortion a "weapon of mass destruction" of humanity: "The Christian feels caught between two ideologies. On the one hand, the ideology that caricatures God with contempt for man. On the other, the ideology that manipulates man in defiance of God.

On one side, declared and recognized adversaries: the terrorists of the bomb, avengers of the Prophet. On the other side, undeclared but well-known adversaries: the terrorists of thought, prescribers of secularism, worshippers of the republic. In which camp should we place ourselves as Christians? We do not want to be taken hostage by Islamists. But we do not want to be taken hostage by the self-righteous. The Islamic ideology has just made 17 victims in France. But the ideology of self-righteousness makes each year 200,000 victims in their mother's womb. The abortion, which has become a fundamental right, is a weapon of mass destruction" [...]. We want to oppose Islamic terrorism without giving reason to terrorism against God."

The bishop thus equates the republicans with the murderous Islamists and compares the deaths, 200,000 on the side of the republic, 17 on the side of the Islamists. Has he been condemned by the Church of France and by Rome for his remarks? No! He is even systematically defended. Thus Radio Notre-Dame explains: "Recalling the doctrine of a religion, when one is under the aegis of the Republic, does not pass. However, the bishop was only recalling the Catholic doctrine in force. It seems astonishing to conceive that the government authorizes religious representatives to exercise the functions of chaplains within its institutions, but that it refuses to recall the religious doctrines in question..."[43]. *La Vie* opens its columns to him to explain Francis' conception of the third world war: "In this 'third world war fought in pieces,' we have to spread the eternal Gospel in a new way. That is why I think that we in the Armed Forces are at the forefront of the new evangelization because we do not have the possibility of clinging to past habits, even less than elsewhere."

Need we remind you that more than 200 chaplains ensure the presence of the Church among the 420,000 military and civilian personnel of the Defense and their families? The Ministry's sanction was certainly immediate, since this publication will no longer be able to carry the Ministry of Defense logo, but it is insufficient. The Church has a long history and a heavy liability in this area, even if it no longer benefits, today as in the past, from the alliance of the throne and the altar, which has always led to that of the sword and the goupillon against the people.

---

43. http://radionotredame.net/2015/vie-de-leglise/monseigneur-ravel-logo-ministere-de-fense-35070/

Pope Francis (really) believes in the devil

Pope Francis rejects the foundations of anti-capitalism and alterglobalism as he condemns any idea of class struggle and advocates collaboration between the 99% who suffer the yoke of the minority and the 1% who dominate and destroy the world. However, we should not make the new pope a lover of dialogue. First of all, because the new Catholics with identity are convinced that truth is not shared and that they do not only carry a part of the truth, like everyone else, but the absolute truth. Secondly, because the belief in the devil makes the Church's opponents not only erring individuals but also Satan's minions, with whom one should not dialogue - ever, says Opus Dei. Vatican experts have noted that Pope Francis differs from the currently dominant preaching in the Church by his continual references to the devil. Why does this belief bother me as an atheist? I remain convinced of the validity of the analysis I produced in a book entitled *The Return of the Devil* (*op. cit.*), in which I showed how diablery and right-wing extremism in the Church always go hand in hand.

This Church of Pope Francis, which is said to be "progressive", is returning to the old temptations by associating, as in the 19th century, anticlericalism, anti-Christianity, Masonry and Satanism, and adding to them, for good measure, libertarian currents, Islamism, homosexual unions, family planning, etc. Cardinal Robert Sarah, prefect of the Congregation for Divine Worship and the Discipline of the Sacraments, even referred to "two unexpected threats (like two "beasts of the Apocalypse") on opposite poles: on the one hand, the idolatry of Western freedom; on the other, Islamic fundamentalism, atheistic secularism versus religious fanaticism. To use a slogan, we find ourselves between 'gender ideology and Isis." Cardinal Sarah points out that "Islamic massacres and libertarian demands regularly occupy the headlines. (Remember what happened on June 26!) These radicalizations stem from the two main threats to the family: its subjectivist disintegration in the secularized West through quick and easy divorce, abortion, homosexual unions, euthanasia, etc. (cf. the gender theory, which has been the subject of a number of studies, and which has been the subject of a number of studies. (On the other hand, the pseudo-family of ideological Islam that legitimizes polygamy, the submission of women, sexual slavery, child marriage, etc. (cf. Al-Qaeda,

Isis, Boko Haram...) [...]. Several clues allow us to guess the same demonic origin of these two movements."[44]

The Church of Vatican II did not speak of the devil or only metaphorically. Pope Francis, by constantly citing the devil, is reviving a distant past. This return of the devil to the Church is primarily the work of charismatic circles, although it is also the delight of Opus Dei and traditionalists. The currents of liberation theology, which the Church pretends to cajole, have, on the other hand, never spoken of the reality of the devil and have probably never believed in it. Other progressive theologians such as the Protestant Paul Tillich (1886-1965) considered demons to be mental structures.

So the Pope believes in the devil, of course, but does he believe in the devil as in the Middle Ages? The answer is unfortunately unequivocal: "But this generation, and so many others, have been made to believe that the devil is a myth, an image, an idea, the idea of evil. But the devil exists and we must fight against him." This position of Francis is in line with those of John Paul II and Benedict XVI even if, it can be considered that it was Paul VI who revived this belief in the devil.

Father Gabriele Amorth, the Vatican's official exorcist, maintains that the devil is not an impersonal entity, that he is not a simple word used to designate what psychoanalysts refer to as an abstract evil existing in society, he is a concrete person and, as St. Peter says in his first letter, he is "like a roaring lion [who] prowls around, seeking to devour"[45]. John Paul II took advantage of a trip to Turin (considered one of the capitals of Satanism) to alert Christianity in turn, but this return of the devil to the thinking of the Church had its moment of glory when the Pope went to Lyon (another capital of esotericism and Satanism) to canonize a small country priest, the Curé d'Ars, who was a true champion of encounters with the devil in the 19th century. Francis thus takes up a tradition that is not specifically South American.

The church has succeeded in making people believe more in the devil. A recent study shows that in the Netherlands, for example, 60% of young believers say they believe in the devil and hell, whereas thirty years ago this proportion was less than one in three. Exorcisms are legion: more than 1,000 per year in Belgium, and France has nearly 120 exorcist priests. In 1999, John Paul II approved a new *Ritual of Exorcism*. Of course,

---

44. In *Liberté politique*, October 16, 2015.
45. In the magazine *30 Jours*, n° 1, January 1996.

Benedict XVI only precipitated the demonization of mental disorders, thus marking an anti-scientific turn, targeting psychoanalysis in particular.

I will not discuss theology but the effects of these beliefs. The Church has sufficiently proven over the centuries how witch hunts lead to the deaths of tens of thousands of popular women. Believing in the devil in the manner of Pope Francis is the best way to develop a pastoral of fear by reminding us that "the door is narrow". The consequence is well known because as Flaubert wrote: "One must never think of happiness; that attracts the devil, for it is he who invented that idea to enrage the human race."[46] However, in order to succeed in the ecological transition, we need a conception of the good life, in the sense of the South American *buen vivir* and of the "more living" of the negro-African philosophy of existence, or of the full life of "poor people's ecology." All these currents are not on the side of "less to enjoy" but of "more to enjoy", including carnally, including sexually. To believe in the devil in the manner of Pope Francis is to denounce the passions of the flesh, "the devil, the world and the flesh", in other words, it is to maintain that human passions "are the wounds of original sin" (sic). I would like to respond by repeating the words of Robert Escarpit in his *Open Letter to God*: "As for the apple affair, you should have planted your tree somewhere else, or not created Adam in your image. In this case, the prohibition was tantamount to an encouragement, as any teacher will tell you. It was not the devil who tempted our ancestor, it was you who tempted the devil.[47]

Believing in the devil in the manner of Pope Francis is also inevitably saying that we must fight against him with the "armature" of the capitalized Truth, that is, with the dogma of which the Church and the Pope would be the only interpreters. The Pope does not say that some people should sometimes confront the devil: he explains that this "continuous struggle" concerns us all at every moment: "We need the shield of faith" because "the devil does not throw flowers at us but flaming arrows", so we must take "the shield of salvation and the sword of the Spirit which is the Word of God", we must constantly watch "in prayer and supplication".

To believe in the devil in the manner of Pope Francis is to take up that detestable tradition which explains all misdeeds, including social and

---

46. Gustave Flaubert, "letter to Louise Colet", May 21, 1853, in *Correspondance*, selection and presentation by Bernard Masson, Paris, "Folio", Gallimard, 1998, p. 227.

47. Robert Escarpit, *Lettre ouverte à Dieu*, Paris, Albin Michel, 1966.

ecological ones, by original sin; it is therefore to engage in the wrong terrain, it is to disarm humans in the face of catastrophes.

Believing in the devil in the manner of Francis is never the best way to begin a dialogue because this belief is fraught with danger. Francis sees the devil everywhere, especially in his political and religious opponents, who are naturally sent by the devil... It's a strange way of preaching understanding to "people of good will", to the faithful of other religions, to Godless people like me, and even to priest-eaters! The Pope affirms that not only does a hatred of the world exist towards Jesus and the Church, but that, behind this spirit of the world, there is "the prince of this world": "By his death and resurrection, Jesus has freed us from the power of the world, from the power of the devil, from the power of the prince of this world. The origin of hatred is this: we are saved and this prince of the world, who does not want us to be saved, hates us and gives rise to persecution, which began in the early days of Jesus and continues to this day."

Believing in the devil in the manner of Pope Francis is a reminder that since the devil, who is behind evil thoughts, is "a liar, the father of liars, the father of lies," it is no longer appropriate to seek dialogue with adversaries. Faced with the devil, it is necessary - the Pope maintains - to react as Jesus did, who "responded with the word of God. We cannot dialogue with the prince of this world. Dialogue is necessary among us, it is necessary for peace, it is an attitude that we must have among us, to listen to us, to understand us. And it must be constantly maintained. Dialogue is born of charity, of love. But we cannot dialogue with this prince; we can only respond with the word of God that defends us. I will leave the final word to Albert Jacquard: "It seems to me that religions already manifest a form of totalitarianism when, beyond an individual, they want to flush out the demon that acts in him, and this, in the name of a doctrine that is interested in the "whole" and not in the elements that compose it. Were not the Inquisitors totalitarian when they tortured a poor devil with the idea of fighting against this All that is everywhere present and acting that is the Devil?"[48]

This return of the devil in the pastoral field allows a return in force of the most right-wing currents such as the Legionaries of Christ[49], Communion and Liberation, Opus Dei, but also a giant step in the direction of traditionalist currents.

---

48. Albert Jacquard, *Petite philosophie à l'usage des non-philosophes*, Paris, Calmann-Lévy, 1997.
49. http://www.regnumchristi.fr/meditations/je-sais-qui-tu-es

Could the good Pope Francis canonize a genocidal priest?

Pope Francis took advantage of his trip to the United States in September 2015 to canonize the priest Junípero Serra (1713-1784), evangelizer of California, considered one of the "founding fathers" of the United States but accused by the North American and Mexican American Indian peoples of being responsible for the destruction of their culture, even of being a genocidaire.

This Franciscan priest, an important theologian who taught in the most important Spanish Catholic universities before embarking for the New World in 1769, was the founder of the first of nine missions created in California to convert the Indians to Roman Catholicism. The work of historians has long since established the indictment: prohibition to speak native languages, obligation to abandon customs such as dress, house arrest in camps, forced labor, chronic malnutrition, mistreatment, etc. Some historians even speak of "camps" where the Indians were not allowed to speak. Some historians even speak of "death camps" and estimate that the indigenous population dropped from 300,000 to 62,000 in one century. There are also academic works that establish the responsibility of this priest, including those of historians Steven Hackel and Elias Castillo. Junipero Serra was the one who decided that it was necessary to create enclaves, not to protect the Indians as his defenders claim today, but to subjugate them and make them obedient and productive "good Christians".

This cursed priest, as the Amerindians say, had already been beatified in 1988 by John Paul II as a symbol of the evangelization of the West. I was among those who hoped that Pope Francis would back down and not dare to canonize this religious, if only to avoid aggravating tensions, especially religious ones, between peoples. How could the Church of Rome canonize this man who crystallizes against him the hostility of a part of the Amerindian peoples? The question is all the more worth asking because the Church of Rome knew what it was doing and that its decision would provoke a wave of protests. The case has been a source of tension for almost a century, since the Cause for the beatification of this priest began in 1934. Francis said Serra would be canonized in an "equipollent" way, a way that "is used when a man or woman has been blessed for a very long time, and there is a veneration of the people of God: there is no trial of the miracle"; in other words, he had to be canonized at all costs.

The Amerindians immediately mobilized against this project. Valentin Lopez, president of the Amah Mutsun people (who occupied the San Juan Valley long before the Spaniards) declared: "The period of the missions was brutal for our peoples.... There can be no doubt that Junípero Serra is personally responsible for the destruction of our culture." The Mexica movement (which brings together members of the Indian peoples on both sides of the Mexican border, which is considered an artificial border intended and thought out in the interests of the whites alone), and its leader Tezcatlipoca (which means "smoking mirror" in the Mahuasi language), is more forceful: "He planned the genocide" and the pope is "prolonging this genocide." Toypurina Carac, spokesperson for the Kizh Gabrieleno Nation, an indigenous people from the Los Angeles area, has similar words: "We strongly denounce the canonization of the one who was the murderer of our people and our culture." Ron Andrade, director of the Los Angeles County Indian Commission, also accuses this priest of being responsible for the genocide of Native Americans in California, etc. Demonstrations, solemn appeals from various peoples and their leaders, and petitions have multiplied in the hope that Francis will listen to reason and abandon his project. But the Pope remained deaf to all the appeals. The day after the canonization, the *Huffington Post* newspaper headlined: "Once again silenced, Native Americans insulted by Pope Francis' decision to canonize Serra.

Faced with numerous protests, Francis awkwardly retorted that if this canonization "revived bitter memories of the treatment of the Indians during the missionary and colonial period", it was also necessary to take into account the fact that John Paul II had asked for forgiveness from the Amerindian peoples in 1992 for all the massacres committed during the evangelization. As if asking for forgiveness would then authorize the canonization of a genocidal priest? He also added that this saint would be "the patron saint of the Hispanic people of the country". Saint for some, devil for others?

Why on earth did Francis want to canonize this contested priest? It is already undeniably the sign of a Church that intends to assume its identity (this famous Church of identity) to better evangelize (and "re-evangelize"). This priest is therefore the symbol of evangelization, as John Paul II already maintained, a *reconquista* of which the Church of Francis intends to make the glory! The pope explains thus: "I prefer a Church that is rugged, wounded and dirty to be taken out by the wayside, rather than a

Church that is sick of closure and the comfort of clinging to its own securities" (*Pastoral Letters* 2013). The pope only seems to "forget" that, as in the pedophilia cases, it is not primarily the Church that suffers, but the peoples who have been massacred!

This affair is unfortunately an opportunity to note that the Church is still not clear on these questions. In 2007, Benedict XVI had already provoked a controversy during a trip to Brazil by denying that the evangelization of the Americas "involved an alienation of pre-Columbian cultures" because he said: "Without knowing it, the Amerindians sought Christ in their rich religious traditions. With the water of baptism, the Holy Spirit came to fertilize their cultures, purifying them." Pope Francis is a much better communicator than his predecessor, for while he asks (again) for forgiveness from the indigenous peoples, he curiously specifies "not only for the offenses of the Church" (sic), he also adds, in the manner of Benedict XVI, that the balance sheet would be positive overall: "I humbly ask for forgiveness, not only for the offenses of the Church itself, but for the crimes against the indigenous peoples during the so-called conquest of the Americas. [I also ask all of you, believers and non-believers, to remember so many bishops, priests and lay people who have announced and proclaim the good news of Jesus with courage and gentleness, respect and peace; who in their passage through this life have left moving works of human promotion and love, often among the indigenous peoples or accompanying their popular movements, even to the point of martyrdom."

How can one not turn against Francis what was said against Benedict XVI? Felipe Quispe, leader of the Pachakuti indigenous movement, former secretary general of the Unified Trade Union Confederation of Peasant Workers of Bolivia, and former candidate for the Bolivian presidential election, declared: "Luis Evelis Andrade, philosopher, former priest, leader of the National Indigenous Organization of Colombia, and senator, added: "To deny that the imposition of the Catholic religion was used as a mechanism of domination over the indigenous peoples is to want to conceal history. As indigenous peoples, if we are indeed believers, we cannot accept that the Church denies its responsibility in the annihilation of our identity and our culture," etc. Many activists and historians urged the pope to reread Bartolomé de Las Casas (1474-1566), the Spanish Dominican who denounced the atrocities committed by the conquistadors and who declared in front of the Church: "A living pagan Indian is always preferable to a dead Christian Indian"!

How the Knights of Columbus are found at work

The canonization of Junípero Serra is a gift from Francis to the Knights of Columbus, which the Church so desperately needs. Carl Anderson was in charge of the eulogy of this genocidal priest, and with the support of numerous Church networks, he took advantage of the opportunity to completely rewrite history. Carl Anderson explains that the accounts of the massacres were a "black legend" invented by the enemies of Roman Catholicism. The legend, he said, was fabricated to slander the Spanish Franciscans who established the California missions for the good of the Indians and lovingly spread Christianity among the natives. His speech at the canonization was soberly titled "Our Lady of Guadalupe, Mother and Guide of Fra Junipero Serra, Honorary President of America", a sign that for him it was not just a matter of giving a patron saint to the descendants of the Spaniards, since Our Lady of Guadalupe celebrates the conversion of the indigenous people through the grace of the Virgin Mary. The canonization was co-sponsored by the Pontifical Commission for Latin America (the same one that defeated liberation theologies), under the patronage of the Archdiocese of Los Angeles. Carl Anderson adds that "we should no longer allow the honorable story of one of our great saints, Junípero Serra, to be slandered; [...] The presumption of the black legend is that the Indians - the indigenous peoples - were treated cruelly, perhaps tortured, were exploited; [...] What drove and motivated Junípero Serra and the other missionaries was the message of Our Lady of Guadalupe, that these people have dignity. When she appeared to Juan Diego, she said, "Am I not your mother? [...] The followers of Our Lady of Guadalupe must understand that [...] evangelization does not mean domination or exploitation. It means bringing the Gospel to the people [...]. The horrible things that happened happened after the Spanish missionaries were driven out of California [...]" The Knights of Columbus, therefore, placed great importance on Francis' canonization of Serra because "we have always been concerned to defend the Church against prejudice and sectarianism [...]. It is time to set the record straight, [...] it is time to pay more attention to Catholic history [...]. As early as the early 1900s, the Knights of Columbus founded the first chair of Catholic history at the Catholic University of America in Washington, D.C., to begin this work and to challenge prejudice." Pope Francis is "the most important spokesperson in the whole world on this subject.

I'm sure he's going to talk about religious freedom when he comes to the United States. And I hope he will generate a new spirit of solidarity among Christians around the world.

The 30,000 participants in the canonization Mass were given a booklet co-authored by Carl Anderson and Vincenzo Criscuolo, general reporter of the Vatican's Congregation for the Causes of Saints. Anderson's text was intended to prove that the direct extermination of the indigenous peoples of California was in fact the work of the Anglo-Saxons after the U.S.-Mexican War and the "gold rush" in the mid-nineteenth century, i.e., the Protestants. This propaganda operation was skilfully prepared during a meeting organized in May at the Pontifical North American College in Rome, by the Pontifical Commission for Latin America, the Pontifical North American College and the Archdiocese of Los Angeles, in the presence, of course, of the Supreme Knight Carl Anderson... How can we be surprised that since this canonization, incidents have multiplied: statues of Junípero Serra and several tombstones in the cemetery where he is buried have been vandalized, the doors of the basilica have been damaged, etc.

Can the good Pope Francis beatify an anti-Semitic priest?

The shock Catholics love Pope Francis who loves the priest Leon Dehon to the point of wishing to beatify him even though the procedure initiated by John Paul II had been blocked by Benedict XVI because of the canon's anti-Semitic remarks. Pope Francis likes to tell this joke: "It's the story of a deeply anti-Semitic priest. At Sunday Mass, he begins his homily by violently attacking the Jews. Suddenly, the Church trembles, the preaching stops... Jesus comes down from the Cross. Turning to Mary, he says: "Come, Mother. We are not wanted here.

Léon Dehon (1843-1925) is the founder of the Congregation of the Priests of the Sacred Heart of Jesus, which symbolizes the Church's desire for political power. The Sacred Heart is never far from the just and holy war against the infidels. Leon Dehon contributed for decades through his writings to the spirituality of the Sacred Heart and to the study of so-called "social" issues in the Church. Pope Pius X already spoke of him as a saint, but his beatification was blocked in 1952. So the good Pope Francis knows nothing of his anti-Semitic writings. He tried to justify his decision by explaining that these words had to be placed in their historical context. I can understand that, because it is sometimes possible to admit that a text is polluted by the dross of the times (in this case, the nauseating air of a still anti-Semitic Catholic Church). But Dehon's anti-Semitic statements are in line with his thinking and the heart of his system! His contentious works, and in particular his famous *Social Catechism,* written by the commission of social studies of the diocese of Soissons under his presidency, had been published with the approval of "his greatness, the Bishop of Soissons", so much so that this book committed the Church of the nineteenth century, so that by beatifying Léon Dehon, he would be committing the Church for eternity. It is not I who says this but the texts of the beatifications themselves. I will only quote an excerpt from a chapter entitled "The anti-Semitic reaction": "Yes! This is still a sign of hope. There may be a little exaggeration in this movement, there is always exaggeration when strength or freedom that has been compressed reacts and rises again. It is certain that the Jew and the Christian are not on equal terms, since the Talmud puts the conscience of the Jews vis-à-vis the Christians on the line. Therefore, in order to restore the balance, some restrictions on the freedoms of the Jews are necessary, and the Christian states have always understood this. France even still has some laws to restrain them, but it no longer applies them. This people has inescapable instincts. They have a thirst for gold, they have Christ as their enemy. Left free and gifted with a great talent for speculation, they have conquered our gold and hold us in bondage. He holds the press and makes the opinion [...]. Our governments are slaves to the High Bank. They can no longer take a measure that displeases the billionaires, without the latter raising their voices and threatening to provoke a crisis on the stock market. We are the slaves, that is understood.

This beatification would be all the more disturbing in the current context where Pope Francis is once again denouncing the Golden Calf and in which we are witnessing a rise in the extreme right and a return of anti-Semitism. I will not be so unkind as to generalize the Polish case, but all the same! Catholic anti-Semitism did not cease after the end of the war: "Redemptorist Father Tadeusz Rydzyk, director of the ultraconservative Radio Maryja station, will be able to continue his work with impunity. On Monday, July 23, his superior, Father Zdzislaw Klafka, openly supported him and cleared him of recent accusations of anti-Semitism. The controversy had arisen two weeks earlier, after the publication by the weekly

Wprost of the transcript of a lecture given by Father Rydzyk in his school of social and media culture in the spring. He had attacked the Polish president, accusing him of being under the influence of a Jewish lobby.[50] This priest, head of a press group, is also known for his defense of creationism and nationalism.

He was received by Pope Benedict XVI in 2007 despite protests[51]. Much closer geographically, we find Father Guy Pagès, a former army chaplain, now a priest without a ministry, who has chosen the Internet apostolate, with some success in terms of audience. Guy Pagès is a particularly fierce anti-Semite and anti-Muslim. The vicar general of Paris explains that there is no imprimatur concerning the videos and that the priest Guy Pagès can therefore continue his provocations. However, nothing would prevent the Church from bringing a lawsuit, as it has done hundreds of times against priests advocating liberation theologies. The Church is not responsible for Guy Pagès' remarks, but why is he regularly invited to Church movements, to TV Liberté, to the Journées chouannes de Chiré in 2015, to the summer camp for becoming a good soldier of Jesus Christ, to the SIEL colloquium and, worse, to the OSCE? The Organization for Security and Cooperation in Europe is the only organization with a generalist vocation that welcomes all the states of the European continent. Is it normal that the Catholic Church is represented, on this occasion, by a priest spewing hatred[52] ? (Is it necessary to remind that Massimo Introvigne, the lawyer of all the bad things in the Church, is the personal representative of the president of the OSCE concerning the fight against racism, xenophobia and discrimination?) Father Pagès praises self-defense for the online TV ripoublik.com (sic): good Christians should not turn the other cheek but use violence[53].

Pope Francis, in choosing to beatify the priest Léon Dehon, would be committing a quadruple moral fault, with regard to the Jews, with regard to the poor, with regard to the Freemasons and with regard to the socialist and emancipatory currents. Léon Dehon was not only an anti-Semite but an absolute reactionary. He certainly loved his poor very much, but in his

---

50. http://www.cicad.ch/fr/le-p%C3%A8re-tadeusz-rydzyk-et-lantis%C3%A9mitisme.html#sthash.LOKxfOev.dpuf

51. http://www.liberation.fr/planete/2007/08/09/le-baisemain-au-pape-qui-choque-la-communaute-juive_10632

52. https://www.youtube.com/watch?v=BhIKAq375aA

53. http://www.islam-et-verite.com/pages/pages-cachees/verite/les-interventions-publiques/l-abbe-pages-evoque-la-legitime-defense.html

own special way: "The Church and the people are made to love each other [...]. The Church loves the little ones because it is compassionate. The little ones love the Church because they are grateful." Translation: the "good" poor must not envy the rich, according to a whole theological tradition! Is this the image of the theology of the poor that Francis wishes to give? Dehon was also a curious democrat (I'm not even talking about being a republican) since he does not hide his love for the Christian Middle Ages: "If this name (of democracy) is given to the arbitrary domination of the mob, the Church cannot favor democracy which disregards the divine laws". He therefore likes democracy under the condition of good Christianity, and, in the face of dictatorships, he invites the people to submit unless the laws of God are betrayed: "The political constitution of each people depends on historical circumstances. Subjects are obliged to accept governments and to do nothing to overthrow them; revolutions are an immense evil that one does not have the right to provoke [...]" Is this the lesson that Francis retained from his long and disturbing experience of the military dictatorship in Argentina?

The priest Leon Dehon does not like Jews, nor socialists, nor atheists, nor Freemasons and he reminds us that Leo XIII and several of his predecessors have stigmatized the perversity of their doctrines and the infamy of their acts. The enemies of the priest Dehon are in the service of Satan, the enemy of God.

Part Two: Will Francis save the planet?

The Church has pulled off quite a media coup with the encyclical *Laudato si'*. This letter published by Francis in June 2015 registered 1,680,000 hits on Google compared to only 327,000 for the IPCC (Intergovernmental Panel on Climate Change) report, which has been around since 1988. The Church of Francis has therefore succeeded in its *greenwashing* operation. It has not spent the church's money unnecessarily on its communication consultants. But what about on the religious and political level?

This text, far from being revolutionary and progressive, in fact recalls the great dogmas of the Church in matters of sin, sexuality, economics and politics. Under the pretext of defending ecosystems and an "Earth for humanity", Francis reminds us that the Church alone holds the absolute truth and intends to impose its dogmas on us in areas that do not concern ecology. Francis denounces the legalization of contraception and abortion, he attacks those who "falsify" marriage with divorce and gay marriage. His ecology also bears a striking resemblance to austerity policies. Francis is not on the side of a "more to enjoy" but of a castrating "less to enjoy". So it is not I who has chosen to return to the favorite hunting grounds of the priest-eaters, but Francis who cannot help but instrumentalize ecology to make it a field of application for a repressive religion. This is a curious encyclical which, with the exception of some "left-wing" Catholics, but also of Catholic-liberals, is praised by all those on the extreme right of God. From Opus Dei to Communion and Liberation, everyone is pleased with this stroke of papal genius. For example, Opus Dei, whose theme for the 2014 university was "Ecology of the Person and the Environment," after participating in the Holy Father's General Audience, promised to carry its appeal for ecology.

The hidden face of the encyclical *Laudato si'*

This encyclical signed by Francis is of course a collective work even if his name will remain permanently attached to this new theology of ecology. An encyclical is technically a letter addressed by the pope to all the bishops, and sometimes to the faithful, but it does not commit papal infallibility.

Each word of an encyclical is weighed at length, so that the average reader often misses the real issues, which only appear at the end of a long period of time and to initiated readers. The leftists and the ecologists are victims of semantic intoxication, because it is not because the bishop of Rome makes the same observations as them on the planetary situation and that he uses the same words... that he says the same thing. The essential of the theses of the ecological encyclical can already be found in the declarations of Aparecida, which acknowledged the defeat of the theologies of liberation and therefore the possibility of a new preferential option for the poor... Ecology in the Vatican sauce is not more emancipating than its popular theology. We are not on the same side of desire and enjoyment!

We will therefore be obliged to deconstruct the text of the encyclical, since it has been skilfully elaborated to allow the greatest number of people to join in, postponing to the middle and end of the text the subjects that make people angry (such as the dogma of original sin), but above all that which gives the true key to its reading. Mario Toso, a bishop who worked extensively on its collective drafting and who was, until January 2015, secretary of the Pontifical Council for Justice and Peace, tells us: "The encyclical, as it is presented to us today, shows a face that is different from that of the first draft. The latter provided for a long introduction of a theological, liturgical, sacramental and spiritual nature. If the original structure had been retained, the encyclical would have been more immediately addressed to the Catholic world. Instead, Pope Francis preferred to modify this structure, moving the theological part toward the middle and end of the text."[54]

---

54. www.standelarminat.com/les2ailes/index.php?...

This obligation to read between the lines in order not to be fooled is also underlined by another Catholic luminary, a great connoisseur of the writing of encyclicals, since he himself participated in the drafting of Benedict XVI's *Caritas in Veritate* as (former) president of the IOR: Gotti Tedeschi explains, in an interview with *La Repubblica* and in a commentary published by another newspaper, *Il Foglio*, that one understands the deep meaning of the encyclical only when one adds to the expression *Laudato si'* ("Praised be you") the words *mi Signore* ["my Lord"]. This need to clarify is doubly strange, because in a Catholic context the expression "Praise be to you" systematically refers to the Lord and "Praise be to you, my Lord" is in fact the real first sentence of the encyclical. Gotti Tedeschi only insists on countering those who would make a profane reading of the text. Because the ultimate cause of the behavior that leads to environmental degradation "is sin, the loss of God", while the proximate cause is "consumerism". This "excessive consumerism" would not be the consequence of capitalist lifestyles or even of advertising aggression, but of "a desire to compensate for the fall in births in Western countries"[55]. The translation of this theological clarification is that we must first fight the deep causes of ecological collapse, such as contraception or abortion, rather than the superficial causes such as capitalism and productivism! Since the destruction of ecosystems can only be stopped by re-establishing the so-called natural laws, i.e. those of God, the priority would be to evangelize the "useful idiots" of profane ecology. This text is therefore not as consensual as the media would have us believe!

However, everyone has access to the pontifical message as soon as it is translated by his own flock in magazines that are less mainstream and therefore less ecumenical. Some have remembered that Francis is a Jesuit, and therefore perfectly accustomed to this system of writing, which is not immediately obvious and allows for multiple readings, even though its truth is totally univocal. This strategy of obfuscation is not specific to the pope, far from it. One can even argue that the more one considers the prose of the soldiers of God involved in ecology, the more diabolically deceptive their literature becomes. Thus, right-wing (even very right-wing) ecologist-Cathos are good at masking themselves, not hesitating, for example, to quote left-wing authors such as Cornelius Castoriadis, Antonio Gramsci, André Gorz, in the good old tradition of Alain de Benoist's pagan New Right, which they used to vomit out before

---

55. http://chiesa.espresso.repubblica.it/articolo/1351074?fr=y

the latter proclaimed his sympathy for this particular pope[56]. Alain de Benoist maintains that for "Pope Francis capitalism is an intrinsically evil system"[57]. But who could believe that the anti-capitalism of the "Pope of the New Right" would in any way resemble ours?

This strategy of confusion is claimed with the famous "everything is linked". Thus the confusion maintained between PMA (medically assisted procreation), GPA (surrogate motherhood) and GMO (genetically modified organism). Let us then note the equivocation of the notion of "social doctrine of the Church", since by "social" one should not understand social justice as we spontaneously understand it, but the Catholic conception of society, that is to say, admiration for the Middle Ages and defense of private property. Finally, let us note the equivocation that consists in speaking of a "culture of waste". The Church is in fact moving imperceptibly from the observation made decades ago on the unsustainable nature of our mode of development to something else. Francis' main thesis is that the culture of waste (material pollution, to put it simply) is only one element of a much more important pollution, that of the heart, that of the spirit, that of the whole of man, as soon as he no longer believes in God, as soon as he no longer submits to the so-called natural laws. The culture of waste would be the consequence of the loss of reference points between good and evil, between high and low, in short between God and the devil. This criticism of the culture of waste incites us to move on to the essential, not the fight against nuclear power and incinerators, not the fight against programmed obsolescence, since all these wastes are only important symptoms, but secondary, compared to the fight against pornography, against degenerate modern art, against contraception, against abortion, against the falsification of marriage by concupiscence, etc.

This strategy of confusion can only lead to scandalous drifts. Thus, Father Hervé Benoît dared to compare the victims of the Bataclan attacks with the terrorists by publishing on the site Riposte catholique a text entitled "The (plucked) eagles of death love the devil" in which he denounces the bobo generation: "Same rootlessness, same amnesia, same infantilism, same inculture [...]. The others, of Muslim values that have become even

---

56. I must admit that I also had the unpleasant surprise to find myself given as a reference on the AF website: http://www.actionfrancaise.net/2007/01/30/le-pari-de-la-decrois-sance/

57. http://www.bvoltaire.fr/alaindebenoist/pape-francois-systeme-capitaliste-intrinse-quement-mauvais, 196913

crazier through contact with modernity: intolerance, dogmatism, cosmopolitanism of hate. This priest describes the Bataclan spectators as "poor children of the bobo generation, in ecstatic trance, 'young, festive, open, cosmopolitan' as the daily newspaper of reference (sic) says... but they are the living dead. Their murderers, these hashashin zombies, are their Siamese brothers." Father Benoît then establishes a connection between the number of victims of these attacks and the 130 or 160 abortions performed, according to him, every day, in France. He concludes by asking: "Where is the real horror? Referring to a song by the group Eagles of Death Metal that was performing that night at the Bataclan where it is about the devil: "You invoke the devil in jest? He takes you seriously. An extraordinary exorcist told me the same day of the attacks: "If you open the door to him, he will be happy to enter". Dear reader, never forget that the ultimate cause of the behavior that leads to terrorism and ecocide "is sin, the loss of God"! Following the protests sent to the bishopric, Cardinal Barbarin, who had initially simply described his remarks as "hurtful to the victims", dismissed him as chaplain of the Basilica of Fourvière in Lyon. Father Benoît regularly publishes in extreme right-wing Catholic magazines such as *La Nef* (alongside ecologist-Cathos Jacques de Guillebon or Falk van Gaver, see *below*). Hervé Benoît quotes the anarchist novelist George Orwell specifying that an ecclesiastic can afford it without blushing (sic). These scandalous positions are only possible because this type of believer believes himself to be the bearer of a capitalized Truth, of a true Christian science.

"Christian science" versus science

The media have promoted this encyclical *Laudato si'* so much that everyone thinks they know it without even having to delve into the text. However, this document is worth the detour because the journey holds some surprises. Not only does the Pope consider that our secular ecology, by not tackling the "ethical and spiritual roots of environmental problems" (i.e. by not submitting to his capitalized Truth), would only confront the "symptoms" and therefore that the struggles against capitalism, productivism But he adds that "the violence in the human heart wounded by sin is also manifested in the symptoms of disease that we observe in the soil, in the water, in the air and in living beings". The destruction of ecosystems would be the consequence of original sin, and profane ecologists would be useful idiots of the system. Who is Francis kidding when he accuses non-believers of considering religions as a "subculture" when it is he who is demonizing us? Not only would our children still be guilty of original sin, responsible according to him for the environmental crisis as for everything else, but it would also be the sin that would prevent the Church from recognizing that it is right when it considers environmental mobilizations as derisory. The Pope, under the title "The Gospel of Creation" (*Laudato si'*, 2), seems, for example, to advocate a new alliance between science and religion and between reason and faith, but it is to better defend dogmas and the idea of a Christian science[58].

Christian science, since it is always the notion of "primitive revelation", developed by the proponents of nineteenth-century Christian science, that can lead to such a close link between pollution and original sin. It will be recalled that the notion of "primitive revelation" concerns what was given by God to Adam with/through language and against which profane science cannot go, because there is no possible knowledge without the help of God. This Christian science is marked by an absolute anti-Cartesianism, since it considers rationalism as the origin of all evils. The Church no longer displays its positions as clearly as in the 19th century, but the heart is still there: scientists must have revealed truth as a guide for their research. This "Christian science" is not only the one that burned Giordano Bruno and censured Galileo and Copernicus (among many others), it is also the one that leads, today, to deny the theories on the evolution of species, or to cobble together (as we shall see later) pseudo-theories on "intelligent design" or "guided evolution", it is still it which, in the name of essentialism, refuses to recognize the equal rights of LGBT people[59], it is still it which fights against "unnatural" contraception and abortion, against desire in the couple and opposes the right to die with dignity.

This "Christian science" is the one claimed, for example, by Fabrice Hadjadj, one of the inspirers of the ecologist-catholic review *Limite*, director of the European institute of anthropological studies Philanthropos, in Fribourg (Switzerland), when he wrote in *La Croix* on February 10, 2009: "The believer must hold that all scientific truth is

---

58. By Christian Science, I am not referring here to the eponymous movement (Christian Science) founded by Mary Baker Eddy and which I reported on in my book *Les sectes à l'assaut de la santé*, Paris, Éd. Golias, 2000.
59. LGBT: lesbian, gay, bisexual and transgender.

compatible with Christian dogma, since it is the same God who is the author of reason and the giver of faith. So the question of the compatibility of Darwinism with Christianity comes down to the question of the scientificity of Darwinism itself."

I intend to denounce both science without conscience and faith without reason. Pope Francis obliges us to remember that religion (and especially his own) has always been opposed to the scientific development of knowledge. The Church has historically been the champion of the crime against reasoning, through the prohibition of verification of facts, through the manipulation of texts, through censorship and self-censorship in order not to end up locked up, tortured, murdered. Is it necessary to recall what happened to the autodafés, etymologically "acts of faith"? Do we need to recall the principle of the Index which established the list of forbidden books? The Church destroyed most of the works of the materialist thinkers of antiquity, which we would have needed so much to think about a society of the good life. Only about 5% of the texts of Democritus, the father of materialism, remain, and the Church has only spared a few dozen pages of Epicurus. It continues to subject its own theologians to censorship and silence.

The great mathematician and philosopher Bertrand Russel (1872-1970) is still alive when he denounces the war of religion against science. Ecology needs "disbelievers" who have "more and more" critical spirit! We will see that it is not by chance that the Jesuits of Quebec are defending, in this autumn of 2015, the science that they say is threatened (cf. *infra*). We are not scientists and we know that other approaches are necessary as long as they are open and do not close us in. We are on the side of the imaginary and of the symbolic in which we will be ready to make a place, at the sides of the arts, to the various spiritualities. We are for the poetization of the thought and the existences because never the poets will claim to speak in the name of a revealed truth to impose to all. Ecology, which calls for the decolonization of the imaginary, does not intend to recolonize it. The Church can believe what it wants within its walls but in the city we must denounce the imposture as soon as it claims to be more than a metaphor. The Church has really believed (and especially imposed to believe to non-believers) for a long time in the creation of the world in six days, some still believe in it. All approaches to God have indeed the same big flaw which is to pass arbitrarily from the definition of the thing to the existence of the thing. The Church is back to the Middle Ages every time it claims to put reason at the service of revealed truths, this "rationalization" of revealed truths has a name, scholasticism, it has a reality, absurdity and intolerance. The encyclical of Francis is, as Bishop Mario Toso admits, a scholastic work in its intuition but also in its construction. It instrumentalizes the cause of ecology, which it intends to put at the service of its power, at the service of Christ the Bridegroom and of his one and only Bride-the Church. This text is therefore falsely addressed to "people of good will" because the secret will of the pope is to bring them back to his dogmas. *Nein Danke!*

The ecologist-cathos at the service of neocreationism?

The Church is moving forward in a hidden way in its fight against science and reason because it must take into account the increase in the level of schooling. This is why its position seems to be constantly changing on these issues. The media likes to oppose Pope Francis and Benedict XVI on scientific matters simply because Francis has declared that the theories of evolution and creationism are similar and that God is not "a magician with a magic wand": "When we read what is said about creation in Genesis, we run the risk of imagining that God is a magician, with a magic wand capable of doing everything. But this is not the case. He created human beings and let them develop according to internal laws that he gave to each of them so that they could fully realize their potential [...] The Big Bang, which we believe to be the origin of the world, does not cancel out the intervention of a divine creator. Evolution in nature is not contradictory to the notion of creation because evolution requires the creation of beings that evolve."

Francis did not become a materialist and Darwinian, but he did understand that the Church would not defeat science by taking up the stories of the mainly Protestant American creationists, who are convinced that the Earth was created in six days less than 10,000 years ago... According to a CBS poll in November 2004, 55% of Americans believe that "God created humans in their present form" (67% of Republicans versus 47% of Democrats). To make Francis a revolutionary in this area would be as aberrant as believing that he will actually liberate sexuality! His remarks before the Pontifical Academy of Sciences in October 2014 are not so different from those of Pius XII, who already welcomed the Big Bang theory, or those of John Paul II, who maintained that the theory of evolution was "more than a hypothesis"... One only rejoices before Francis because one ignores that the Church has long admitted that "evolution in the sense of common ancestry may be true, but evolution in the sense of Darwin's - an unguided and unplanned process - is not accurate"[60]. One only marvels at Francis because one does not understand that he is implementing the strategy defined by Benedict XVI during a closed-door seminar held from September 1st to 3, 2006, in the Pope's summer residence, after the publication of an article by Cardinal Schönborn in the *New York Times*, which encouraged a rethinking of the Darwinian explanation of evolution. This article was considered providential by Benedict XVI because it sought to "recover in a new form a dimension of reason that we had lost. Without it, faith would be exiled to a ghetto and would thus lose its meaning for the totality of the reality of the human being"[61].

This strategy is that of Catholics like Patrice de Plunkett or Jean Staune, to whom I have been opposed for several years. They claim to be massive supporters, certainly not of North American-style creationism, but of "guided evolution" or "intelligent design"[62]. These pseudo-theories, although they seem less grotesque than those of the classical creationists, have the same political effects, because once the existence of a designer at the origin of the world is postulated, it becomes very easy to pass laws against contraception, abortion, etc. The pontifical knight Patrice de Plunkett has the great merit of doctrinal consistency. Pretending to question himself ("Is creationism a crime?") and to be offended that the media could accuse the Pope of adopting *Intelligent Design* (ID) after the meeting held behind closed doors from September 1st to 3, 2006, he explains that neocreationism should not be confused with ID: "*Intelligent Design* is a scientific hypothesis of paleontologists: they believe, in the current state of knowledge that the theory of evolution "chance" does not explain certain observed phenomena, which seem the signs of an internal logic that would be at work in the mechanisms of evolution. "Patrice de Plunkett, faithful to the new temptation of the Church, plays the victim: he claims that the proponents of

---

60. Words spoken in 2005 by Cardinal Schönborn.
61. http://benoit-et-moi.fr/2014-II-1/benoit/creation-et-evolution-la-reflexion-de-benoit-xvi.html
62. Cyrille Baudouin and Olivier Brosseau, *Les créationnismes*, Paris, Syllepse, 2008. And by the same authors, *Enquête sur les créationnismes. Réseaux, stratégies et objectifs politiques*, Paris, " Regard ", Belin, 2013.

unofficial scientific theses would be considered heretics and slandered. He explains about ID that "scientists who consider this hypothesis are reviled by 'hard' materialists. Catholic Christians believe that man is not an 'accidental product deprived of meaning' (Benedict XVI)... and that life and the universe are a creation of God: a notion compatible with the observed phenomena of evolution... It is as if the scientists of the Pontifical Academy and the crazy Texans think the same thing [...]. One can refuse the idea that life is the work of God, but what right do we have to impose this idea on others? What right do we have to disqualify a paleontologist on the scientific level, under the pretext that she is a member of the Teilhard de Chardin Foundation? Perhaps because a race for speed is underway, the biotechnology lobby has a lot of money to make: it is therefore in its interest, before certain scientific deadlines, to silence those who protect the dignity of the human person. The idea that the human person is the work of God is the absolute guarantee of this dignity. This idea must therefore be discredited.

Thus, the conspiracy theory (diabolical?) is put forward as a massive argument. Those who are opposed to "intelligent design" are said to be henchmen of the biotechnology industry, which would like to put an end to human dignity. It should be remembered that this dogma of "intelligent design" is a watered-down version of creationism born in the ultraconservative networks of North America and that, in many states, creationists are trying to have the theory of "intelligent design" (sic) introduced into the school curriculum.

Jean Staune, one of my opponents on a November 2015 television show[63], is a recent convert to Catholicism, who, like any convert, is particularly feisty; he is the founder of the misnamed association "Université Interdisciplinaire de Paris" (UIP), often denounced as one of the main tools of neocreationism in France and in Europe. This collaborator of the Pontifical Council for Culture is also a great adept of "green capitalism" and private enterprise. This shocking anti-Darwinian and anti-materialist is an advocate of "guided evolution". Under this pretty nickname lies a current that refuses to be confused with the North American madmen of creationism (the Earth was created in six days) and even with the proponents of "intelligent design", but his theses are just as effective in blurring the lines of thought, probably with more talent. The objective of Jean Staune and the anti-materialist currents is to reintroduce spirituality

____

63. http://www.francetv.fr/evenements/cop-21/diffusions/13-11-2015_434056

into the scientific field, no matter how. This so-called "Interdisciplinary University of Paris" (for it is of course not recognized by the Ministry of Higher Education and Research) has become an essential vector of "religiously correct" science. This famous IPU is naturally promoted by religious institutions such as the program *Le Jour du Seigneur*, or Radio Notre-Dame, and supported and financed (to the tune of about one million euros per year according to *Le Monde*) by the North American John Templeton Foundation (see *below*), but it seems to have lost a good number of its sponsors such as L'Oréal, Auchan, EDF, Air France and a few other "green" multinationals. Among its partners are the Pontifical University Regina Apostolorum, the Pontifical Gregorian University, the Pontifical Lateran University, etc.

These theses are not only chimerical but dangerous at a time of climate change and the right decisions to be taken. They forbid understanding the deep nature of living beings and reduce biology to a vitalism that denies the emergence of living beings from inanimate structures. This teleology has only one goal: not to save the planet but the Christian confession of faith: "I believe in God, creator of Heaven and Earth", even if it means not understanding anything about the evolution of species and missing the planetary stakes. The Church, while maintaining its doctrinal basis, is thus navigating at sight, as its successive tactical positions prove. Thanks to the work of Guillaume Lecointre, a professor at the Muséum national d'histoire naturelle, we discover that the Church is following the developments of the Templeton Foundation: "If the UIP in France and the John Templeton Foundation (JFT) in the United States of America are explicitly on the same line, both distance themselves loud and clear from the intelligent design (ID) movement. However, there have been links between ID and JFT. A report dated September 1st, 2000, available on the American website Science & Theology News, mentions a conference entitled *The Nature of Nature* sponsored jointly by the JTF and the Discovery Institute. The main theme of the four-day conference was *Intelligent Design*. This clear collaboration between the two institutions completes the conclusions of Philippe Boulet-Gercourt's investigation of the relationship between JTF and ID: "The Templeton Foundation, which promotes the reconciliation of science and religion, has offered to fund research projects in the field of ID. The work of these two structures has not always been as different as the JTF now claims. Let's recall that ID supporters lost a high-profile lawsuit in December 2005. This bad publicity led structures like the IPU and the JTF to try to distance themselves from a spiritualist movement that had lost credibility in the eyes of public opinion, after having gone some way with the ideas or promoters of ID in the past. The Templeton Foundation now clearly relies on the IPU to extend its worldview to Europe, but changed its tune *on* ID when it realized that ID was discredited in the media.

Let us note the paradox that the Church seems to be following in the footsteps of a foundation directly linked to the fundamentalist movement... Protestant. So much so that in March 2009, the Discovery Institute (the parent company of the "intelligent design" proponents) accused the Templeton Foundation of blocking its involvement in supporting the Vatican. Perhaps we can resolve this paradox by opening the official Directory of Vatican Foundations. The latest foundation listed is the Science and Faith Foundation (STOQ), formed on January 10, 2012, at the suggestion of Cardinal Gianfranco Ravasi, president of the Pontifical Council for Culture. The acronym STOQ stands for "Science, Theology and the Ontological Quest," a program with the goal of dialogue between science, philosophy and theology, implemented in some of the Pontifical Universities of Rome under the patronage of the Vatican and with the support of the Templeton Foundation... I would add that the Templeton Foundation, which finances, to the tune of more than 60 million dollars a year, "scientific" research on big *questions,* including the future of the planet, is naturally denounced in the United States for its very right-wing and ultraconservative positions. Its founder, John Templeton, was a leading member of the Presbyterian Church all his life, and is one of the richest people on the planet (one hundred and twenty-ninth place in 2006), having made his fortune through his investment fund. This great Christian philanthropist renounced his American citizenship in 1968 to avoid paying income tax and ended his life in the Bahamas...

Scientists therefore rightly accuse neocreationists of undermining the skepticism necessary for any scientific approach worthy of the name, by wishing either to reintroduce faith into the scientific approach, or to achieve a forced compatibility of the results of science with their dogmas. I would add that the ecologist-cathos, by questioning what they call "the relativism of values", undermine the very conception of an open and democratic society in which truth is shared.

The ecologist-cathos against the freedom of thought

In the name of defending the planet, eco-church members have become the champions of the fight against what the Church has chosen to call "relativism". This thesis has long been the property of the most conservative currents such as Ichtus (also known as the Center for Training in Civic Action according to Natural and Christian Law), which believes that liberalism automatically leads to the relativism of values, and therefore to the loss of God. This movement, long marginalized within a church worked by the left, has recently regained some color since its general delegate, Guillaume Dumouchel de Prémare, was the first president of the Manif pour tous. This thesis is also taken up by the ideologists of Catholic ecology (whose portraits we will draw up in a future chapter). Thus Tugdual Derville, general delegate of the association Alliance VITA (against women's rights), spokesman of the "Manif pour tous", co-initiator of the current for a human ecology, reminds us that if "everything is worthwhile, nothing is worthwhile", which allows him to denounce the intellectual bankruptcy of "relativist bioethics"; Vincent Cheynet, the Catholic editor-in-chief of the monthly *La Décroissance*, opposes Serge Latouche, an atheist economist and one of the fathers of the degrowth movement, whom he accuses of opening "the way to a total relativism of values"; Gaultier Bès de Berc, co-author of the bible of integral ecology, also denounces this "tyranny of relativism", to use the formula of the Jean Ousset collective (named after a Mauretanic Catholic intellectual). For this Church, Freemasonry continues, as in the 19th century, to be the symbol of this relativism of values. Thus Mgr Rey, the bishop of the diocese of Fréjus-Toulon, explains that one cannot be a Freemason and a Catholic because "belonging to Freemasonry is adherence to a system of thought that is part of relativism, in a negation of the place of God's grace." The same estimated about the attacks against *Charlie Hebdo*: "When Mohammed is represented in the form of a turbaned turd, Benedict XVI sodomizing children, the Virgin Mary with her legs spread in a suggestive way; when one indulges in provocation, in obscenity on what touches the most intimate consciousness, that of faith, of the sacred, of religious symbolism...This new iconoclasm inevitably generates, by ricochet, and of course, without ever justifying them, revenge, other violence even more unbearable in an almost mechanical spiral, and of which the current events offer us the horrible spectacle. The sacredness of derision and insult can only produce hatred in return. Marion Maréchal Le Pen gives the political version of this thesis: "For me, equality does not take precedence over freedom, and children do not take precedence over parents. I reject the software of May 68, which itself rejects the words value, identity, principle, or master."

John Paul II reminds us that in the face of a "society that is losing its traditional references and that voluntarily favors a generalized relativism", our "first duty is to make Christ and the Gospel known". He denounced in a speech delivered the day before his election "a dictatorship of relativism that recognizes nothing as definitive and gives as its ultimate measure only its own ego and desires." Pope Francis, receiving the diplomatic corps accredited to the Vatican on March 22, 2013, also strongly attacked the relativism of values...

The mass is thus said: we would have lost all reference points by losing our faith! We would be incapable of constructing our own definitions of good and evil since we would have chosen the rights of man against the rights of God. The ecological crisis, even before being the result of extractivism, would be the consequence of the freedom unduly granted to humanity... Society could not be founded under the symbol of the freedoms to be conquered, because this posture of the Enlightenment would maintain the illusion that man is all-powerful, whereas, says Francis, only God and his spouse, the Church, would be all-powerful

However, ecology must advocate absolute freedom of thought because it can only praise doubt, and question all dogmas, those of "really existing socialism", i.e. Stalinism, those of capitalism and productivism or those of the great ideologies and religions. I would not care about this dogma if it did not have tangible consequences. Thus, in his spiritual testament, *Memory and Identity: Conversations in the Passage Between Two Millenniums* (Flammarion, 2005), John Paul II writes: "The law established by man has precise limits that cannot be crossed. These are the limits set by the natural law, by which God himself protects man's fundamental goods. Francis, speaking on the subject of the cartoons published in the press, considers that in religious matters freedom of expression has limits: "One cannot insult the faith of others, one cannot make fun of it"[64]. This same pope who recognizes that killing in the name of God or imposing a religion is an aberration does not find it aberrant to insult billions of human beings

---

64. http://www.la-croix.com/Religion/Actualite/Le-pape-Francois-on-ne-peut-insulter-la-foi-des-autres-2015-01-15-1267821

by putting on the same level anti-Semitism which is a crime and atheism which is a fundamental right... Pope Francis speaks a lot about the refusal to offend one's neighbor but he has a variable geometry conception of what is an offense!

Mgr Jean-Pierre Batut considers that "the culture of derision has shown its limits: Western societies dishonour themselves if they present it as the ultimate *in* thought and if they put the whole world on notice to adhere to it". I admit that I consider it a sign of good republican health to claim the right to blasphemy. But it must be specified that for the Church blasphemy is not only and simply the fact of mocking God because "to deny the existence of God or his Providence, to deny the mystery of the Holy Trinity or of the redemptive Incarnation, are blasphemies; and they are as much and even more so than insulting God, insulting him or dishonoring him. Father Hervé Belmont continues: "We are in a society in which blasphemy has become institutional (in France, it is even constitutional); it is permanent, it contaminates all public life and becomes for each member of society a formidable peril that insinuates itself into hearts as if without their knowledge. The apostate social order is thus a particularly serious form of blasphemy. Here too, we must not stop at the outward appearance: the hidden blasphemy is more serious and more perilous.[65] Francis, like John Paul II, considers that "the sin against the Holy Spirit is unforgivable.

Pope Francis talks about respect and the possibility of speaking freely but without provoking and this for all religious grounds or not, but some dogmas are a provocation for billions of humans. I don't know if this blasphemous book insults the faith of Francis, but his dogma that makes a child just born a sinner, because of Adam and Eve, is an insult to humanity; his vision of marriage in which it is enough to look at one's spouse with desire to be accused of being a falsifier is inhuman, his assimilation of atheism and anti-Semitism is scandalous, etc. What to think of Francis' famous quip during his plane trip from Colombo to Manila in January 2015 when he explained to reporters, "It is true that we should not react violently, but if Mr. Gasbarri [in charge of the trip, standing next to him] who is a great friend says a swear word about my mother, he should expect to get a punch! It's normal... You can't provoke, you can't insult the faith of others, you can't make fun of faith!"[66] This is quite irresponsible when

---

65. http://www.quicumque.com/article-les-catholiques-face-au-blaspheme-101276513.html
66. https://www.youtube.com/watch?v=FAvASiHXyeQ

we are witnessing the rise of religious violence! Proposals that are quite revealing, moreover, of the papal unconsciousness that passes from the insult to the mother, worthy of the playground, to the insult to beliefs!

The question is not whether the Church should be forbidden to reaffirm values, but whether it should always claim to forbid humans to choose their values. This is why, even before being anti-liberal on the economic level, Rome first condemned religious, philosophical and political liberalism. It is true that the Church has since put republican water in its mass wine, but beware of the return of the repressed, as certain statements attest: "One cannot provoke, one cannot insult the faith of others, one cannot make fun of the faith!" said Francis about *Charlie Hebdo*[67].

The Church today speaks of "value relativism", as do all the champions of the world conservative revolution[68] (which shows once again who its political allies are), while in the 19th century it spoke of "indifferentism" (another word but the same content), which was, according to Pope Leo XIII, the cause of all evils: "Indifferentism [is] that perverse opinion which has spread as a result of the deception of the wicked, according to which the soul can obtain eternal salvation by professing any belief. " Leo XIII called freedom of conscience a "pestilential error" and Pius IX an "absolute evil" that corrupts youth "pouring into it the gall of the dragon of Babylon", with first rationalism that "never ceases to exalt the strength and supereminence of human reason", with then "the belief in the progress of mankind which is exalted with no less audacity and artifice by these enemies of revelation." The solution was "the infallible authority of the pope". This dogma is a supreme confession: a proclamation of the powerlessness of all and the omnipotence of one! The vocabulary has changed: one no longer dares to attack reason so openly, so one denounces the omnipotence of man, man who thinks he is God, "unfettered enjoyment", May 68 and Cohn-Bendit, etc. The solutions are always the same: to fall back on the conception of the "good life", to advocate austerity in the name of ecology and degrowth, as in the past the patronesses preached abstinence to the poor, and always to affirm obedience to the authorities as an absolute principle, unless something contrary to God's laws is ordered. Do we need to recall the words of Gregory XVI referring to the verse in

---

67. See also *above* the teaching that Bishop Rey retained from the attacks against *Charlie Hebdo*.

68. Paul Ariès, *Misère du sarkozysme. Cette droite qui n'aime pas la France*, Lyon, Parangon, 2005.

the Epistle to the Romans (Rom. 13.2.): "He who rebels against authority rebels against the order established by God"? The Church is naturally on the side of authority, while the growth objectors are spontaneously on the side of the leaderless mob. Consistent environmentalists are in fact convinced that there is an intimate link between the destruction of the planet and the existence of a strong and uncontested power! It is not a question of replacing the power of the State and of corporations by that of religions. They are on the side of the objection to power, whatever it may be. We must not accept the papal accusations without reacting, because it is not because we do not adhere to the dogmas of the Church (which have changed greatly over the centuries) that we do not have equally strong values. The Church does not have a monopoly on values, nor on morals! Identity Catholics like to quote Leo Strauss' formula, "If everything is equal, cannibalism is only a matter of culinary taste." Francis also maintains that "Without truth everything is permitted" and that "The culture of relativism is the same pathology that pushes a person to exploit his neighbor and treat him as a pure object, forcing him into hard labor, or making him a slave because of a debt. It is the same logic that leads to the sexual exploitation of children or the abandonment of the elderly who do not serve personal interests." This thesis is unacceptable because it locks humans into a Cornelian choice, either to submit to divine, natural and Church laws, or to recognize themselves as bastards.

Now we know that we can create, beyond our philosophical, political and religious convictions, a human society, that is to say, a society that gives itself its own laws... without giving birth to the monster that Francis rightly denounces by speaking of pedophilia, abandonment of the elderly, destruction of ecosystems, slavery, transhumanism, etc. I readily accept that there is a link between all the facets of evil. In 1997, I even wrote three books in this sense that *Le Monde diplomatique* had listed, emphasizing the interest and originality of this thesis[69]. We are indeed facing a systemic crisis (economic, ecological, social, political, anthropological, cultural) but what links us is not the death of God, but the death of man due to capitalist omnipotence. I am ready to admit that our time knows an inversion of the sacred and the profane: it does not cease to sacralize the most profane (money, growth, techno-science, the spirit of gain) and profanes the most sacred (the living, the values that we gave ourselves like freedom, equality, fraternity). It is the logic of capitalism and productivism that

---

69. http://www.monde-diplomatique.fr/1998/05/BIHR/3742

leads to evil, too quickly confused with the logic of atheism and philosophical materialism! I remain convinced that an emancipatory political ecology must guard against any pretension to totalization, a priori or a posteriori. We also know too well that there can be no absolute truth without authorized interpreters of this truth, thus without an absolutist religious apparatus. The (ecological) way will be made by walking as the poet Antonio Machado says.

The Church of Francis has a vocation to participate in the construction of collective values, but on an equal footing with the others... This is precisely what the soldiers of God, who have the wind in their sails today, refuse to do, in contrast to the old currents of Catholic Action that are more open to democratic debate. Thus François-Xavier Bellamy, one of the founders of the Vigilantes, naturally politically committed to the right but wishing that the right was no longer "a slower version of the left"[70], explains that Catholics do not have to participate in the democratic debate on values, because the ideas of the Church would not be values among others but the good in itself: there would be one and only one truth which would be theirs. François-Xavier Bellamy goes even further by explaining religiously that Christians do not constitute one family of thought among others. As a consequence, the democratic game of values would not concern them! How can we not contrast this with what Leonardo Bof, the great liberation theologian, said, on the contrary, that the Church "must renounce the status of exclusivity and no longer act as if it were the sole guardian of the truth. The Church must listen to other voices, become more humble and no longer be afraid. What opposes faith is not atheism, but fear.[71]

François-Xavier Bellamy also explains that it is not enough to believe that one is a Christian because there is only one good reason to adhere to Christianity and this only reason is the certainty that Christ tells the truth (sic), the whole truth and nothing but the truth concerning the conception of society, the human person, sexuality, money, ecology, etc.[72] Let us beware of those enlightened people who come claiming to hold the truth and who consider their values to be of a different nature. When they claim

---

70. http://www.lefigaro.fr/vox/politique/2015/05/30/31001-20150530ARTFIG00001-francois-xavier-bellamy-la-droite-ne-doit-plus-etre-une-version-plus-lente-de-la-gauche.php
71. http://www.lemonde.fr/international/article/2013/05/23/leonardo-boff-Benoît-xvi-a-ete-un-eminent-theologien-mais-un-pape-qui-a-decu_3415869_3210.html
72. https://www.youtube.com/watch?v=PIcpZL2uRkw

that they are not defending convictions but the good of society, it is a way of referring their opponents to evil, and therefore to the Evil One!

The ecologist-cathos, soldier-monks of austerity

Catholic ecology betrays its reactionary character best when it confuses degrowth (sobriety) with austerity. The idea is not new: Leo XIII explained that the law of natural justice dictates that "the salary must not be insufficient to support the sober and honest worker" and that to demand more from a boss would be "a violence against which justice protests" (sic). The lady bosses, including those of the austere monthly *La Décroissance*, will therefore never cease to hunt down the useless object of the month (sic) and to explain to people of little means how to do without the pleasures they cannot afford. A drawing in the monthly *La Décroissance* gives the lie to this: we see an employee begging for a salary increase and his boss replies: "Take this book instead, which will explain to you how to do without" (sic)[73]. The Catholic philosopher Émilie Tardivel, a regular at the Académie catholique de France, a columnist on Radio Notre-Dame (author of *Parole dans l'air : 40 chroniques d'écologie intégrale*, Cerf, November 2015) explains (with good reason) that Francis' degrowth has nothing in common with that of the growth objectors, because for the pope it concerns the material degrowth of existences (living simply) and not global economic degrowth, that of the GDP[74]. Catholic degrowth has had its master: the Portuguese dictator Salazar who imposed austerity and repression on the people in the name of the Catholic Church. The good Salazar, who intended to implement the social doctrine of the Church, would have been happy to become an ecologist if ecology had been in vogue and if it had allowed him to further repress the consumerist "baser instincts" of the people. We have seen the organization Tradition Family Property make the same speeches in Brazil, and Chileans remember its apostolate of austerity.

Paul Ryan, who became *Speaker* of the House of Representatives after having been Chairman of its Budget Committee, a Republican member of Parliament located on the right of the party, the poster boy for conservative

---

73. http://confusionnisme.info/2015/10/26/dans-la-decroissance-une-bd-qui-fait-fuhrer/
74. https://www.youtube.com/watch?v=AJlGGw3jPsI

Catholics, claims, in the name of St. Thomas Aquinas, Friedrich Hayek and Ronald Reagan, whom he cites as his three main references, an economic program based on austerity until 2040! In the eyes of American Catholics, Paul Ryan appears to be the right antidote to Barack Obama, since he plans to cancel the health care reform that the Church has furiously opposed, to overhaul essential federal services such as Medicare, the medical coverage for the elderly, which he promises will be at least partially privatized, and Medicaid, the coverage for the poor, which would become a prerogative of the federal states... As a good Catholic, he promises a tax reform in favour of the richest. A good Catholic, he opposes abortion, even in cases of rape of the mother or incest. A good Catholic, he explains that his desire to cut all government spending was inspired by the Pope: "The Holy Father, Benedict XVI, has accused governments, communities and individuals with high levels of debt of living at the expense of future generations and not living in truth."[75].

So we have good reason to be cautious when the Church speaks of simplicity or material degrowth and praises sobriety. Francis writes that "it is important to assimilate an old teaching, present in various religious traditions, and also in the Bible. It is the conviction that 'less is more'. Indeed, the constant accumulation of opportunities to consume distracts the heart and prevents us from evaluating each thing and each moment. On the other hand, being serenely present to each reality, no matter how small, opens up many more possibilities for understanding and personal growth. Christian spirituality proposes a growth through sobriety, and an ability to enjoy with little. It is a return to simplicity that allows us to stop and appreciate what is small, to be grateful for the possibilities that life offers, without becoming attached to what we have or saddened by what we do not have. This means avoiding the dynamics of domination and the mere accumulation of pleasures.

We, who never stop repeating that degrowth is everything but doing the same thing in less, that the program of political ecology is not to invite people to tighten their belts a little, a lot, passionately or madly, we can only be shocked, in our ecological convictions, when we read that Francis' project is summed up in the formula "less is better". This has never been the principle of ecology, which advocates "less is better", because it is not "less" in itself that is "better" (go and ask the Greeks and the poor, for

---

75.	http://www.rfi.fr/ameriques/20120829-paul-ryan-atout-choc-charme-republi-cains-presidentielle-americaine-romney/

example, if "less is better"!) but to do something else, differently, that is to say, to multiply the steps aside. The objectors to growth have always said that they do not only want to distribute the same cake (GDP) differently, but also to change its recipe, because it is not a question of better distributing products of programmed obsolescence. We do not want children in school canteens to have "less", we want them to have a relocalized, re-seasonalized food, less water consuming, ensuring biodiversity, made on the spot, served at the table, etc. We are not only telling users of the public water service that they should learn to turn off the tap ("less is more"), we are advocating free use of water (water for cleaning) in the face of rising prices or the prohibition of misuse (water for filling a private pool). We are not telling citizens that they will have to learn to stay locked up in their suburbs, we are saying that we can have, at the same time, the right to travel and the ecological transition, with, for example, the generalization of free public transport as already practiced by some cities. To say that "less is more" is to lack imagination and to trivialize the capitalist way of life, because it is to be incapable of thinking of another society, it is to call on people to accept austerity in the name of God and the Church! No, Francis, the planet is not dying from the unreasonable thirst of fallen humans, it is dying from the fact that capitalism imposes impossible ways of life. We can earn in France much more than the planet could bear, if eight billion people lived like we do, but this purchasing power does not even allow us to live well and be happy! This is why we do not want to "live less" but to "live differently", that is to say to invent collectively other styles, other genres, other ways of life, in short we want to put an end to the capitalist imagination, without sinking into recession, without making the renunciation of life our religion!

This "less is more" proves that Catholic ecology remains anti-popular, that it is, in fact, only a version of Malthusianism, pregnancies excepted. This Catholic Church can only relish this austere perspective, for it would allow it to legitimize once again its two-thousand-year-old love of sacrifice. The only thing this Church forgets (or remembers only too well) is that there can be no sacrifice without an ideological and repressive apparatus. For centuries the Church promised heavenly paradise and gave us the Inquisition, fundamentalism, human rights violations. Stalinism promised an earthly paradise for tomorrow and produced the gulag. We exchange your singing tomorrows for happy mornings. This dogma of "less is more" represents a danger for democracy, because it justifies all "enlightened tyrannies" as Hans Jonas proposes in his book *The Principle of Responsibility* (*Das Prinzip verantwortung* [1979], trans. Jean Greisch, "Champs Essais", Flammarion, 2013) and all "governments of the wise" as suggested by Dominique Bourg (a Christian environmentalist philosopher in vogue). The growth objectors who love the good life claim that they no longer believe in a singing tomorrow because they want to sing in the present, and if they want to sing in the present, it is because they know that this ecological and social good news has objective and ideological foundations.

We can sing in the present tense because the planet is already rich enough to allow eight billion people to live well without being subjected to these dogmas. The United Nations reminds us that it would be enough to mobilize 30 billion dollars a year for 25 years to solve the problem of hunger in the world and that 80 billion dollars a year, still for 25 years, would solve "great poverty". The world's military budget reaches 1,600 billion dollars per year. The ICP (International Criminal Product) is 1,000 billion dollars, i.e. 10 to 15% of the world's GDP, compared to the (not even) 1% granted for development aid. The North American food waste represents 100 billion dollars per year, three times what we need. Above all, we can sing in the present tense, because there are already other ways of life, other ways of thinking, dreaming and acting than those of the enriched. In South America they speak of *buen vivir* ("good living"), in the negro-African philosophy of existence of "more living", in India of "full life"... so many ways of saying that the solution is not in a lesser enjoyment, but in a "more to enjoy" made possible by the existence of popular ways of life, by what Joan Martínez Alier calls the ecologism of the poor[76]. Catholic ecology cannot fundamentally believe in this pre- and post-capitalist "already there", which we should "simply" develop, because it remains trapped in its pessimistic anthropology, in its dogma of original sin. I am sad to say that by his motto "less is more" Francis is doing a dirty job and is aligning himself with the ecology of the rich.

Francis could only be converted to the ecology of the poor if he adopted the theses of liberation theologies, because the preferential option for the poor does not consist in speaking in the name and place of the poor, but in recognizing that they are already bearers of a part of the answer, not precisely because they are economically poor, but because they have other

---

76. Joan Martínez Alier, *The Ecologism of the Poor. A study of environmental conflicts around the world*, Paris, Éd. Les Petits matins, 2014.

cultures. The followers of liberation theology explain that it is precisely by walking alongside the poor that one can hope to meet God, and so, although I do not belong to the same chapel (or even to any chapel), I can find myself in full human fraternity with these Christians. The Church of Francis advocates austerity. With the publication of the apostolic exhortation *Evangelii gaudium* (the joy of the Gospel), we discover with sadness that for the new bishop of Rome "the financial crisis has its origin in an anthropological crisis", in the forgetfulness of God, in the return of the devil, and not in capitalism and productivism. We already know that it was not by chance that Francis had appointed, in 2013, Msgr. Filippo Santoro, muse of the Communion and Liberation movement to reflect on what could be these new "religiously correct" ways of life[77]. How can we not be worried because if popular ecologists are on the side of a "more to enjoy", since it is only by giving desire, by arousing desire that we can set society in motion, the conception of the "good life" that the Church has been developing, since the beginning of time, camps on the side of sacrifice!

The ecologist-cathos instrumentalize anthropology

The Church congratulates itself by defining itself as an expert in humanity. The worst thing is that this honorable label is not contested by any media. Yet the facts are stubborn enough for us to ask for a little modesty with regard to the crimes against humanity that it has committed in history, and for which some popes have even had to ask for forgiveness. Often, today, the Church advances masked, preferring to speak of anthropology and symbolism rather than of natural laws and divine laws. The declarations at the time of the Manif pour tous on the supposed transgression of hypothetical symbolic invariants constituting the family, the individual and society give a good insight into this functioning, which forced the psychoanalyst Roland Gori, initiator of the Appel des appels, to remind us that psychoanalysis is not a guide to morals and a set of moral prescriptions, and the anthropologist Maurice Godelier to explain that it is not the end of the family, but rather "the metamorphosis of kinship".

What is at stake behind this game of fools around anthropology and the symbolic is the return of a revanchist Church, the idea of a Christian

---

77. http://www.zenit.org/fr/articles/italie-promouvoir-des-styles-de-vie-durables

society, the choice between the traditionalist current of *La Nef* and the monarchist current of Action Française, but in all cases, under the guise of a "Christian May 68", i.e., a "May 68 in reverse", the promotion of an authoritarian, moralistic and castrating system[78].

The ecological stakes are only a pretext to lead an anthropological fight against what is presented as a generalized decadence. Yvan Blot, a member of the Catholic Academy of France, who has been involved in the extreme right throughout his political career (Groupement de recherche et d'études pour la civilisation européenne (GRECE), Club de l'Horloge, Front national, Mouvement national (Bruno Mégret's MN), la Droite forte, etc.), denounces the decadence of the Americanized West.He explains in a text that would not be denied by many ecologist-catholics that four idols have led to decadence: utilitarianism, that is to say the ideology of the domination of technology over ourselves, money or Mammon, the masses as raw materials and the ego against transcendence... Mgr André Vingt-Trois, cardinal and archbishop of Paris considers that "French society is "not yet completely" decadent but the risk exists..." The Socio-political Observatory of the diocese of Fréjus-Toulon, that of Mgr Rey, defends under the pen of Falk van Gaver, the book *Decroissance ou décadence* and its author Vincent Cheynet, speaking of an "objective alliance of the partisans of nature and the disciples of grace against the society of the unlimited, against the cancer of growth, against the excessiveness of man, his hybris, his will to power."

Minute, under the title "Chouanneries", draws up the anti-decadence argument for the extreme right-wing militants mobilized on the ecological front: "When disorder reigns at the top of the State, it is logical that there is also disorder in the streets and in the countryside. This is not a novelty. In the last few months, there was the episode of Notre-Dame des Landes and its useless "Ayraultport". There was also the "1,000 cows" farm in Picardy, quite indecent at a time when small farmers in France are going to be victims of the reform of the Common Agricultural Policy (CAP). With its productivist vision and its submission to the lobby of the big supermarkets, the Ministry of Agriculture, whose portfolio is now held by a close friend of François Hollande, Stéphane Le Foll, is pursuing its planist policy inherited from the 1950s (when it was useful), whereas it should come down to the level of the realities on the

---

78. Cf. *below* the developments devoted to the family, love, contraception and abortion.

128

ground and give priority to short circuits, those that go directly from the producer to the consumer."[79]

Action française, a follower of the "neither left nor right" but royalist, calls for these new fronts to be the tomb of the... republic: "The "French Spring" is an example, but there are many organizations, such as the Veilleurs, the mères veilleuses, but also the patriotic movements and groups that we see reborn today, secular and confessional associations, all seem to converge towards the same goal: to fight creeping totalitarianism and to straighten out the country through the primacy of the values that constitute the human [...]. Our followers still do not see that they have awakened a French force that was flowing like lava in the depths of the earth and that could well turn into a raging volcano. With the leaders of Action française first, and then with our most constructive partners, we are going to propose a reflection this summer and in the autumn, with a view to setting up a mechanism capable of federating this force. A kind of "national council of resistance" based on the spontaneous revolt of those who are the salt of the earth in France. The republic is dying of having denied France, let's pull the plug.[80]

The soldier of God Bès de Berc, champion of integral ecology, justifies his commitment to the Manif pour tous and then to the Veilleurs movement, explaining: "We are the Pope Francis generation"; interviewed by Philippe de Saint-Germain, he explains that the Taubira law or the ecological questions are only different fronts of the same anthropological and civilizational "war"[81]: "We know that this is a long-term war, an anthropological and civilizational war, which for not being military is no less a question of life and death. From artificial procreation to euthanasia, the Vigilantes are there, discreet but determined, to watch over fragile and beautiful life." *La Vie* (Catholic) of June 27, 2014 quotes Gaultier Bès de Berc evoking "radical ecologists opposing PMA-GPA in the continuity and logic of their environmental struggles."

Axel Rokvam, co-author with Bès de Berc of the bible of the ecolos-cathos, in charge of the association Liberté politique, founding member of the Veilleurs will speak from the top of the podium of the Manif pour tous

---

79. Antoine Ciney, *Minute*, October 28, 2014.
80. Olivier Perceval, secretary general of the Action française.
81. The association "Liberté politique" which is on the right of God and which was a partner of the Catholic University of Fréjus-Toulon with Marion Maréchal Le Pen, claims the friendship of big bosses like François Michelin.

in the name of the Veilleurs to denounce the commodification of everything with the PMA and the GPA. This activist of integral ecology will be in charge of violently apostrophizing the minister Christiane Taubira during a conference at the Sorbonne: "But who are you, Madam, to change my civilization? Is it up to the Minister of Justice to legally suppress biological filiation? Does it belong to the legislator to tell me who my parents are? Do not abuse your power, Madam, you would risk making us into merchandise, re-establishing a slavery of which I will be an eternal enemy. You know very well that this project only serves you. You keep the French busy by using a homosexual community that is not inclined to marry and even less to "have children". You would therefore be honored to withdraw it now, because only pride can hold us back from reason."

This hatred of Christiane Taubira is common to Catholics of the right and the extreme right. Thus, the traditionalist Abbé Beauvais said during a demonstration organized by the Civitas movement against alleged Christianophobia: "It's good to have Banania, but not good to have Taubira! "This good father was released by the courts of the Republic, which accepted his defense system: he would have neither cell phone nor computer, would not read newspapers and would not watch television, so he was not "necessarily informed that the wording used is not only criticized for several years by several associations because of its colonialist overtones and racist stereotypes that it would convey, but prohibited since a decision of the Court of Appeal of Versailles on May 19, 2011. This entrenched abbot is however the one who negotiated with the police the release of another cleric during the violent incidents that took place during the Manif pour tous at the Invalides.

Another friend of Bès de Berc, the right-wing Catholic Vincent Cheynet, also chanted the new dogma: "Degrowth raises first and foremost an anthropological issue. His opponent, or rather lifelong rival, Nicolas Hulot, Hollande's "special envoy", who also multiplies trips to Rome and appeals to religions to save the planet, recites, in his preface to the encyclical *Laudato si'*, alongside Cardinal Philippe Barbarin, Archbishop of Lyon (a so-called "friendly" personality of the association Liberté politique and who is also found alongside the order of the Knights of Columbus on August 5, 2015[82]), the catechism: "The climate crisis is not simply an environmental crisis. It is the visible symptom of a profound anthropological

---

82.   http://www.leprogres.fr/lyon/2015/08/13/l-infernal-agenda-de-mgr-barbarin-en-aout-interroge-certains-fideles

crisis." Guillaume le Carbonnel, an activist in the identitarian movement, while confiding, despite everything, his tenderness for the monthly *La Décroissance*[83] and claiming to be of the "Neither Right nor Left" also explains that "The anthropological anchoring of *homo economicus* must disappear for the benefit of a more human society, [...] radical ecology and the degrowth movement integrate perfectly with identitarian issues. Through its concern for relocalization, redistribution, and regaining a sense of limits, political ecology is deeply ethno-cultural in essence."

Samuel Maréchal, the father of Marion Maréchal Le Pen, former leader of the FNJ, now leader of Europe Finance et Industrie, author of a book entitled *Ni droite ni gauche (Neither Right nor Left)*, was a theorist of ecology as seen from the extreme right (on the occasion of the 1997 summer university devoted to the theme "Ecology, let's depollute the minds"): "Real ecology is respect for the natural order of the world, respect for the implicit hierarchies that it entails, respect for man, his heritage and his environment", he added on the subject of the question of identity and immigration: "It is not a question here of knowing who will one day pay the pensions of future generations, but simply of noting that European man is a species that we will have to protect closely one day or another [...]. To be an ecologist is to protect our living environment, which is first and foremost cultural, human, social or familial.

First remark: we can therefore speak of (the crisis of) the symbolic by designating very different things and by drawing totally opposite conclusions... Is it a question of thinking about the "new subject of capitalism", its symbolism and religiosity (with the centrality of money as the primary symbol), with its new dogmas (the cult of the market and of growth), its high priests (advertisers and economists), its objects of worship (the department store), its rituals (the sales), its excommunications (the people of the "without"), its acts of grace (carbon offsets), as many of us are trying to do? On the contrary, is it a question of deploring the decline of religions but also of identities (we are no longer in a Greco-Roman

---

83. "The monthly magazine, directed by Vincent Cheynet, is in its tenth year of existence and has maintained a totally invigorating tone and critical approach. Last March, Cheynet published a small booklet entitled *Décroissance ou décadence* in which he returned to all the themes linked to the hybris (excess) that we are currently experiencing. If he cannot reasonably be classified among our friends, Cheynet, as a man concerned with debate, did not consider it useful to spit on Alain de Benoist, which is already not so bad. Moreover, he shows himself to be an admirer of Jean-Claude Michéa, which is not to our displeasure. In short, the man is worth a look. " http://fr.novopress.info/novopress-actu/decroissance/

world, nor European, nor even Indo-European), which motivates the hardening of identities (the nationalist ones of the National Front and the identitarians or the religious ones of the new Catholics). For my part, I define myself as a citizen of the world, which is why the monthly *Les Zindigné(e)s* is a partner of Emmaus International, of the Danielle-Mitterrand Foundation and of the Utopia movement to demand, with the Organization for Universal Citizenship, the universal passport[84]. The crisis of the symbolic is not a banal "desymbolization" (a revival of the old right-wing Catholic theme of the 19th century of decadence) but, as Christian Laval brilliantly analyzes, a mutation of the symbolic. Capitalism tends to produce a new, properly symbolic construction in which the general equivalent of money plays the role of mediator of social relations. As long as we have not finished with this general equivalent, with this symbolic construction, we will continue to go to the wall. I am even very afraid that Christian anthropology is of little help because (as we shall see) it makes a pact with capitalist anthropology quite easily.

Second remark: convictions - religious or atheist - are not in question, because what we refuse is the will to oppose the rights of God to human rights. These Catholics have even invented a new acronym: DHSD, i.e. human rights without God[85]!

Ecological Catholics in the service of a pessimistic anthropology

Growth objectors keep saying that we will not escape climate collapse as long as we rely on guilt or on appealing to responsibility (because knowing is not enough to believe what we know, and even believing what we know is never a sufficient condition to act). We can only change society by making people want to change. This is why Gilles Deleuze said that only the desire (to live) is revolutionary. The choice of the Church is the opposite, even if John Paul II called to no longer be afraid. Why do the polls show that Catholics are the most afraid, that they look more askance at those who receive minimum social benefits, why do Catholics vote more to the right? Catholicism remains a machine that scares its flock by

---

84. http://www.o-c-u.org/fr/
85. http://www.chire.fr/A-154268-les-droits-de-l-homme-sans-dieu-dhsd.aspx

repeating that "the door is narrow" and that one must earn one's place in heaven. The new reactionary faces of the Church awaken even more this pessimistic dimension that sticks to it and that does not even manage to channel its "good news" of the forthcoming resurrection of the dead... Should we not fear a coupling between this old apocalyptic pessimistic Catholic background and the speeches on the end of time that work on its ecology? On the contrary, we need people to be less afraid in order to consume less but better, because hyperconsumption is also an opium of the people. This is why we demand an "income for all, even if they don't have a job"! The strength of capitalism and religions is on the contrary to maintain fear. We are not growth objectors, lovers of the good life, ecologists because the planet is on fire, but simply to live well.

Catholic ecology does not manage to be positive despite the efforts of its followers who, like the austere monthly *La Décroissance*, only have the phrase "joie de vivre" in their mouths, in order to mask their fear, because their vision of man is soiled by the fundamental dogma of original sin. Catholic ecology cannot be positive because its anthropology is based on a representation of a world intrinsically corrupted by women. The way to escape this evil is to rely on a theocratic conception of authority, hence its desire to impose its order. This pessimistic vision of human "nature" (if there is such a thing as "nature") is mobilized to justify its societal choices and to constrain the individual. Paul VI condemned contraceptive methods not in themselves but because of the fatal effect that a lax position would have on human weakness: "It is to be feared [...] that man, by becoming accustomed to the use of contraceptive practices, will end up losing respect for woman and, without any further concern for her physical and psychological equilibrium, will come to regard her as a mere instrument of his own selfish enjoyment"[86]. One discovers that it is the fear of the human in the man and the woman, that it is the absence of confidence in the humanity which founds its choice of the repression. Certainly, the Church has the right to evolve (and its main dogmas are quite recent) but I do not believe that we should understand Francis' words as an incitement to sexual liberation, when he writes that we must not come to consider women "as mere selfish instruments and no longer as respected and loved companions". Let us note that the construction of the sentence could lead us to think that the situation of women was better before (before the right to contraception and abortion) and nothing

---

86. In the encyclical *Humanae vitae*.

allows us to think that the church has revised (if not worse) its theology of the couple and of love[87]. It is therefore quite logical that the popes have never ceased to appeal to the rulers to impose liberticidal legislation, it would be up to the princes to apply the retrograde laws of God and of the Church. How could this austere and liberticidal Church in the field of morals be on the side of human emancipation?

The eco-cathos against emancipation

Catholic ecology intends to mobilize us to defend the so-called natural laws because their transgression would lead humanity straight into the wall. We must take the time not to let ourselves be misled by formulas that do not say what each of us is entitled to understand spontaneously. The laws of nature, of which Francis speaks, are not the laws of life that lead us to choose, for example, permaculture against productivist agriculture, or to defend farmers' seeds against the desire to patent life, or to wish to develop the circular economy (where, as in nature, everything is transformed). The laws of nature, according to Francis, are not the defense of ecosystems against climate change or the sixth great extinction of species. The laws of nature, which the ecologist-cathos talk about and which they use as a smoke screen, are the difference between the sexes and social inequalities. I confess that I do not want to be embroiled in the crusade against gay marriage and the defense of sexual stereotypes in the name of the defense of the planet. Francis considers sexual difference to be a law of nature: "Human ecology also implies something very profound: the relationship of the life of the human being with the moral law inscribed in his or her own nature, a relationship that is necessary in order to create a more dignified environment. Benedict XVI affirmed that there is an "ecology of man" because "man also possesses a nature that he must respect and that he cannot manipulate at will". The valuation of one's own body in its femininity or masculinity is also necessary to be able to recognize oneself in the encounter with the one who is different. In this way, it is possible to joyfully accept the specific gift of the other, man or woman, the work of God the Creator, and to enrich each other. Therefore, the attitude that claims to "erase sexual difference because it no longer knows

---

87. See *below*, "Healing the couple to heal the planet".

how to confront it" is not healthy." So would I be a bad ecologist if I reject sexist clichés in society and in school? Would I be a good environmentalist if I agreed to march against equal rights? We see how the Church, which, despite its terrible history, qualifies itself as an expert in humanity, is also trying to appropriate the notion of human ecology... Do we need to remind the ecologist-cathos that the first human ecology was founded at the beginning of the 20th century by sociologists from the University of Chicago who intended to transfer the models of biological ecology to the human race, thus producing a naturalization of social phenomena, the better to make ecology a non-issue of social struggles?

My ecologism of the poor is nourished on the contrary by the class struggle, including the definition of the good life and the ecosocialist existential anguish dissolvers that will have to be opposed to those of capitalism/Catholicism! We need dissolvers of existential anguish because the headlong rush into productivism and consumerism is also a bad answer to our own finitude, so we need to transmit to humanity reasons to live and to hope elsewhere than in the race to "always more". These new dissolvers are not a product of our imagination because we recognize them in the uses and struggles of the impoverished against the enriched, it is the primacy of the commons against lucrative private property, it is the construction of the commons against the confinement in structures, it is the importance given to free time (thus to the reduction of the working time) and to the festival allowing the passage of the *homo economicus* to the *homo ludens*, it is the recognition of the right to the beautiful in front of the enlaidification of our existences (" pubtréfaction " of the landscapes, These are "spiritual exercises" (to use a jargon dear to the Jesuits) allowing the development of the spirit of solidarity, cooperation, enjoyment of being, by refusing, for example, the "sportivation" of existence by the suppression of the spirit of competition at school, by developing cooperative games (we all win or lose together, not against each other), these are methods of conflict management, of de-escalation of violence, it is the refusal of new management methods, of generalized policing, etc. We can see that with these few proposals, we are very far from guilt and repentance and its procession of deprivations. Moral ecology? Of course! One must be at least a right-wing Catholic to imagine that the morality of a teacher cannot be worth that of a priest or an imam as Sarkozy maintained[88]. Our morality

---

88. Paul Ariès, *Misère du sarkozysme. Cette droite qui n'aime pas la France*, Lyon, Parangon, 2006.

---

is not only atheist, but it is also that of the joyful passions against the sad passions that religions cultivate by maintaining fear. It is essential to think morality in an incarnated way (to speak like the Church) by freeing the body from the constraints of institutions and in particular from work and also from sexual repression (two themes dear to the Church). We are very far from the religious medieval moralism that condemns sexual liberation and advocates frustration and sacrifice as a model of life. We are on the side of a popular eutopic ecology, knowing that eutopia is the right place, the country of happiness, and that it is not necessary for that to believe in an unchanged human nature, that of the laws of God, of nature and of the Church. What are these laws of nature? The ones that justify that the big eat the small? The ones that have served the Church for centuries to justify slavery, presented as a law of nature and a will of God? The ones that justified the domination of women by men for so long? Those that still justify today the maintenance of social inequalities willed by God, those that order certain good sexual positions and condemn others, those that define the purpose of sexuality? Should we recall the strong words of Bishop Bergoglio regarding Christina Kirchner's candidacy for the presidency of the Republic of Argentina: "Women are naturally unsuitable for political tasks, the natural order and the facts teach us that only man is a political being par excellence, the Scriptures show us that women have always supported the reflection and creation of man, but nothing more than that.[89]

Healing the couple to heal the planet

It is generally imagined that the Church is simply natalist. However, it is enough to go back to the interventions during the last synod dedicated to the family to glimpse the ideological background: Dr. Anca-Maria Cernea declared, for example, in the name of the Association of Catholic Doctors of Bucharest: "Material poverty and consumerism are not the first cause of the crisis of the family. The first cause of the sexual and cultural revolu-

---

89. http://www.gauchemip.org/spip.php?article20490; the church is now contesting the authorship of these words. Are they symptomatic of what the left thought of the bishop of Buenos Aires? We can see that he was very far from being considered a left-wing, progressive, feminist pope, etc. However, the idea of a specific charism for men and women can explain this provocation.

tion is ideological. Our Lady of Fatima said that the errors of Russia would spread throughout the world. This was done first in a violent form, classical Marxism, which killed tens of millions of people. Today it is mostly done through cultural Marxism. There is continuity between Lenin's sexual revolution, through Gramsci and the Frankfurt School, and the contemporary ideology of gay rights and gender. Classical Marxism claimed to redesign society through the violent dispossession of property. Today's revolution goes deeper; it claims to redefine the family, sexual identity and human nature. This ideology calls itself progressive. But it is nothing more than the old proposal of the serpent, that man should take control, that God should be replaced, that redemption should be organized here on earth, in this world. It is an error of a religious nature, it is gnosis."

The ecology that I love is on the side of "more to enjoy", the only condition to pass from the enjoyment of having to the enjoyment of being. The Church certainly proposes its own form of enjoyment of being with spirituality, but I confess that I prefer love, friendship and the social link. I am therefore on the side of the liberators of love, not the censors. Now, according to Francis, the planet is sick because of original sin and therefore also because of the "falsification" of conjugal love, whether it be contraception, abortion, gay marriage and fornication, and therefore the "tyranny of desire", including between spouses[90]. Pope Francis thus takes up again in all things the "theology of the body" founded by John Paul II and under which he classified the 130 or so catecheses pronounced on this theme between 1979 and 1989. This theology of the body, "a gift of John Paul II to the Church", a real "treasure that is not yet sufficiently known in France", would reveal the true "plan of God on human sexuality"[91]. The Church is not in fact becoming more and more tolerant in this area, as is believed, but more and more intolerant and dogmatic. This is why the famous synod on the family of September 2015, which some considered a lost opportunity was only a cover-up. Indeed, the only solution put forward by Francis to allow remarried divorcees to be able to receive communion again was, in the wake of John Paul II and Benedict XVI, and in conformity with religious tradition, to have their first marriage annulled by an eccle-

---

90. The notion of original sin was created by Saint Augustine around 397 to designate the state of sin in which every man finds himself because of his origin from a sinful race. It was only later extended (then reduced?) to the sin of Adam.
91. Yves Semen, author of numerous works on these questions will be our guide for this chapter, especially his book *La Sexualité selon Jean-Paul II*, Paris, Presses de la Renaissance, 2004.

siastical tribunal under the false pretext that the spouses had not made a true marriage before God because they were not ready, because they did not measure all the consequences. This solution is immoral because it is based on the denial of the real history of the real people, it forces them to lie by denying the reality of their first marriage, it leads them to think (or to let believe) that they would have lived for years in a lie. Francis' objective was not to help (love?) those who suffer but to save Christian dogma in the face of modernity. This is why the Church has been keen, for only a few decades, to canonize couples as couples, not for the sake of "democratizing" the character of sanctity by conferring it on mere laymen, but to remind us what Christian marriage should be: John Paul II opened the ball in 2001 with the canonization of Luigi Beltrame, a deputy attorney general of the Italian state, and his wife Maria Corsini, a stay-at-home mother, a model couple who attended Mass every day; the parents of St. Therese of the Child Jesus (Louis Martin and Zélie Guérin in 2008) were the second couple to be canonized; and the third couple soon to be canonized is that of Paquita Dominguez and Thomas Alvira, both members of Opus Dei.

Yves Semen, president of the Institute of Theology of the Body, member of the Philanthropos Institute (like Patrice de Plunkett), author of numerous works on sexuality and marriage, is recognized by the Catholic media as the great specialist in the theology of the body (from Radio Notre-Dame to KTOTV, including *La Croix* and *La Vie*). He himself knows how to choose his preface writers since his book, *La Sexualité selon Jean-Paul II*, was prefaced by Mgr Dominique Rey, the famous bishop of Fréjus-Toulon, the one who gives the short shrift to Marion Maréchal Le Pen.

Citizens (even those who are Catholics) know very little about the Church's true thinking on couples and sexuality. As a result, people think that Catholic marriage would simply be a little more solemn, would simply oblige them not to remarry after a divorce, would simply encourage them to have more children, etc. This presentation misses the point entirely. The sacrament of marriage is not a way of saying that the family would be important to the Church as the foundation of society, since it would introduce a real supernatural dimension: the married man and woman would no longer be human beings like the others but more comparable to priests and nuns. Only when we understand that Catholic marriage is conceived as a repetition of the marriage between Christ the Bridegroom and the Church the Bride can we understand why marriage must be forbidden to homosexuals, why divorce must remain illegal, because if the Church recognized even the possibility of divorce, it would be admitting that God could divorce her... Only when we understand that, for the Church, adultery does not concern only and primarily the relationship between a man and a woman who is not his wife, but the relationship between a husband and a wife, as soon as the gaze they have on each other is made of desire, that we will be able to understand why chastity, between spouses, should be the best principle of cohabitation, otherwise the couple would not be the cross that it must be for each of its two components and nothing would justify that Christ died on the cross for his Church. Only when we understand that for the Church men and women have "different charisms" that make men "beings of reason" and women "beings of love" can we understand why John Paul II no longer says only that women must be dominated by men, but that they must dominate each other, since men must obey their wives in matters of love and women must obey their husbands in matters of reasoning, for if women and men were equal, not only would Christ the Husband be equal to the Church the Wife, but mere humans, priests. Only when we understand that for a couple the greatest gesture of poverty and charity is to "make one more child" than reason dictates and not to divest themselves of their possessions (except for the benefit of their children), because God's law imposes on each one the obligation to build up a patrimony and to defend his or her private property, can we also understand why the Church, the spouse of Christ, must also increase her own wealth and private property. Finally, it is only if we establish an analogy between the Christian couple who must give birth to children and the Church/Christ couple who must convert that we can understand what is at stake in the new evangelization (the *reconquista*).

All the Church's positions derive from this dogmatic background. Thus its mobilization against what it calls the gender theory, which leads it to defend sexist clichés (such as "daddy reads, mommy sews") is only a consequence of its belief in original sin. The first effect of this sin would be "sexual shame", which does not so much lead to the need to hide one's sexual organs as to "hide everything that has to do with the sensitivity, psychology and affectivity specific to masculinity and femininity"[92]. This inability to communicate in difference would be a sign that humanity is fallen, because man before sin was differentiated. Spouses should, says the head of the Institute for the Theology of the Body, consider their relationship in marriage "in the light of the nuptial relationship of Christ and

92. Yves Semen, *La Sexualité selon Jean-Paul II, op cit*, p. 154.

the Church". We can therefore already deduce the principle of submission of the woman to the man in the image of the submission of the Church to God. John Paul II modernizes the Church's thesis by speaking of the reciprocal submission of the two spouses, in the sense that marriage would be the cross that would already consist in "immolating one's own will". Each of the two spouses should obey the other according to the charisms proper to the man and the woman: "The male psychology is rather marked by rationality, the submission of the wife must take into account this sign of the male vocation [...]. If the feminine psychology is rather dominated by the heart which, according to the word of Pascal "has reasons that reason does not know", it means that the husband must recognize in his wife this authority of the heart which is his privilege [...]. These differences in mentality and psychology which characterize femininity and masculinity are inscribed in the very vocation of the body made for giving, and this obedience which the spouses owe each other is a requirement of the mutual gift to which they are called by their marriage."[93]

Francis and John Paul II do not question the teaching of Pius XI, but they express it in a more modern way: "The husband is the head, the wife is the heart, and since the former possesses the primacy of government, the latter can and must claim as her own this primacy of love.[94]

The second effect of original sin according to the Church would be that man and woman see their sexuality only in a similarity with animal sexuality, and only Christian marriage, which is not, contrary to popular belief, the place of the connection between pleasure and procreation, but "the way to the redemption of the body" (John Paul II), would allow man and woman to be more perfect than before original sin (since it is a sacramental reality). Let us note that this dogma is based on an absurdity since human sexuality is the most different from the hormonal cycles (gestation periods) that characterize animal sexuality. To proclaim with the Church that contraception is "intrinsically bad"[95], is precisely to fail to see that contraception de-estializes/humanizes sexuality! The third effect, again according to the Church, of original sin is that the woman's desires will be towards her husband, but he will dominate her (cf. Gen. 3:16). In other words, the domination of the husband over his wife would be inevitable as soon as the spouses look at each other with desire, with passion. The

---

93. *Id.* at 418-419.
94. *Encyclical Casti connubii.*
95. In the Catechism of the Catholic Church.

140

only way to be saved from this tyranny of desire and domination would be for the spouses to reproduce in their married life the attitude of Christ the Husband towards the Church the Bride; therefore, the spouses must accept to "crucify their flesh with its passions and lusts", it is a matter of "burning out the roots of concupiscence". Human marriages, like Christ's marriage to the Church, must repeat "the immolating marriage of Christ and the Church". That is why, as Semen maintains, "the celebration of the sacrament of marriage is completed only on the nuptial bed, just as Christ's consent to the Church in the offering of himself is confirmed only by the redemptive offering of his body on the Cross. "The Cross is thus revealed as the nuptial bed of Christ the Bridegroom and the Church the Bride. The indissolubility of the couple, the refusal of contraception and abortion, the submission to sexist clichés, the refusal of the "tyranny of desire" are therefore not thought of in the superior interest of the spouses and their children but in that of eternal salvation... and of the Church. Finally, Christian marriage is a way of reminding us that there is a chosen people: humanity as a bride has betrayed its divine spouse through sin, but God marks the renewal of his covenant with the chosen people (the Church). The Church insists on the fact that the Christian couple is not a couple like the others, it has God with it, to guarantee its salvation. The new Catholics with a sense of identity are therefore right in this respect to recall that the Church does not reduce women to their wombs, contrary to the Manichean tradition which opposes body and spirit. This would explain Francis' famous line, which has delighted some feminists: "Some people think that to be good Catholics, you have to behave like rabbits, but that's not the case"[96]. Yves Semen is right: "This papal outing does not constitute a change in the Church's teaching." Duly noted. But is what the Church says about humanity any better? For example, when she reminds us that true evangelical poverty would be achieved "by having one more child than would be reasonable" because, in her eyes, true charity is to "increase the number of the chosen ones in the heavenly Jerusalem in order to extend it to the measure of God's heart." Christian couples are therefore responsible for multiplying the number of Christians, and it is in this capacity that they are "missionaries of life" complementary to the apostolic mission of priests.

---

96. Pope Francis during the press conference held on the plane returning from his apostolic trip to the Philippines.

The family, for these ecologist-Cathos, is not you or me, as long as we choose not to submit to the criteria of the "good Catholic family", which have strictly nothing (and fortunately) to do with ecology! The idea of a threatened family does not date from the proliferation of divorces. Already in the 19th century, the Church proclaimed the family to be in danger and did not yet denounce television or "marriage for all" but rather public schools and social assistance: "By substituting the providence of the State for that of the father, the socialists go against natural justice and break the bonds of the family. Francis, in his praise of the Catholic family, also forgets to specify that his conception of the family is that of only a small part of humanity: our human brothers have, in history, lived much differently.

The eco-cathos against women's rights

The ecologist-cathos explain that one could not be an ecologist and accept to question the Christian conception of the family, nor admit the freedom of contraception, nor, of course, the right to voluntary interruption of pregnancy. It is therefore no coincidence that the integral ecology magazine *Limite* has dedicated its first issue to "Decrease and multiply..." I would therefore be, according to the Church of Francis, a bad ecologist, and the traditionalists of the Society of St. Pius X or the followers of Opus Dei would make excellent ones.

The Church has never totally renounced (can it without denying itself?) the realization of what Diderot called "empire", that is, absolute power over everyone. Religion wants spiritual power only in order to exercise temporal power. Its fundamental dogma is not the distinction of powers (the famous "render to Caesar what is Caesar's and to God what is God's") but the full pontifical power, according to the formula of Thomas Aquinas. Practical consequence: the law of men must always be inspired by the law of God interpreted by the Church. The area of sexuality is the one where the Church still exercises the most power. It would not take much for it to claim to create the "empire" again. The Church is stuck with its dogmas and cannot be on the right side of the struggles. Growth objectors who love the good life are convinced that "woman is the future of man" (according to Aragon's formula), not only because domination over women (like domination over animals) is intrinsically linked to the domination of nature and to human exploitation, but also because the solution lies in the development of the feminine part of each of us, in the recognition of our bisexuality.

Many have been misled by Francis' latest statements (September 2015) in which he seems to take the side of Eve against Adam, even daring to say "the temptress woman? Now that's a hurtful idea," as if this thesis had not been the thesis of his Church for 2,000 years! Francis' new dogma is, in this respect, not all that new, since it simply reminds us that "through the words addressed to the serpent, God surrounds the woman with a protective barrier against evil, to which she can have recourse - if she so wishes - at every stage of her existence." In other words, God can save women as much as men, but only to the extent that they too submit to the divine will. The Church can then, with Francis, take the lead in the emancipation of women, but an emancipation that brings them back into the fold. Francis can then denounce "machismo, whose goal has always been to dominate women. We are in danger of making the same mistake as Adam did when God said to him, "Why did you eat the apple?" and he replied, "The woman gave it to me. It is always the woman's fault. Poor women! We must defend them![97]

This new theology innovates only in a formal way, because women in the dominant doctrine have always been saved on an equal footing with men, which implies that they accept to submit to pseudo-natural and divine laws. Francis' stroke of genius is rhetorical: to present the emancipation of women, not as opposed to the institution of marriage, but to the desire of man, including - as we shall see - the desiring gaze of his spouse.

We must oppose the pope on the right of women to self-determination and for this reason we must remind him that nothing will be possible on the ecological level without resuming and deepening the movement for the liberation of women! The Church has been, is and will remain profoundly misogynistic as long as it continues to profess that man is made in the image of God and that woman comes from a part of man, because the part is always inferior to the whole. St. Paul will reinforce this inequality, present in the Old Testament, by explaining that the woman was made for the glory of man and the man for that of God. Each saint (or almost) will add his part to this macho and misogynistic anthology. Saint Ambrose defined "woman as the source of evil", Saint Jerome said

---

97. http://www.huffingtonpost.fr/2015/09/17/pape-francois-eve-adam-bible_n_8152988.html

that "woman is the principle of all evils", Saint John Paul II dared to say "the vocation of woman is motherhood: yesterday, today and always".

Let us not believe that these sexist declarations were without consequences: in history, including the history of France, as long as the Church remained dominant, the civic non-existence of women and their eternal civil minority were known. The Church will only be able to truly open itself to ecology the day it puts an end to the dogma according to which the woman is the door of the devil (sic) and that she is responsible for having lost the human race by corrupting Adam (sic). She will only be able to truly speak of human ecology the day she draws the consequences for herself (the place of women in the Church). As long as the Church does not accomplish this Copernican revolution, the ecologist-cathos will continue to call for economic decrease in order to have more children and will call for "fucking without fucking the planet" (cf. *below*). The Church has not changed its natalist discourse because it cannot, except by changing itself, because the family is built on its own model, with the marriage of Christ the Husband and his Church the Bride to multiply the flock. The Church cannot ignore the fact that its natalist choice is counterproductive, because how much would we have to decrease materially if we all had Christian families with four or five children, when we already exceed the planet's regenerative capacity every year on August 26, while the North Americans exceed it in mid-February, the Germans in mid-March and the French in mid-April. Let's be precise: there are not too many humans on earth, but there are already enough! On the other hand, there is a lack of equal rights between men and women, there is also too much machismo/sexism. I would add that Paul VI's encyclical *Humanae vitae* on marriage and birth control was far from unanimous in the Church: 650 North American theologians had rejected the pontifical thesis! To speak of natural law concerning the family is above all to defend the power of the Church. It is enough to read the encyclical of Paul VI to discover this truth: "No member of the faithful will want to deny that it belongs to the magisterium of the Church to interpret the natural moral law. It is indisputable, in fact, that [...] Jesus Christ, in communicating his divine authority to Peter and the apostles [...] constituted them authentic guardians and interpreters [...] not only of the evangelical law, but also of the natural law" (*Humanae vitae*, 4). In this area, as in many others, it is a call to submission. The idea of submission is so deeply rooted in the Catholic Church that the Pope can calmly explain that it is not a question of obeying him because of the quality of his arguments but only because of his infallibility. So why submit? "Not so much because of the motives alleged, but rather because of the light of the Holy Spirit which the pastors of the Church enjoy in a special capacity to expound the truth..." This so-called natural law in the Vatican sauce is a prescientific view of nature. It postulates, for example, an "indissoluble link, which God has willed and which man cannot break on his own initiative, between [...] union and procreation". Thank God, billions of us break this bond every time we make love for the simple pleasure of meeting and not of giving birth! This natural law would be eternal because God would have created it for eternity... To submit to this natural law would simply be to submit to God. This natural law is only a metaphysical principle inherited from the scholasticism of the Middle Ages, a metaphysics subordinated to the magisterium of the Church. I was talking about a pre-scientific conception of nature because the scientific revolution consists precisely in dominating nature by discovering its laws. Have we ever seen a doctor passively waiting for the "natural law" to be fulfilled!

This Christian conception of the family is not only based on the obligation to procreate (one can however live in a couple and not legitimately want children) but also on the centrality of private property. The present conception of the Catholic family (for the first Christians did not give birth in the imminent expectation of the end of the world...) depends directly on the conception of the Church as the bride of Christ... Remove this belief in the sacredness of the Church, and thus this belief in structural inequality, and the Christian conception of the family falls by itself! The Church does not defend the family out of love for its neighbor but to protect its own power over other human beings, including its own flock. The Christian family is not historically a love story but a matter of childbirth and the constitution of a private patrimony. The key words of Christian marriage are sacrifice, dedication and renunciation. The left has long wanted to change the family and eliminate inheritance. Let's dare to say that a Catholic couple with children from a good social background pollutes much more than a popular couple with the same number of children! The figures prove it: it is not the Christian character of marriage that explains why some are more "ecological" than others, but their lifestyle! What right do we have to maintain that the first are in the culture of life and the second in the culture of death? What kills humanity today is the productivist and capitalist system, and the relationships of domination!

Francis, contrary to the other themes addressed in his encyclical, returns several times to the question of abortion. This is to make it clear that many bad environmentalists kill embryos. He explains that "it is worrying that some environmental movements that defend the integrity of the environment and rightly demand certain limits to scientific research do not sometimes apply these same principles to human life. In general, it is justified to exceed all limits when experimenting on living human embryos. They forget that the inalienable value of the human being goes far beyond its degree of development". Thus, "since everything is connected," "the defense of nature is not compatible with the justification of abortion. An educational path to welcome the weak people around us, who sometimes disturb and are inappropriate, does not seem feasible if we do not protect the human embryo, even if its arrival causes discomfort and difficulties"; [and] "the valuing of one's own body in its femininity or masculinity is also necessary in order to be able to recognize oneself in the encounter with the one who is different. In this way, it is possible to joyfully accept the specific gift of the other, man or woman, the work of God the Creator, and to enrich each other. Therefore, the attitude that claims to "erase sexual difference because it no longer knows how to confront it" is not healthy."

Yet the media has hailed as a great advance for women the power Pope Francis has given priests, on the occasion of the Year of Mercy, to forgive abortion in confession. This much-publicized announcement is not only a pseudo-new development, it is also very bad news for the cause of women. It is not an innovation because, although the lifting of an excommunication is in principle reserved to the Pope, this power has long been delegated to bishops and priests. On the Vatican website, one can find a vade mecum for confessors dating from 1997, which explains that "as regards absolution for the sin of abortion, [...] if repentance is sincere, and if it is difficult to address the competent authority to whom the remission of censure is reserved, any confessor can absolve the sinner". This document was signed by the ultra-reactionary Cardinal López Trujillo, who was at the time head of the Pontifical Council for the Family. African Cardinal Philippe Ouédraogo, not exactly a progressive either, recently recalled that bishops "can delegate this ordinary power to absolve from the mortal sin of abortion to deanery priests, or to all parish priests [...] or to all priests, with certain provisions. So Francis is not innovating, but he is succeeding in a sleight of hand that consists in making the simple reminder of an ultra-reactionary dogma seem like a gesture in favor of

146

women. The theology of the Church remains totally unchanged: an abortion is always punished by a *latea sententiae* excommunication, *that* is to say, it is automatic: by committing the act, the person excludes himself from the communion of the Church, and therefore from the chosen people of God. However, the Pope is not content to simply reiterate the dogma; as a good reactionary, he intends to impose a return to the practice of confession and penance, which has long been neglected. The "progressive" Francis is again the worthy heir of the "reactionaries" John Paul II and Benedict XVI, because this return was undertaken at the end of the pontificate of John Paul II and really developed under the pontificate of Benedict XVI. Francis is therefore also a reactionary bishop in this area, believing in sin as the devil and wishing to impose confession and the sacrament of forgiveness.

The ecologist-catholic Tugdual Derville is not mistaken, which is why he is delighted with this decision by Francis, which will make it possible to "de-analyze" abortion by recalling, according to the classic argument, that it is not a simple medical act[98]. This delegate general of the association Alliance VITA, spokesperson for the Manif pour tous, co-initiator of the Courant pour une écologie humaine, compares the words of Francis with those of John Paul II and notes a complete analogy: "Pope Francis has just declared, with regard to women who have had an abortion: 'I know well the conditioning that led them to this decision. I know that it is an existential and moral drama. I have met many women who carry in their hearts the scar of this difficult and painful choice. What has taken place is deeply unjust." In 1995, in article 99 of his encyclical, Pope John Paul II already wrote to them: "The Church knows how much conditioning may have weighed on your decision, and she has no doubt that in many cases this decision was painful, even dramatic. It is likely that the wound in your soul has not yet healed. In reality, what happened was and remains deeply unjust."[99] Father Guitton, director of the Socio-political Observatory of the Diocese of Fréjus-Toulon, contributor to Famille chrétienne, Boulevard Voltaire, activist of the Manif pour tous, shock ecologist-catho is the author

---

98. We know in particular since the work of Georges Canguilhem that not only is there no stable border between the normal and the pathological, but that medical acts are never "simple" medical acts. The human being is also fully involved in a prostate removal, a mastectomy, but also in most pathologies and therefore in most treatments. Editions La Ville brûle has published, among other things, *J'ai avorté et je vais bien merci* by the collective Les filles des 343 salopes and a comic book, *Le Choix*, by Désirée and Alain Frappier.
99. http://www.france-catholique.fr/L-avortement-et-la-misericorde.html

147

---

of a prayer… for the aborted: "Lord, we ask you to forgive these mothers who have had an abortion"[100]. We cannot advise these drifting Catholics enough to follow the methods of the Union of European Christian Nations (UNEC), which organized pilgrimages to Auschwitz in order to "make Europeans aware that a genocide even more monstrous in terms of the number of its victims is underway." Unless they prefer to prosecute, with God's truce, the guilty for crimes against humanity[101].

The ecologist-cathos, soldier-monks of the social doctrine of the Church

The Church is not only reactionary in matters of morals but also in its conception of society, work, business and social relations. The eco-cathos have rediscovered the misnamed social doctrine of the Church as a "good for all" in the face of environmental collapse.

This so-called "social" Catholicism is not a softer version of socialism. It was born in the 19th century against the Revolution and in reaction to "Christian socialism. Social Catholicism is to be linked to the "intransigent" current, as historians Jean-Baptiste Duroselle and Jean-Marie Mayeur have shown, a current that was at first openly counter-revolutionary and that asserted itself with Gregory XVI and the condemnation of Lamennais, a current that developed with Pius IX and his *Syllabus* condemning modernity, a current that regressed in the 20th century in the face of the red peril, but that came back in force with the right-wing movement of society. This current is based on a triple refusal, that of the Renaissance, that of the Reformation and that of the Revolution, three historical cuts dominated by individualism and the secularization of the State, of reason and of science[102].

The social doctrine of the Church was thus born in opposition to everything we love: humanism, the rights of man and citizen, social progress! However, it all began well because the 1864 encyclical *Quanta cura*

---

100. site-catholique.fr/index.php?post/Priere-de-Louis-Marie-Guitton
101. Claudie Lesselier (ed.), Fiammetta Venner (ed.), "Préférence familiale" et "préférence nationale" : le programme du FN", in *L'extrême droite et les femmes*, Villeurbanne, Golias, 1997.
102. On the Catholic historian Jean-Marie Mayeur (1933-2013) see www.lemonde.fr/…/ jean-marie-mayeur-historien-du-religieux-et-du-laique_ 3494806_3382.html

148

was anti-capitalist: "Who does not see and feel very well that a society removed from the laws of religion and of true justice can no longer propose any other goal than to amass and accumulate wealth." We have forgotten this reactionary anti-capitalism because in the 20th century the Church chose a tactical alliance with capitalism in the face of its principal adversary. But in the context of the new global balance of power, after the collapse of the Soviet bloc and the implosion of liberation theologies, it can return to its old reactionary and nostalgic anti-capitalist background. I say nostalgic because the golden age for/of the Church remains the Middle Ages, which is why it has preserved its ritual, its ways of being, its main dogmas. The Church, having the feeling that it has nothing to fear on its left, no longer needs to give the change and can even afford the luxury of beating up on the capitalists, just to remind us that outside the Church there is no salvation! I will borrow from an article in the *Annales a* few quotations which show that Catholic anti-capitalism is not new[103]. The Catholic counter-revolutionary philosopher Antoine Blanc de Saint-Bonnet (1815-1880) wrote in the 19th century that "the spirit of the word consumption must disappear"... Father Droulers recalls the moral imperatives that must be the basis for the condemnation of the "unquenchable thirst for gold" and of an economy of enrichment, growth and profit (sic). Louis de Bonald calls for the perfection of men rather than the perfection of machines... According to Jean-Marie Mayeur, this uncompromising social Catholicism dreams of an incarnated religion that would regenerate the world corrupted by the revolutionary fault and would lead to the myth of the rural society (the famous "the earth does not lie" of Pétain, borrowed from the Catholic Charles Maurras) opposed to industrialism, to anti-capitalism associated (at the time) with anti-Protestantism and anti-Semitism, to the idea of an "organized society" made up of bodies and associations, and to the rejection of political, economic and religious liberalism. I understand that the Church was forced in the 20th century to pollute the purity of its dogma with social positions that were more to the left than to the right, and I understand that it had to accept at one point working-class priests who were involved in the CGT and the PCF and fought with the people. However, the Catholic left has never liked to talk about the social doctrine of the Church. It is not by chance that they invented the preferential option for the poor! But today (almost) all the

---

103. Jean-Marie Mayeur, "Catholiques intransigeants, catholiques sociaux" in *Annales*, 1972, vol. 27, p. 483.

reactionary theses of the social doctrine are flourishing again within a part of the Church, which, freed from "intrinsically perverse" collectivism, can rediscover them with jubilation.

But this was without Leo XIII (1878-1903), the author of the encyclical *Rerum novarum*, who was nostalgic for the Middle Ages, when political and religious powers were still intrinsically intertwined. This pope used "Catholic science" (medieval scholasticism) to explain what should be the principles of a social order capable of saving capitalism (the rich and property) from the revolutionary threat. This doctrine was so "revolutionary" that Emperor Wilhelm II asked the pope to take part in the Berlin conference on the condition of workers in order to find a way to counter the popular movements. The Church has certainly modified its social doctrine on some points, especially in its choice of corporatism after the fascist, Franco and Salazarist experiences, but the essential theses remain the same. One of them is of particular interest to us because it is taken up again for ecology: "According to the opinion of some people, what is called the 'social question' is only an economic question. It is absolutely certain, on the contrary, that it is a moral and religious question that must be solved in accordance with the laws of morality and religion." The reader may recall that this is exactly the reasoning used regarding the ecological situation (as if the writers of the "revolutionary" *Laudato si'* had the text of the very reactionary *Rerum novarum* before their eyes). The consequences of this papal blindness will be dramatic in the 21st century on the ecological level, as they were in the 19th century on the social level: "Increase the worker's salary, reduce the hours of work, reduce the price of food, if at the same time you allow him to hear certain doctrines and see certain examples that lead him to lose the respect due to God and to follow corrupted morals, his work itself and his profit will be ruined. Daily experience teaches that many workers who lead depraved and religionless lives live in deplorable misery even though they get better wages with less work."[104]

This rejuvenated Church sees in this doctrine the answer to the ecological crisis, as evidenced by the colloquium organized on September 19, 2015 "at the request of the bishops of France," a forum opened by Bishop Brunin in charge of the family (we already know that this familialist/natalist choice owes nothing to chance) with two major moments: "Understanding the social thought of Pope Francis" and "Understanding

---

104. Encyclical *Graves de communi re* (1901) of Leo XIII.

the ecological thought of Pope Francis", followed by a round table: "In what way can the thought of Pope Francis move French society", with as a guest star the Catholic ecologist... Cécile Duflot. Let's hope that the former minister will have been able to remind us that Catholic ecology cannot be used as a cover for the refusal of abortion and marriage for all!

Solving the social question was to silence the bad doctrines (collectivists), it was to submit humans to the laws of God and the Church. To solve the ecological question is also to silence the bad doctrines (they are always the same, those that the Church denounces as egalitarian), it is to submit the human beings to the laws of God and of the Church.

The ecologist-cathos, soldier-monks of private property

The social doctrine of the Church and therefore also its ecological doctrine are articulated around the defense of private property, especially lucrative property. The theology of the family makes the constitution of a private patrimony an ardent obligation born of (pseudo) natural law. This fixation on property is native, since historians specializing in prehistory have shown that the monopolization of wealth first had a priestly religious foundation. If "property is theft" as Proudhon wrote, we should add a religious theft[105]!

Let's not forget that the Church has built its colossal fortune over the centuries, through plundering and well-understood agreements with political power. The wealth of the Church would not exist without the alliance of the throne, the sword and the goupillon. On the eve of 1789, the Church of France was the main landowner, well before the nobility, so it is understandable that it did not appreciate the partageux. Leo XIII is becoming fashionable again among ecologist-catholics. Let us recall that he maintained, in accordance with the canons of the Church, that "the right of property was given to man by nature" and that it is a "stable and perpetual" right. In *Quod apostolici muneris* of December 28, 1878, he denounced "the sect of those men who call themselves variously by almost barbarous names, socialists, communists, nihilists" and who attack "the right of property sanctioned by natural law. The same insisted

---

105. Paul Ariès, *L'alimentation de la préhistoire à nos jours*, Paris, Max Milo (September 2016).

that the social solution through equality and the abolition of private property would be "greatly unjust" for the workers themselves because it would deprive them of "their dearest desire, which is to become [...] capitalists. Egalitarianism (sic) would thus be an evil work because it would cause "disturbance in all ranks of society, an odious and unbearable servitude for all citizens, the door open to all jealousies, to all discontents, to all discords, talent and skill deprived of their stimulants and, as a necessary consequence, wealth dried up in its source ; finally, in place of this much dreamed-of equality, equality in destitution, in indigence and in misery"[106].

The Church is itself immensely rich and has always defended its properties. It never ceases to seek tax exemption or tax advantages whenever the balance of power allows it. It prefers to be financed by the compulsory tax levied by the State rather than by the voluntary contributions of its flock... judged insufficient. In this area, it forgets its love of the principle of subsidiarity (see *below*). The French situation is, moreover, largely an exception, including in Europe[107]. The German bishops have just decided that German Catholics who do not pay the obligatory tax for the Church will henceforth be considered excommunicated (from September 2012).

However, since St. Thomas Aquinas in the thirteenth century, the Church seems to have harmoniously combined two principles, that of the universal destination of goods and that of private property, which would nevertheless always remain subordinate to it... This compromise is in reality a fool's game, because although the Church officially opts for a wide diffusion of private property and not for its restriction, it has historically opposed, as long as it has been able, taxes on income and wealth. Its philanthropic champions do not hesitate to choose their nationality based on tax rates (like John Templeton). It has always taken the view that "Thou shalt not steal or covet what belongs to thy neighbor" as condemning the envy of the poor toward the rich; it has argued, as long as it could, that wage earners could not demand more from business owners than was necessary for their mere survival (see *above*). This compromise is a fool's game that serves the interests of the powerful!

---

106. Encyclical letter *Quod apostolici muneris* of Pope Leo XIII (On modern errors) of December 28, 1878.

107. With the exception of Alsace and Moselle, where, because of the Concordat of 1801, which is still in force, priests, pastors and rabbis are paid by the State. The local law of worship has been validated by several decisions of the Council of State since 1924 and the Constitutional Council in February 2013.

Francis is not discovering the moon when he calls for the fight against financial capitalism, while defending, tooth and nail, private property. His predecessors already attacked the "dreadful usury", the notion of the productivity of capital and reminded us that all wealth comes from work. Pope Francis, like his predecessors, still defends private property even if he reminds us that the rich must make good use of it... In other words, the rich must not forget the share of the poor! The bad tongues would say that the Church loves the poor so much that she does not want them to disappear, first because they allow the rich to earn their place in paradise by doing charity, then because the poor are poor by virtue of natural laws and divine laws, and finally because they would be the living figure of (the suffering of) Jesus crucified... Exaggeration? No, not at all! The Church of Francis reminds us that both poor and rich are called to eternal beatitude and that what matters is not wealth or poverty but the use you make of it... The Church therefore calls for a marriage between the "just possession of wealth" and its "legitimate use". To the question of how much to give, the Church answers that "no one should live contrary to the propriety" of his or her status, so those of a rich person are not those of a poor person. It is not a question of keeping what is necessary but of keeping what is proper. What remains must be given in alms (especially not in bad taxes), because giving is not a duty of justice but of Christian charity, the fulfillment of which could not be pursued by legal means (sic). Christian charity, before being a good deed, is a bad deed against taxes. The Church adds a supreme argument to defend the natural right of property: poverty would not be an opprobrium because the true dignity resides in the morals; or the virtue would be the common heritage of the mortals, within reach of the poor as well as of the rich, only the virtue and the merits would obtain moreover the reward of the eternal beatitude. Fraternal charity is well thought out in the Church, with the exception of true liberation theologies which consider that the poverty of some is the consequence of the enrichment of others, as a war machine against the class struggle.

The identity Catholicism of Francis, like the intransigent Catholicism of Leo XIII, can recognize the existence of social classes but with the objective of uniting social classes through/in the love of God. The Church still advocates the bringing together of classes through property and charity because God would have wanted there to be rich and poor. This socially unacceptable reasoning becomes absurd from an ecological point of view. We know that the rich are destroying the planet by their way of life but also by the bad example they give to the whole society. Fortunately, working-class people have other ways of living, of thinking, of dreaming, they have other relationships to work, to consumption, to time, to space, to nature, to illness, to aging, to death, and therefore to life. The working classes, not because they lack financial resources, but because they have another wealth, are an opportunity for the planet. It is therefore impossible to continue to refuse to choose between the rich and the poor, impossible even to send them back to back in the name of mercy! Francis' encyclical is pitiful because it has nothing else to say but to hope that the rich will not behave too much like the rich. The fear of God would be the only brake on the uncontrollable passions of their nature (sic). The Church hierarchy has to choose: either it keeps its dogmas and cannot be green, or it adopts the point of view of liberation theologies. If it chooses the camp of the impoverished, it must stop confusing lucrative private property (that of the means of production) with private property for use. The Church has never stopped playing with this ambiguity since the dawn of time, acting as if capitalism allowed the generalization of private property, whereas this system does not guarantee property for all, but its monopoly. The Church must recognize that the first wealth of the working classes, which are the most ecological social classes, is not their bank account, it is not their private property but the public services and the common goods. 50% of the human beings have less than 5 000 euros of patrimony and this amount is also the average patrimony of a worker in France. The Church also speaks of the common good, but with a very different meaning from ours.

The Common Good versus the Commons

The ecolos-cathos put forward the notion of the common good, but their conception of this common good has strictly nothing to do with that of the left and ecology. Our common good is that of the Universal Declaration of the Common Good of Humanity, adopted at the People's Summit in Rio de Janeiro in 2012: "The paradigm of the common good of humanity or 'living well' as the possibility, capacity and responsibility to produce and reproduce the life of the planet and the physical, cultural and spiritual existence of all human beings in the world." Our common good is thus conjugated in the plural since it is a series of rights/credits allowing shared access to resources. Our common good is to give everyone something to live on in the sense of *buen vivir*, it is to guarantee access to vital water and food sovereignty, it is to imagine what a real energy shield could be, it is to consider that the slogan "a roof is a right" must become a reality, it is to begin to think collectively about what a universal citizenship could be, etc. Our common good is therefore a human construction, and therefore necessarily random. I would add that its conception will always be in debate since it is a matter of politics, and that in a democracy the truth is put to the vote and does not depend on any revelation. As a human being, I claim the right to make choices and even very bad choices. Catholics participate actively in this construction but the Church, as an institution, defends a completely different conception of the common good, since it is always in the singular because it corresponds to its revealed dogmas. This is why it is a capitalized Common Good. Let's remember that a capitalized Truth is always a way of making humans smaller!

The Common Good that this new identity-based Church, enemy of dialogue (cf. *above*), would like to be able to impose on us for our own good is the questioning of the right to contraception and abortion, the refusal of egalitarianism and the defense of lucrative private property, and the condemnation of spouses who have the mistake of looking at each other with desire. These holders of the Common Good in capital letters are also exceptional soothsayers. Thus the right to abortion will soon become an obligation, as François Billot de Lochner, head of *Liberté politique* and of the Association pour la Fondation de Service politique (AFSP), predicts: "The right to abortion could become an obligation, or a duty. Saint John Paul II said it over and over again: the legalization of abortion, which is the worst of laws, would open the door to a succession of complementary and deadly laws. At the rate things are going, the fundamental right to abortion could one day be accompanied by an obligation to abort, according to criteria defined by the political decision-makers of the moment: malformed fetus, birth control policy, mother judged not capable of raising a child, family too large, and so many other arguments.

How can we not ask this advocate of the Common Good in the face of absolute evil, this great banker, boss of the Financière Saint Louis, who believes that "inviting Marion Maréchal Le Pen was not an option, but a duty", if the FN responds to his Catholic vision of the Common Good? "Marion Maréchal Le Pen, on the so-called "societal" subjects, is part of those national elected officials, so few unfortunately, who have not ceased to fight with a rare courage and a rare tenacity against the deconstructors of all sides, at the bottom maneuver since 2012. [...] Marion Maréchal Le Pen's party is the only major political formation to take positions consistent with what the Church says on a number of fundamental issues, such as the Taubira law, of which she seems to be the only one to demand the pure and simple repeal." The Vatican's Common Good can therefore lead to the National Front! The latter is multiplying the signs of allegiance: if it has long preferred Latin Masses, its mayors know how to be "religiously correct".

Thus Robert Ménard, elected mayor of Béziers with the support of the FN, imposed in 2015 a mass at the Béziers bullring for the opening of the feria; David Rachline, FN mayor of Fréjus, also organizes his mass in the open air and prays in the street as part of the Port Fréjus festival in July 2015.

Thus Laure Fouré, leader of Souveraineté, Identité et Libertés (SIEL) - a party close to the FN (whose main leader, Karim Ouchikh, is a special adviser to Marine Le Pen for cultural and Francophone affairs) - defends a conception of the Common Good that is faithful, according to her, to that of the Church: "Yes, the French people are of white race and Christian religion" (sic). This columnist of the poorly named Boulevard Voltaire and close to Riposte laïque calls out to parishioners: "Catholics, don't be afraid of the National Front"! She then launches into a long demonstration aimed at proving that the FN program is in conformity with the Common Good and the social doctrine of the Church: "A brief study of the National Front's project would have led our self-proclaimed censors to recognize that the values it defends appear more respectful of the Gospel message than those of its main competitors. To be convinced of this, let us recall some fundamental points of the Church's social doctrine. First of all, private property, considered as a natural right of the human person, but whose purpose is also social: if it makes it possible to ensure civil peace, the right to property must be exercised in respect of the universal destination of goods, i.e., the person who possesses must make his goods bear fruit and practice charity towards his relatives. This is a far cry from the collectivization imposed by Marxist theory, to which the Front National has never subscribed. [...] Another essential principle is that of subsidiarity, evoked in these terms by John Paul II: "A society of a higher order must not intervene in the internal life of a society of a lower order by taking away its competences, but must support it in case of need and help it to coordinate its action with that of the other elements that make up society, with a view to the common good. Approving the institutions of the European Union is obviously contrary to the respect of this rule, which only the sovereignist parties really defend. [...] Finally, the family, the basic cell of society, which - the Church teaches us - must be founded on indissoluble and freely consenting marriage between a man and a woman."

The search for the Common Good would also be the FN's policy on immigration: "In reality, ignoring for the most part Christian doctrine, Marine Le Pen's opponents seek to oppose her firmness on immigration to the duty of charity advocated by Pope Francis. Yet, Benedict XVI reminds us: "States have the right to regulate migratory flows and to defend their borders, always guaranteeing the respect due to the human person. Moreover, immigrants have the duty to integrate into the host country, respecting its laws and national identity. The National Front says no different."[108]

Laure Fouré says out loud what many new identity Catholics think out loud. She claims the identity of extreme right because fascism and nazism would be fundamentally left-wing doctrines since they are based on the ideology of progress whereas "the extreme right corresponds on the contrary to a conservative, even reactionary current of thought in the proper sense of the term [...]. Particularly attached to the sovereignty of the nation and its independence, to the defense of French traditions and culture, to patriotic and family values, to individual freedom exercised for the common good and more generally to the Christian and Greco-Latin roots of Western civilization [...]. If political inculture had not become the most widespread thing in the world in France today, real or supposed membership in the extreme right would no longer be used as anathema to neutralize one's opponents, but could be legitimately claimed by those who defend convictions still shared, despite the dictatorship of "political correctness", by a good number of our compatriots "[109].

I understand that one can be a practicing Catholic and not approve of the conception of the common good put forward by the National Front! The fact remains that the common good, according to Saint Thomas, is to affirm that if man is indeed a political being who lives in/through society,

---

108. http://www.bvoltaire.fr/laurefoure/catholiques-nayez-peur-front-national,206303
109. http://www.francepresseinfos.com/2013/05/quest-ce-que-lextreme-droite-par-laure.html

then it is appropriate to bring an antidote to this omnipotence of politics since citizens should never be totally masters of their laws. The disagreement of the democrats with the Church then takes on its full meaning. We cannot accept that the common good is a matter of revealed truth and therefore of authorized interpreters, and therefore of a position of authority within society. Thus, Father Yannick Bonnet explains that this truth is the one inscribed by God in the conscience of man, but whose conscience is obscured by the awareness of original sin... The Church would be (thus) Mother and educator of humanity (sic).

The Common Good, as Rome of Leo XIII reminds us, is the refusal of the class struggle because all humans are members of the same humanity. The Common Good is social justice, but understood as the fair share that should go to each person while respecting "natural" inequalities. The Common Good is the set of rights that should remain beyond the reach of the collectivity (i.e. of democratic power), for example, the impossibility of recognizing the right to abortion or gay marriage. The Common Good is to recognize that the source of temporal power is divine. Jesus said to Pilate: "You would have no power over me if it had not been given to you from above" (John 19:11). The Pontifical Council for the Laity reminds us that one of the missions of the Cooperators of Opus Dei is to look after the common good of humanity (sic). We also know that Francis praises the Knights of Columbus for the same reason. This is why this new identity Church intends to do politics again, but in the sense of Communion and Liberation, of Opus Dei, of the Knights of Columbus. The Common Good, in the Vatican style, is the principle of subsidiarity, so misunderstood by many.

The ecologist-cathos, soldier-monks of the principle of subsidiarity

The eco-Cathos put forward the principle of subsidiarity that some ecologists, regionalists and libertarians want to hear in their own way, "decentralized", "self-managing", "anti-authoritarian" above all, which does not correspond, of course, to that of a Church that holds a revealed truth. The trap is all the greater because Rome can legitimize its thesis by taking advantage of the crisis of institutions, that is to say, the crisis of the State and of politics. The Church would be on the side of what emerges within civil society in a depoliticized way and in respect of the natural right of persons and social bodies, against a State and a politics given a priori as totalitarian. The Church thus calls for a transition from a vertical society to a horizontal society in which there would not be "less power", but a monopoly of power by those who are the only interpreters of the truth. This principle of subsidiarity was thought against the human rights of 1789 because it rests on the refusal of an organization known as "artificial" and more still on what Rome will name for a long time the "collectivist society" (the various socialisms). There are so-called "fundamental" intermediary bodies such as the family, local communities, professional bodies (companies and corporations) and intermediary bodies "by deliberate agreement" such as associations. The Church differentiates, however, between "good" associations whose purpose is to vivify natural communities and all the others... The existence of intermediate bodies is to be seen in relation to obedience to natural authorities, since the ideal city would have a body with a head and members (Leo XIII). This thesis of subsidiarity is therefore not another way of talking about self-management and direct democracy, but a war machine against the political conception of society that bases legitimacy on political legality. This thesis is above all the criticism of the politics understood as conflict (notably conflict of classes including on the definition of the "good life"). To the political and symbolic rationality it substitutes the technical and economic rationality, in short, the supposed efficiency of the life understood as "market". This is why Europe, from Maastricht to Barcelona, takes up this principle of subsidiarity, because it evacuates the political and disarms the conflicts on the stakes!

It was under the mandate of the very Catholic Jacques Delors that the principle of subsidiarity was enshrined in European legal texts (the Single Act and then the Maastricht Treaty). This thesis, presented today as part of the answer to the ecological crisis, was developed as early as 1931 by Pius XI, in line with the thought of Saint Thomas Aquinas and in reaction to the secularization of the State, in order to allow the Catholic Church to adapt to the democratic fact while continuing to reject liberalism. This principle has a sympathetic appearance but an unsympathetic reality. The individual (as defined by the Church) and society (as defined by the Church) would be absolute values that the State should respect by forbidding itself, for example, to intervene in matters of sexuality (abortion, contraception) but also of economic and social organization (what about the labor code[110] ?). This principle of subsidiarity allows the Church to think of itself as superior to the State and not to apply internally the basic democratic principles (such as the election of leaders).

This principle of subsidiarity in the Catholic style is a war machine against the State, not so much against its economic interventions and its policies of large-scale works (notably the "large useless projects imposed") but against the very idea of a social State. This is why the most "progressive" fathers of social Catholicism, such as Frédéric Ozanam (1813-1853), spoke out against the very idea of a progressive tax, since the owner would no longer have any interest in improving a property of which half of the fruits would belong to the State. Even Albert de Mun and René de La Tour du Pin only admitted the welfare state on a provisional basis while waiting for the restoration of the Christian corporate social order.

The principle of subsidiarity is also a war machine against equality. Chantal Delsol, an eminent Catholic philosopher, editorialist for Le *Figaro* and *Valeurs actuelles*, who likes to define herself as "primary anti-communist", wife of Charles Millon (the ex-minister and ex-president of the Rhône-Alpes region elected in 1998 with FN votes), opposed to the PACS as well as to gay marriage, is a great specialist in the notion of subsidiarity. She explains that an anthropological background "marks the 'subsidiary' society with specific values: for example, one cannot apply subsidiarity without believing in the primacy of autonomy over equality. [...] "The principle of subsidiarity de-states the common good as the goal of politics. Consequence: the general interest must be ensured above all by private initiative, that of individuals but also of churches and companies. Another consequence: "The society that assists too much makes its citizens weak. [...] "The idea of subsidiarity defines the right from the good, while the welfare state defines the good from the rights." The principle of subsidiarity is indeed a way of denying rights/entitlements. Chantal Delsol has become a reference for ecologist-catholics since she established a relationship between the destruction of the planet and the destruction of fetuses: "By what failure of reason, we reject Promethean man when it comes to nature and the earth, and crown Promethean man when it comes to sexuality or procreation"[111]. The only way to avoid being

---

110. It is not by chance that the very Catholic Emmanuel Macron, trained by the Jesuits, before studying at Science Po and ENA, ex-banker at Rothschild, defends the reform of the Labor Code wanted by the Medef.
111. *Valeurs actuelles* of February 3, 2014.

trapped is to recall with the theologian and pastor of the Green House, Stéphane Lavignotte, that sexuality is above all a fact of culture[112], without forgetting to recall that small chefs are no better than big chefs.

Against technicist hybris or against atheism?

Ecologists fight against the submission of humanity to technoscience and megamachine, but they do not look for the solution in religion, but rather in convivial tools, according to the good word of Ivan Illich (1926-2002), a catholic priest, but above all a follower of a profane ecology and a critic of a perverted Christianity. We must not leave the criticism of technoscience or of the ideology of progress to the religious currents of the extreme right, because one can refuse transhumanism or the adaptation of the planet to the needs of capitalism/productivism without refusing the conquest of new human rights or without advocating submission to a so-called natural order.

Jean-Paul Besset had published a book in this sense, *Comment ne plus être progressiste sans... devenir réactionnaire* (Fayard, 2005). The denunciation of technicist hybris by the Church is not the same as that of the ecologists, even if we can cross paths on questions such as the refusal of the adaptation of the planet to the needs of capitalism/productivism and the refusal of the adaptation/division of the human being with transhumanism[113]. I accuse however the ecologist-cathos of instrumentalizing the ecologist fights to smuggle their reactionary theses as regards morals.

Ecological-Catholic circles believe that the strongest attack against technicist hybris is currently the one launched by the Jérôme-Lejeune foundation around the play, *Jeanne et les post-humains*, by Fabrice Hadjadj, close to Communion and Liberation, director of the Philantropos foundation in Fribourg (Switzerland), and adviser of the ecologist-catholic magazine *Limite*. The Lejeune foundation is well known for its anti-IVG, anti-euthanasia, anti-GPA and PMA positions, anti-marriage for all, against the new law on organ donation (with its presumption of implicit consent)... Fabrice Hadjadj, as a good Catholic, refers this perspective to the loss of God and

---

112. *Les Zindigné(e)s*, n° 20.
113. We must not leave the criticism of transhumanism, that is to say the adaptation of humanity to the needs of capitalism/productivism, to religions: see Paul Ariès, *La Simplicité volontaire contre le mythe de l'abondance*, Paris, La Découverte, 2010.

not to capitalism. These ecologist-cathos do not only say that God would be the right answer to technicist hybris, they also attack atheism and other (bad) religions.

Jean-Michel Castaing, a theologian in vogue, is a pen of the ecologist-cathos circles. This enraged member of the Manif pour tous, who sees in the equality of rights before marriage the sign of the revolt against the natural order and even more against God (the one who would symbolize heteronomy), is a regular in the columns of *Causeur, Liberté politique, Cahiers libres* and even Aleteia, a site launched in 2012 to "evangelize the media" and whose editor-in-chief is Jesus Collina, a long-time important member of the sinister Legion of Christ. Jean-Michel Castaing claims, like Bès de Berc or Vincent Cheynet, that "the ecological crisis has deeper roots than the vulgate of ecological thought would have us believe. Its main causes are spiritual, and its first origin is practical atheism". Dear republican, democrat, ecologist, leftist reader, by approving Pope Francis, you therefore agree to become an opponent of atheism and its human rights versus God's rights! For as the unfortunate Castaing claims: "To consider the ecological crisis only from a technical and political point of view is in fact to lock oneself into a pure immanentism. However, to err on the side of observation is de facto to err on the side of ecology, and to maintain the evil that we are trying to avoid. Bastard ecologists, you who think you are saving the planet by proclaiming your atheism! This virulent criticism of atheism has once again found its way into the Church. Francis, contrary to appearances, is not different from John Paul II... He is only more clever in the way he presents the damnation of atheists. *The General Directory for Catechesis* maintains that "atheism is one of the most serious facts of society". Benedict XVI declared at the World Youth Day in Spain that "experience proves that a world without God is a hell in which egoism prevails, divisions in families, hatred between persons and peoples, lack of love, joy and hope. The admiring media thought Francis was more generous because he said in his homily on May 22, 2013, that atheists could also be redeemed by the blood of Christ. Vatican spokesman Father Thomas Rosica, however, explained the deeper meaning of this papal message: people who know the Catholic Church "cannot be saved" if they refuse to enter or stay in it, unless they lead a "right and holy life" (according to the Church's criteria), because in that case they would be Christians "in spite of themselves," which the Church calls "anonymous Christians." The newspaper *La Vie* of March 29, 2013, therefore, rightly titled "Atheists will still go to hell"... Word to the wise!

The good Pope Francis did it again on April 20, 2015, when he received the Conference of European Rabbis at the Vatican and declared that "anti-Semitism and atheism" were "two threats that concern Jews and Christians"! This assimilation of anti-Semitism and atheism is totally scandalous. Anti-Semitism is not an opinion but an offence punishable by law: the perpetrator is liable to up to one year's imprisonment and a fine of 45,000 euros. On the contrary, atheism is a fundamental human right in the Republic and the offence of blasphemy, which was once punished, disappeared from French law for the first time with the French Revolution in 1789, and for a second time in 1881[114], because it had been re-established under the Restoration. Discrimination against atheists has even become a form of religious intolerance against non-believers and is referred to as atheophobia. Nearly one out of two countries in the world still punishes blasphemy! The crime of blasphemy still exists in Germany, Denmark, Italy, the Netherlands, Ireland and Greece, but it is no longer applied, except in Greece. However, calls to strengthen coercive legislation and to punish blasphemers are multiplying, first of all, of course, among the enemies of Vatican II: "In a Catholic State, it is quite obvious that such publications [*Charlie Hebdo*] would have been immediately censored, blasphemy being a crime against the Creator, a crime much more serious than homicide, according to St. Thomas Aquinas, since the blasphemer attacks the divine honor. Blasphemy against God, punished by law until the Revolution, therefore inevitably attracts the divine wrath. "It is the law of history and a customary order of Providence that, in order to punish perverse peoples, God makes use of other peoples who are even more perverse; and this mission, Islamism was invested with it for a long time" affirmed Cardinal Louis-Édouard Pie in 1859."[115]

Ichtus filed a complaint against my Femen comrades and friends for "the crime of public insults against a person or a group of persons because of their belonging to a specific religion, in this case, the Catholic religion, by exposing themselves in a public place on the occasion of a demonstration organized by/and grouping together Catholic associations, with their

114. The local law applicable in Alsace and Moselle has preserved an "offence of blasphemy" inherited from art. 166 of the German penal code of 1871 (*Bürgerliche Gesetzbuch*) and still existing in the legislation specific to the three departments. It states that "anyone who causes a scandal by publicly blaspheming God with outrageous words [...] shall be punished by imprisonment for up to three years."
115. www.catholique-sedevacantiste.com/article-la-liberte-de-blasphemer-une-abomi-nation-damnable-125367546.html

backs and torsos naked, on which were painted the inscriptions "*In gay we trust*", and holding in their hands an aerosol can with the inscription "*Holy Sperm*"; said inscriptions representing outrageous expressions, terms of contempt or invectives against Catholics and not closing the imputation of any fact".

However, we are not (yet?) in the situation of the Muslim countries. In 13 of these countries, atheism is even punishable by death, but elsewhere atheists are sentenced to prison for apostasy or blasphemy. Moroccan students have just been sentenced to one to three years in prison! A Palestinian poet, refugee in Saudi Arabia, Ashraf Fayad has just been sentenced to death in November 2015 for praising atheism (sic). Already detained in 2013 for blasphemy, he had been released because of his fame, he represented Saudi Arabia at the Venice Biennale in 2013, he was arrested again in January 2014, sentenced to four years in prison and 800 lashes, a second court has just sentenced him to death for the same facts. A new law passed in early 2015 labels atheists as terrorists (sic). Unless I am mistaken, I have not heard Francis or the "specialist" in "religious freedom," Massimo Introvigne, initiate a protest movement. The Church does intervene, however, at the highest level, when Christians are accused of blasphemy and condemned, for example in Pakistan.

A report entitled *Freedom to Think: A Report on Discrimination against Humanists, Atheists and Non-Practicing People* is published annually by the International Humanist and Ethical Union (IHEU). According to the report, from the Christian West to the Islamic Middle East, atheists face discrimination, and persecution includes execution, life imprisonment, revocation of citizenship, and denial of education and access to health services. The report examines laws affecting freedom of conscience in 60 countries and lists numerous individual cases where atheists have been persecuted because of their non-belief. The report cites discriminatory laws that deny atheists "the right to exist, curtail their freedom of thought and expression, revoke their citizenship rights (and) restrict their right to marry."[116]. The holy alliance of religions against atheism is one of the main threats today on a planetary scale. Yet atheists are legion: 85% of Swedes, 40% of French, 40% of British, 14% of Americans according to the CIA - about 12% of humans.

Yet the Church still refuses to recognize atheism for what it is. It continues, in the 21st century, to maintain that its true nature is idolatry

---

116. http://iheu.org/

because there are always idols when one does not recognize a unique God. The atheist would be a paganist who ignores himself and who would count among his divinities the cult of the ego, which would lead him to want the human to take the place of God. This doctrine is a way of reminding us that "outside the Church there is no salvation! The atheist could only save himself if he conforms to the so-called "natural law". Thus a couple (even an atheist couple) could enter paradise if they reject unnatural contraception, abortion, if the spouses do not look at each other with desire, if they build up a patrimony and defend their private property, etc.

The soldier of God, Jean-Michel Castaing, finally clears technoscience because the real culprit would not be technology but "practical atheism": "Everyone agrees on the fact that this excess is at the source of the serious ecological crisis which threatens the survival of our "common house". However this hybris does not result only from the intrinsic possibilities to the findings of the technoscience, nor from the simple submission of the man to its logic. Certainly, science and technology impose their models, and try to make us take the possible for the desirable and the desirable. But before becoming an idol whose feet man kisses, the Technique sat its reign on the oblivion of God, on a practical atheism ". Consequence: the destruction of the planet is the oblivion of God, it is practical atheism (not even militant), a clever way to clear capitalism/productivism and those who serve it! The soldier of God, Jean-Michel Castaing, thunders moreover that the enemy is not only the convinced atheist but the indifferent one, the one who forgets God: "The forgetfulness of God is the fruit of man's freedom, to whom God addresses himself and asks for his assent. God has never cultivated the perverse project of leading the history of the world by organizing his own eviction by men!" Mankind would therefore be free, since God has willed it so, but it is nevertheless in conditional freedom like the prisoners, a freedom with chains on its feet, a freedom in a straitjacket, in short a Catholic freedom!

Jean-Michel Castaing finally wonders about the consequences of atheism. First consequence: faced with their oppressors, the dominated could not appeal to any transcendence. It is true that atheists have more faith in social struggles and the construction of power relations and that they expect more from an increase in democracy than from any divinity. The second consequence that this modern-day Torquemada asserts is that if only the "respiritualization" of humanity can save the world, it is still necessary for humanity to turn to the right religion, to Catholicism. I feel like saying to this eco-catho salesman: "Fuck your religious brand![117]" Drop your bigotry and accept that there are a thousand ways to make values flourish. The ecology of the Vatican sauce thus marks the return to the "holy war" against atheists but also against bad religions: "The ecology to which these gnostic sects initiate their members is more similar to that of the New Age than to the one whose riches Pope Francis invites us to discover in Christian wisdom throughout the pages of the encyclical *Laudato si.*" It is an undeniable fact: to err on the side of caution is to err on the side of ecology. Faced with such a challenge, reflection is never enough. To cite only the example of the "New Age", it is never superfluous to specify what type of ecology is at stake in a debate of ideas. The adversary is therefore not only atheism, but also the "false" religions including those that question monotheism. The Church will never stop lighting bonfires and burning witches! "The ecology that this current of thought conveys is closer to esoteric and spiritualist superstitions than to a structured and coherent political thought. According to the "New Age" in fact, "Nature is a living being traversed by sympathetic impulses and animated by a secret fire that human beings seek to master. Men can enter into contact with the superior or inferior worlds through the imagination (an organ of the soul and the spirit), or through mediators (angels, spirits, demons) or rituals" [...]. As we can see, the "New Age" is not far from substituting Nature for God! A god who merges with cosmic energy. We are far from the personal God of the biblical revelation. Thus the observation that we established at the beginning is confirmed: ecology looks as much, if not more, at the spirit, at spirituality, than at politics. In order to avoid the reflection being parasitized by gnoses of all kinds, it is not useless to specify the understanding and the extension of the concept of "ecology", that is to say the definition that one can give of ecology as well as the whole of the objects that this concept designates or concerns closely.[118]

These ecologist-cathos, who speak of human ecology and of the Church as an expert in humanity, are definitely not sympathetic or confraternal. They denounce the superstitions of others but do not see the beam in

---

117. Paul Ariès, *Putain de ta marque, la publicité contre l'esprit de révolte*, Villeurbanne, Golias, 2003.
118. http://www.libertepolitique.com/La-revue/La-revue-Liberte-Politique/Vieillir-une-vocation

their own eye: I don't care if the followers of Amerindian pachamamism confuse the personal God of Christians with esotericism, but I notice that they don't canonize a genocidal witch of Christians and that instead of subjecting nature to the laws of the economy as capitalism does with its project of carbon money and increased commodification, they intend to subject the economy to the laws of the living (with permaculture)!

Philippe Oswald is another enraged member of the Manif pour tous, he too denounces materialism and atheism, he too calls, with Frigide Barjot, for Catholics to get involved in politics, he too speaks of a "May 68 in reverse", he too feels himself growing ecologist wings since this hunting ground is open: "It is a profound movement, of human ecology, which totally rejects the liberal-libertarian drift stemming from May 68, of which too many political leaders and opinion leaders, especially journalists, are the heirs and propagandists. By announcing that the Manif pour tous would present candidates for the next municipal elections, Frigide Barjot has outlined a long term strategy of which this unprecedented spring, a sort of "May 68 in reverse", delivers the first signs. Undoubtedly, the month of May will be hot... We must do everything possible to make it, in the strong sense, edifying.[119]

This former head of the very right-wing association Famille de France, who accompanied the Marches in the Desert, organized by Ichtus, explains that "after the French Revolution, the Civil Code cut the family from its Christian roots"... Homo marriage would therefore be only a vile pretext! This editor at Aleteia, who wrote in the aftermath of the massacre "Being Charlie, no thank you", has just been awarded by Francis the highest papal award by becoming a knight of the Order of Saint Gregory the Great. Benedict XVI had already awarded the medal of Commander in 2012 to Patrick Buisson, this far-right activist, adviser to Sarkozy, a great defender of Christian values but a specialist in clandestine recordings of the presidential couple, indicted for misuse of corporate assets and misappropriation of public funds in the affair of the Elysee polls.

---

119. http://fr.aleteia.org/2013/04/22/manif-pour-tous-des-veilleurs-qui-annoncent-lau-rore/

The ecologist-cathos against political ecology

Political ecology was born alongside scientific ecology but against the current of "human ecology" in the American sense[120]. We must remember this if we do not want ecology to be used one day to cut off heads under the pretext of saving the planet according to God's plan. Democracy will always imply leaving the gods in their churches! The ecologist-cathos, as good disciples of the extreme right-wing Catholic Charles Maurras, believe in politics first, even though they are fervent papists. However, their very conception of ecology makes them followers of a falsely political ecology because their ecology is first and foremost religious. Their supreme deception consists in claiming to belong to the current of political ecology because, no more than a Muslim or Protestant ecology, papist ecology cannot be a political ecology in a republican framework. The worst political mistake is the false consensus, the agreement masking the disagreement. We are on the side of a "more to enjoy", they are on the side of a "less to enjoy". We consider that there is no possible limit to democracy and therefore to the power of citizens to make the law, even if it means being wrong; yet for the ecologist-cathos, the ultimate cause of ecological disasters is not capitalism or even productivism but the immorality of humans in the face of divine laws. One of the theorists of this pseudo-ecological Church, Bès de Berc, is therefore right: Pope Francis is basically just updating the Church's discourse! We are no more right to speak of a "green pope" than we were with John Paul II. In 1991, John Paul II closed the relationship between Catholics and ecology by speaking of "human ecology" and he even added "authentic" (in *Centesimus Annus),* thus disqualifying all other forms of ecology. Catholic ecology is above all a matter of moral submission insofar as humanity should accept "its own natural and moral structure" (sic). Political ecology is thus refocused on the natural man and... the family. Pope Benedict XVI already developed this idea in his speech to the diplomatic corps (January 9, 2012) following the climate conference in Durban. Ecology thus acquires a new central concept: the family. Ecology would thus become a moralism with its procession of penances. It is easy to understand why Vincent Cheynet titles his latest book *Decroissance ou décadence,* even though this term has always been specific to the hard Catholic right, and why he puts at the

---

120. http://www.cairn.info/revue-societes-contemporaines-2003-1-page-167.htm

heart of degrowth the refusal of gay marriage (Vincent Cheynet has always been keen to distance himself from the National Front, but his right-wing Catholic identity ideas lead him to cultivate dubious friendships). The ever pontifical knight Patrice de Plunkett is not mistaken when he publishes on his blog a glowing review of the book by the degrowthist Cheynet without mentioning his religious commitment: "Its content (let's rejoice) should surprise many Catholics, who will discover many similarities between the degrowth sensibility and the social thought of the Church, perhaps with words and references that are sometimes quite different, but with a fundamentally convergent anthropological perspective. Some signs already seem to indicate this in the "cathosphere": this book could well contribute to a profound transformation of the Catholic view of degrowth, and simultaneously to the awareness of the promising potential of a rapprochement between radical ecologists and Christians freed from the liberal imposture. The very Catholic and very right-wing *La Nef* website, which also reports on the latest book by the ever-right-wing Catholic Vincent Cheynet, is enthusiastic: "In his latest book, we discover how deep this convergence between radical ecologists (quickly called extremists) and integral Catholics (quickly called fundamentalists) is."

If Vincent Cheynet is indeed not very radical in social matters (his confusion of degrowth and austerity; his refusal of an "income for all, even without a job" ; his refusal of free public services and common goods, his condemnation of the Indignés and Anonymous movements), it is true that he explains in *La Vie* (Catholic) of April 17, 2014 that "the law of marriage for all contributes to opening the Pandora's box of all the demands that lead us to the *Brave New World* described by Aldous Huxley [...]. The law of marriage for all [...] is a pure product of utilitarian and capitalist ideology." He adds in the (not really leftist) magazine *L'Écologiste* that "gender theory is an avatar of liberalism" and that "we are facing a murderous utopia". The reader will allow me to remind you that certain political-religious connections are not new. Let us remember the good relations between Teddy Goldsmith's magazine *L'Écologiste* and Joseph Ratzinger, the future pope Benedict XVI... Patrice de Plunkett maintains, before God, that the journal *La Décroissance* (by Cheynet) is on "the same line as *L'Écologiste as far as* anthropology is concerned".

It is easy to understand why the new magazine *Limite* puts the question of man "being of nature" at the heart of its fight, since this man "being of nature" necessarily has "a daddy, a mummy and children"... Do we have to think that the little ecologist girls dress in pink and the boys in blue! This ecology, instrumentalized to defend the Christian conception of the family (even before questioning the relationship between man and nature) is natalist: "Have children, not shopping" in the words of Eugénie Bastié, editor-in-chief of *Limite*, a journalist at *Le Figaro*, close to Mgr Rey. This new magazine makes its front page on "Decrease and multiply" with a text entitled "How to fuck without fucking the planet", a racy version of "Be fruitful, multiply, fill the earth" (Gen. 1.28.).

The ecologist-cathos still confuse the issue of politics, because if they call for politics, it is not in the sense of political ecology - which intends to lead the fight about the definition of the good life and which knows that there is a struggle between the enriched and the impoverished, without possible compromise -, but in the sense that the bond between a man and a woman is the fundamental political bond, forgetting that the first political division probably appeared when the first clerics, in prehistoric times, appropriated the monopoly of the communication with the dead and the beyond: "The individual is first and always the effect of a cause. The union of a man and a woman, this fundamental political link, precedes and founds it. Everything is therefore going to be subordinated to this "fundamental political bond", hence the dubious analogies (for example, GMO equals contraceptive pill) which "upset, not without impact on human health, the rhythms and laws of nature"[121].

The ecologist-cathos and the "neither right nor left", therefore right-wing

If many openly display their membership to the right, the most "clever", like Bès de Berc, claim to be "neither right nor left", therefore of the right according to the formula of the philosopher Alain, because these notions would be outdated today (sic). Vincent Cheynet is a right-wing man with a complex concealing his convictions. Both of them display, however, the same hatred of a libertarian ecology (Bès de Berc in his book and Cheynet with the character of Stef le Décroissant), both vomit May 68, its

---

121. Quoted by Étienne Grésillon and Bertrand Sajaloli, "L'Église verte? La construction d'une écologie catholique : étapes et tensions", to be read on the site https://vertigo.re-vues.org/15905

emancipating ideal and its promise of enjoyment. I certainly don't like Cohn-Bendit who went from black to red, then from red to green, then from green to blue, they don't like Dany le Rouge and slogans like "enjoy without hindrance" or "it is forbidden to forbid"[122]. I repeat once again: the growth objectors are not followers of the reactionary "less to enjoy" but of the emancipatory "more to enjoy". Moreover, capitalism does not offer a "more to enjoy" to eight billion people! We are against economic and religious unlimitedness but for the unlimitedness of human rights in the face of capitalism and the rights of God. The denunciation of the cult of omnipotence and the call to accept limits are nothing but falsehoods to defend the omnipotence of God, of his spouse the Church and of the Pope (considered infallible since the 19th century). It is scandalous for them to say that the earth is dying from the fantasy of omnipotence, when more than a billion people do not have access to drinking water, when one person in seven goes to bed every night on an empty stomach, when almost three billion poor people, that is to say almost one person in two, lives on less than two dollars a day, that 30,000 children under the age of five die every day from diseases that could have been avoided, that one third of the world's population does not have access to basic medicines, that 100 million children are still not enrolled in primary school, 55% of whom are girls, that the two urban forms that are developing the fastest are slums and private cities! We do not have the right to denounce the cult of omnipotence and the idea of a world without limits if we do not explain at the same time that 20% of human beings appropriate 90% of the resources and that 1% consume 50%. The Church, its God and its Pope, like capitalism, are only all-powerful because the majority of humans are thought and formatted as powerless. The ecologist-cathos do not cease to shrink humans when they should be grown. It is therefore necessary to put an end to the omnipotence of the powerful, including the Church, in order to generalize the power to live among more than eight billion humans. The world without limits that the Pope denounces is that of the 1% against the 99%, but the Church cannot go to the end of the analysis, for lack of recognizing that the enrichment of some is only the other face of the impoverishment of others, for lack of admitting that the conception of the good life is not first of all a private matter, of good and bad taste, of the Christian family or not, but of class struggle, including within the

122. See Gaultier Bès de Berc, Marianne Durano, Axel Rokvan, *Nos limites, pour une écologie intégrale*, Paris, Éd. Le Centurion, 2014.

Church. There is no possible compromise between the rich and the poor, except of course on the backs of the poor. The "neither right nor left" is the refusal to choose the impoverished against the rich.

The ecologist-catholic magazine *Limite* thus claims to be "neither of the right nor of the left" (despite its networks and ideology, which we will analyze in detail later), but it admits its love for Phillip Blond, under the racy title "The British Michéa who believed in Heaven" (poor Jean-Claude, recuperated in all winds!). This theologian, presented as the "promoter of the *Big Society* against *Big Brother*" is the leader of the think tank Respublica Radical Orthodoxy, furious follower of an interventionist and communitarian conservatism. It was he who brought the very conservative and religious David Cameron to power, around this notion of *Big Society*, whose first effect was to break up what remained of non-private education in England and who wishes to make many trade union activities illegal and restrict the right to strike[123]. This guru of neo-conservatism, champion of the Common Good in the Vatican style, has only one idea in mind: to destroy public services and collective goods! Some people even speak of "red conservatism", not because he is "socialist" or even social, but because he is interventionist, in the manner of the new global anti-liberal right (often Catholic) that is on the rise.

The ecologist-catholic networks at work

The eco-Cathos are certainly not yet totally marching in step, but among the many divisions ("the pope, how many divisions?" said Stalin) let's stop at the networks that make up the new catho-ecolo magazine *Limite*, launched in September 2015 with the support of the watchdogs of the system. Only the newspaper *Libération* published an excellent paper entitled "Des réacs en vert et contre tous" under the pen of Bernadette Sauvaget. Georges Feltin-Tracol, a far-right activist, knows the *Limite* team well. He explains that this magazine is "the result of the meeting between the generation of the Vigilantes and the older generation that animated the royalist sovereignist magazine *Immédiatement* in the 1990s. *Limite* is positioned on the Christian bioconservative niche. Among the

---

123. http://www.lemonde.fr/europe/article/2015/07/16/david-cameron-veut-restreindre-le-droit-de-greve_4684943_3214.html

contributors to *Immédiatement were* many of *Limite*'s writers (of whom we will speak at length) such as Fabrice Hadjadj, Jacques de Guillebon and Falk van Gaver, who was even its editor for a time. The links between the review *Immédiatement* and the monarchists appear clearly on the site of the Action française[124].

The theoretician of the journal *Limite* is the Catholic philosopher Gaultier Bès de Berc (who, in order to be popular, forgets his particle in most of the texts), who is denounced in particular by gay circles as the bearer of an "ecology of hatred"[125]; and the site StreetPress presents him as "catho-pop and eco-reactivity"[126]. He can console himself by consulting the extreme right-wing press, which loves him[127]. Bès de Berc and his cronies use all (good) causes to defend the divine order. They demonstrated in the middle of the unions on May 1st with a banner: "It is not filiation that must be weakened, it is unemployment and precariousness."[128] This does not prevent him from worshipping Phillip Blond... who has become public enemy number 1 of the English workers.

The fight against unemployment, GMOs, Notre-Dame des Landes, Sivens, AMAP, liberation theologies... everything is good for muddying the ideological waters, with the sole aim of condemning abortion, contraception and gay marriage. This strategy, undoubtedly sincere, appears to be confusing because it is based on two principles, "respect for life" and the famous "everything is linked", which are very present at the heart of Vatican thought. The philosopher Bès de Berc is not a second-rate member of this reactionary right. It was he who, in the aftermath of the Manif pour tous, launched the Veilleurs movement and took charge of the preparation and animation of the march in the summer of 2013, an operation that aroused a great deal of opposition from activists in favor of equal rights but also from the ecologists of Notre-Dame des Landes, who refused to accept any confusion by launching the slogan "Neither Vinci nor Veilleurs". Bès de Berc is the assistant director of the magazine *Limite.*

---

124. http://www.actionfrancaise.net/mouvement-evenements-20041111_commemoration.htm
125. http://vendeursesdehaine.yagg.com/2014/07/19/gaultier-bes-de-berc-une-ecologie-de-la-haine/
126. http://www.streetpress.com/sujet/1445856179-gaultier-bes-catho-pop-et-ecolo-reac#
127. http://www.libertepolitique.com/Actualite/Decryptage/Gaultier-Bes-de-Berc-Les-Veilleurs-attaquent-le-mal-a-la-racine
128. Quoted by the newspaper *Le Pèlerin.*

The director is Paul Piccarreta (a former member of the newspaper *Causeur*, which our friends at *Politis* and the MRAP rightly consider to be on the extreme right). The latter gives the history of the concept of integral ecology taken up by the pope. According to him, it was Falk van Gaver (about whom we will speak later) who first used the expression, then Gaultier Bès de Berc in his book, then Fabien Revol, a theologian from Lyon, author of a thesis on "continued creation", then "the word arrived on the wings of who knows what angel, up to the ears of Pope Francis". Paul Piccarreta ends his article in *Causeur* of June 19, 2015 with a call to read... Patrice de Plunkett. This same Paul Piccarreta proclaims "we are at odds with the liberal Catholic right" but his anti-liberalism does not lead him to be an Attac activist and he can be found on the Action française website. Paul Piccarreta claims to be part of a very old current, that of the revolutionary anarchists who were never contradictory with the magisterium of the Church. Is it necessary to recall what was the role of the libertarian companions not only in the fight against the priests but in favor of contraception and abortion? Piccarreta is an anarchist in the manner of Jacques de Guillebon and Falk van Gaver (see *below*), that is, in the same way that Guillebon is also a socialist.

Eugénie Bastié, a Web journalist for Le *Figaro*, is the political editor-in-chief (and therefore a sort of political commissioner) of the periodical *Limite*. Among her references are the Action française (according to *Libération*), Mgr Rey (the one who invites the National Front in the name of the Church), "who is an interesting person", she says, and whom she accompanied to Rome. She fully assumes the fact that the magazine *Limite* is an (adulterous?) child of the Manif pour tous "which wished to continue the fight in a cultural and integral form, which goes beyond the question of the Taubira law to become part of a global critique of the liberal-libertarian civilization"[129]. The blog Fdesouche (sic) announced on October 5, 2014 that Radio Courtoisie (a far-right radio station run by Viscount Henry de Lesquen du Plessis-Casso, boss of the Club de l'Horloge) was hosting Eugénie Bastié, a journalist at Le *Figaro,* Pierre Tordi, a member of Action Française, and Gaultier Bès de Berc, a philosophy professor, on the theme "Is the future in degrowth?"

Among the masters of thought of the magazine *Limite*, we find Patrice de Plunkett, Fabrice Hadjadj and Olivier Rey.

---

129. See the site of the Action française, le Rouge & le Noir, which has nothing libertarian about it despite its colors: http://www.lerougeetlenoir.org/mot/action-francaise

Patrice de Plunkett is a former royalist militant, once close to Alain de Benoist's New Right. Ex-editor of *Figaro Dimanche*, ex-codirector of *Figaro Magazine*, reconverted to Catholicism in 1985, columnist at Radio Notre-Dame, member of the Philanthropos committee (to "re-evangelize" Europe!), Commander of the Order of the Holy Sepulchre of Jerusalem, pontifical knight, defender of Opus Dei, lover of John Paul II, thanks to whom the Church would have from now on a combative manifesto of political ecology. Patrice de Plunkett likes to present himself today as a radical ecologist close to social movements and hostile to the mummies of anti-Bolshevik Catholicism, a great reader and promoter of the right-wing dwindler Vincent Cheynet and the soldier of God Bès de Berc[130]. Patrice de Plunkett sometimes confides, on more confidential sites, such as Liberté politique (n°42, autumn 2008, site of the Fondation de Service politique charged with defending Judeo-Christian values) that "if ecologists today call themselves Darwinians, or anti-Judeo-Christians, it is because they breathe the air of the times more than that of ecology". So what are "anti-Darwinian ecologists"? Supporters of anti-evolutionist currents, as we have already demonstrated?

Fabrice Hadjadj, member of the Pontifical Council for the Laity, director of the Philanthropos Institute (founded to respond to the call of John Paul II to defend the Christian values of Europe), official editorial adviser of *Limite*, is close to the conservative movement Communion et Libération (very hostile to the left) and on which Pope Francis is increasingly leaning[131]. Fabrice Hadjadj is a very big name in this new identitarian, reactionary and (re)conquering Church, the opposite of liberation theologies. It was he who gave the closing speech at the Rimini meeting organized by Communion and Liberation in 2010, before more than 25,000 people[132]. He was also in charge of a governmental seminar with the Italian Ministers of the Interior, Justice and the Armed Forces. It is not known whether he shared with them his usual theses: the women's liberation movement qualified as "contraceptive and abortive militancy" and Islam

---

130. Patrice de Plunkett defends Opus Dei with a question: "Aren't we trying to reach the Catholic Church through Opus Dei? Don't we see in Opus Dei a "concentrate" of everything that our era reproaches the Roman Church for? In this case, to shed light on the daughter (Opus Dei) is to shed light on the mother (the Church) [...]".

131. http://www.christianismesocial.org/spip.php?article351

132. For the record, I got trapped a few years ago when I went to give a conference against "McDonaldisation", a left-wing and ecological guarantee for this annual meeting in Rimini organized by Communion and Liberation.

175

considered as the dialectical term of a techno-liberal Europe that would have rejected its Greco-Latin roots and its Jewish and Christian wings[133]. Fabrice Hadjadj fights of course against Darwinism: "To say that man is a beast among others is precisely to make ecology impossible, since man must have a special dignity in order to be responsible and guardian of creation...". He also explains for *Famille chrétienne* (not really on the left) that the encyclical *Laudato si'* aims to break the lame coupling between Catholicism and the techno-liberal world of unlimited growth, in order to challenge the technocratic paradigm from the Mysteries of the Church. The only solution to the crisis (including the ecological one) would be communion and belonging (hence perhaps the reminder of Greco-Latin roots and the appeal to Europeans?)

As for Olivier Rey, he is the one by whom degrowth was confused for the first time with austerity in the monthly *La Décroissance* of June 2012, debater with Alain de Benoist, Gaultier Bès de Berc on the extreme right-wing Web TV, TVLiberté, a great defender of equal rights before marriage, a militant neo-creationist who argues that "original man does not descend from the monkey"[134]. Patrice de Plunkett invites us to savor Olivier Rey in addition to Cheynet and Bès de Berc. This Catholic right-wing is incapable of thinking of anything other than doing the same thing in less, because what interests it for thousands of years is mortification, the denunciation of greed (the *gula*) which consists in desiring above one's social condition.

Fabrice Hadjadj as well as Gaultier Bès de Berc were naturally the guests of the Assises de l'écologie humaine co-organized in 2014 by three central figures: Tugdual Derville, Pierre-Yves Gomez and Gilles Hériard-Dubreuil. Tugdual Derville, whose brother is spiritual director of Opus Dei, heads the association Alliance VITA, which, under the slogan "in solidarity with the most fragile", defends the positions of the Church on abortion, end of life, GPA, etc., he was one of the spokespersons for the Manif pour tous, general delegate of VITA (formerly the Alliance for the Rights of Life of Christine Boutin). Tugdual Derville, to whom the Action française opens its columns, sees in the Manif pour tous a movement of human ecology in the process of being formed (sic)... Tugdual Derville does not hesitate to display himself with the Legionaries of Christ and with Mr. Introvigne's Alleanza Cattolica (the best defender of sects according to the associations

---

133. http://www.lefigaro.fr/vox/societe/2015/02/10/31003-20150210ARTFIG00397-fabrice-hadjadj-les-djihadistes-le-11-janvier-et-l-europe-du-vide.php
134. https://sniadecki.wordpress.com/2014/03/20/rey-homme/

that fight them)[135]. The anti-sect association CCMM (Centre contre les manipulations mentales) knows Tugdual Derville well and the networks of this gentleman who is very much in vogue today within the Church: "M. Mr. Derville, who lives in the Vendée, is also in contact with the Italian branch of the fascist sectarian movement Tradition Family Property (TFP), Alleanza Cattolica, a movement that has been widely denounced by the French government, and which is directed in Italy by Massimo Introvigne, who is also in charge of the powerful international prosectarian lobby, the Center for the Study of New Religions or CESNUR. Massimo Introvigne, a notorious prosectarian lobbyist, has distinguished himself in France and elsewhere by his systematic interventions in favor of sects brought to justice: Jehovah's Witnesses, Scientology, the Order of the Solar Temple, etc. Thus, Mr. Derville participated with Mr. Introvigne in a colloquium of TFP/Alleanza Cattolica, in Italy. This colloquium was also an opportunity to take stock of the "dynamics" of the European movement Un De Nous, animated in France by Caroline Roux, also of Alliance VITA, and whose goal is to bring back the States on the right to abortion. Spain is leading the way. In France, the first step is to obtain its de-reimbursement. The New Acropolis, another fascist sectarian movement originating from Argentina, constituting with TFP one of the main pillars of CESNUR, also recommends reading the writings of Mr. Tugdual Derville."[136]

As for Pierre-Yves Gomez and Gilles Hériard-Dubreuil, they advise the big economic firms, notably to bypass the population's resistance in the framework of the "Large Unnecessary Imposed Projects" against which ecologists are mobilizing. The Catholic ecologist Gilles Hériard-Dubreuil directs MutadisConsultants, a firm officially "neither for nor against nuclear power" but very much in favor of it, according to the Sortir du nucléaire network, which brings together hundreds of groups. It is known for its work trivializing Chernobyl, maintaining that people could live in irradiated areas[137]. The journalist Marie Astier revealed on the site Reporterre that his firm also helped Center Parcs to concret Poligny (Jura)[138]!

The Assises chrétiennes de l'écologie of August 28, 29 and 30, 2015, co-organized by the diocese of Saint-Étienne and the hebdo *La Vie* (Catholic),

---

135.		https://www.youtube.com/watch?v=yckfMYaomsw&list=PLbRb8mZxyq6yJGP-pL1oAY-RjinS7MX7FM
136. www.ccmm.asso.fr/spip.php?article5555
137. https://infokiosques.net/imprimersans2.php?id_article=207
138. http://www.reporterre.net/Un-des-fondateurs-du-mouvement

heard, alongside some left-wing ecologists, Patrice de Plunkett, Gaultier Bès de Berc, Father Dominique Lang of Pax Christi and journalist at Le *Pèlerin*. A few days apart, some of them, like Paul Piccarreta and Patrice de Plunkett, found themselves, this time without a left-wing endorsement, at the Sainte-Baume university organized by Mgr Rey (presented as a "green bishop" who would have moved the Church according to Falk van Gaver in *La Nef* of April 2012) in the company of Marion Maréchal Le Pen. The magazine *Challenges,* not very suspicious of leftism, recognizes him a "dark catho-royalist temptation" (June 23, 2015). She, who says she does not understand "the obsession with the Republic" (see *Charles* magazine No. 14, June 2015), certifies that she is afraid that "the Republic will erase France," hence the revival of the old slogan of the monarchist right "neither left nor right."

Two other ecologist-catholic personalities are worth a look.

Jacques de Guillebon and Falk van Gaver, both followers of degrowth (not ours) and promoters of a "Christian anarchism". Behind this term hides a right-wing that is all the more wicked for being hidden. These two "obedient sons of the Church" have two enemies: the State and liberalism. They don't like gays either, and they express it in a Christian way: "Homosexuality is a disorder: a mental, behavioral, moral, social disorder, a sentimental disorder, a love disorder. Homosexuality is an evil, a social evil, a spiritual evil, an existential evil, and nothing will stop us from thinking and saying it - like thinking and saying that two and two make four."[139]

A friend of Marion Maréchal Le Pen[140], presented by the Observatory of Journalists (OJIM) as a probable pen of Charles Millon and Christine Boutin, Jacques de Guillebon, a royalist anti-liberal Catholic, has collaborated with the monarchist review *Immédiatement,* the *Figaro Magazine, Valeurs actuelles, Causeur,* the journal of the Action française, he was director of the traditionalist Catholic review *La Nef* (between 2005 and 2009), author of *L'impasse : du mariage laïc au mariage gay* (without secular marriage no gay marriage) and of a dossier on a certain degrowth taken up by Alain Soral (alias Alain Bonnet de Soral)[141], he was however

---

139. lesalonbeige.blogs.com/my_weblog/2012/09/04/

140. http://www.lexpress.fr/actualite/politique/fn/marion-marechal-le-pen-l-effrontee-nationale_1661947.html

141. Alain Soral, who doesn't really appreciate my criticism, publishes a virulent "Paul Ariès ou la critique décroissante au ras des pâquerettes" (Paul Ariès or the decreasing criticism at the level of the daisies), to be read at the address: http://www.egaliteetreconciliation.fr/Paul-Aries-ou-la-critique.html

offended that I dared to present him as being "very right-wing". Jacques de Guillebon is a sanctimonious ecologist, but this father-righteousness is one of the first 19 signatories of the appeal "Touche pas à ma pute! Manifesto of the 363 bastards"[142]. Jacques de Guillebon writes in *La Nef* of April 2011 a revealing little text: "What Marine Le Pen's figure manifests is perhaps, let's be optimistic, the effort of these inhabitants of France to reform themselves as a people, to rebuild a peaceful and great nation." It is true that he does not hide his admiration for Philippe Muray (the one that Elisabeth Lévy presents as "the hidden imam of free spirits", that is to say, puffers of "leftists" and great worshipper of Roman Catholicism) and Chantal Delsol (Catholic philosopher of shock, wife of Charles Millon)[143]. Jacques de Guillebon declared to *Causeur* in March 2013 his love of Pope Francis: "No one was expecting him and it was him, Pope Francis. Not Hollande, not I, not Desouche, but Francis, like everyone else and like no one else. Francis as the Poverello, of course, but also as the Xavier, evangelizer of the Far East and founding figure of the Society of Jesus; Francis also as the de Sales, the immense pastor of Savoy and, by the way, patron saint of journalists." He develops his vision of ecology as follows: "The good ecologist is Benedict XVI [you read that right!], my friend Falk van Gaver, or the consequently Christian partisans of degrowth [Cheynet for example?] The bad ecologist is the big redhead whose name has been filling the pages of the news since 1968.[144] Logical with himself Jacques de Guillebon belched in *Causeur* of December 2014: "The abortion: no to the permanent state of exception. The right to abortion is untenable!"

Its co-author, Falk van Gaver, also proclaims himself to be a Christian anarchist, a radical anti-capitalist, an anti-industrialist, a Luddite, a populist, and he even proclaims to have participated "among other things, in

---

142. On the other hand, the monthly *Les Zindigné(e)s* is a partner of the call "Nous n'Irons pas au bois" with the Zero macho network.

143. Jacques de Guillebon took the trouble to respond to my accusations on the Action Française website: "Mr. Paul Ariès deduced, a few years later from the presence of this file on this site, that there was a diminishing axis of the extreme right. I don't know what he means by this term, I only know that it is not at all the definition that I give of my thought nor of my political ideas. My political ideas are those of social Catholicism, of distributism and close to those of the original socialism, which was, let us remember, mainly Christian and which, inspiring the first French Action, constitutes one of the points of agreement that I can have with this movement. If I am of the extreme right, I am with Novalis, Frédéric Ozanam, Proudhon, Thoreau, William Morris, Chesterton, Gandhi, Péguy, Orwell, Lanza del Vasto, Ellul, Illich and Michéa.

144. https://www.lanef.net/t_article/le-capitaine-cochet-jacques-de-guillebon-25131.asp

the violent actions of the Black Blocs"[145]. Luc Richard (director of the monarchist magazine *Immédiatement*), who traveled with him to Genoa to participate in the counter-G8, was present two meters away from Carlo Giuliani when he was shot by the police, as can be seen in the photographs published in *Paris Match*.

Falk van Gaver naturally claims to be influenced by Bernanos and Orwell, but also by Ivan Illich, Jacques Ellul, Bernard de Charbonneau... However, he was director of the monarchist review *Immédiatement* and contributes to the reviews *La Nef, Causeur, Famille chrétienne*; he is also a delegate of the Sociopolitical Observatory of the diocese of Fréjus-Toulon (the one that gives a short shrift to Marion Maréchal Le Pen). Falk van Gaver defends the good Pope Francis in the name of the Sociopolitical Observatory of the Diocese of Fréjus-Toulon under the title: "Is the Pope left-wing?" He naturally answers in the negative: "Anticapitalism, ecologism, populism..., is the pope of the left? If his two predecessors were classified rather on the right, this one is rather on the left, it seems... He himself has already answered the North American accusation of "Marxism", but if Francis is of the left, Jesus was of the extreme left, it is enough to open any gospel to be convinced of it. And the very first Christians, communist and pacifist revolutionaries who lived in autonomous communities where everything was shared - let's reopen the Acts of the Apostles..."[146]. The Christian anarchist Falk van Gaver gives his own definition of anarchism: it would be enough to go from Blanqui's "Neither God nor master" to "One God, (therefore) no masters"! Falk van Gaver naturally recognizes himself in Francis' encyclical: "I am very happy that the term and concept of 'integral ecology', which I introduced in Christian circles about ten years ago, has been progressively taken up by Christian ecologists and even by the Pope, since it is even the title of one of the chapters of his encyclical, in which he defines it in terms almost similar to mine. I am not saying that there has been a direct influence, even if perhaps indirect impregnation by oil stain, but that it is in the air of time, and that it was necessary to have a term more federative and more "integral" than the only human ecology to speak about a plenary ecology which is addressed to all men."[147]

---

145. http://philitt.fr/2015/09/14/falk-van-gaver-lanarchisme-chretien-cest-lesprit-de-le-vangile-qui-bouscule-les-societes/
146. http://osp.frejustoulon.fr/le-pape-est-il-de-gauche/
147. http://osp.frejustoulon.fr/franc-succes-de-la-journee-decologie-integrale-osp-limite/

It's a pity that Cheynet forgot to denounce the eco-tartuffe, Falk van Gaver, guilty of a car expedition from France to China (sic), but it's true that if he's the one who gave the pope the concept of integral ecology, it's worth an indulgence! The journal *Limite* has joined forces with the Socio-political Observatory of the Diocese of Fréjus-Toulon, under the leadership of the "Christian anarchist" Falk van Gaver, to organize the first day of integral ecology on November 21, 2015, in Toulon, with American stars Olivier Rey, Paul Piccarreta, Thierry Jaccaud and Bishop Rey! The Observatory website, returning to "Bishop Rey's initiative" in the face of the FN, gives the floor to Jacques Bagnoud: "One can only rejoice at this step of reconciliation brought about by Bishop Rey, admittedly small but symbolic, and hope that it will be followed by many others so that the Christian presence in politics will be a source of freedom, dialogue and a consideration of all citizens and all aspects of reality."[148]

The ecologist-cathos and the National Front

The Catholic Church in France has long stood in the way of extreme right-wing ideas. This is a tribute to the Catholic Church, which is much less true in the majority of other nations, including European ones. Its history with the Leagues of the 1930s and with Vichy had given it antibodies. Something extremely serious is happening, however, because those Catholics who used to vote less for the National Front than the rest of the population are now voting more for it… and in particular young churchgoers[149]. The first explicit declarations of the Catholic Church in France against the FN date back to 1985, when Jean-Marie Le Pen obtained 11% of the votes in the European elections, and skilfully tried to seduce the Christian electorate. Bishop Decourtray and Bishop Lustiger denounced this attempt to take over the Catholics and became the bêtes noires of Le Pen, who had them booed at his meetings. Bridges have always existed between the extreme right and a certain Church, but it was mainly the traditionalist circles of Bernard Antony, alias Romain Marie. Bernard Antony, Jean-Marie Le Pen's old Catholic guarantor, founder of Chrétienté-Solidarité, former FN European deputy, former regional councillor of Midi-Pyrénées, former

---

148. http://osp.frejustoulon.fr/marion-marechal-le-pen-linitiative-de-mgr-rey/
149. The only exception is the European elections, especially those of 2014.

megretist, former member of Carl Lang's Party of France (former FN secretary general), director of the newspaper *Présent*, proclaimed, as early as the end of the 1980s, that "the National Front does not disagree on any point with the doctrine of the Catholic Church, which has firmly condemned communism, freemasonry, socialism, even moderate socialism, and doctrinal liberalism. " One should also mention among the traditional bridges the Club de l'Horloge, which became the Carrefour de l'Horloge, founded in 1974 by Yvan Blot and Henry de Lesquen, and which has made a specialty of working to bring together the right and the extreme right by giving a large place to Catholicism: "Sovereignty is a hollow idea if it is not based on a preserved identity. It is not enough in this respect to defend and promote the French language, although this is very necessary, it is also and above all necessary to re-establish the unity of the nation by fighting the Islamization of society and its melanization, that is to say the explosion of the populations of the congoïde (black) race, because France is a people of the white race, as General de Gaulle said excellently."[150] Viscount de Lesquen is opposed to any rapprochement of the Church with Islam.

However, we are no longer faced with such bridges to the extreme right, but with a shift of a large part of Catholics. This shift, which occurred in less than two years, between 2013 and 2015, is a consequence of the Manif pour tous and the Catholic identity movements that surrounded it, notably around the issue of sexism. The Church thus bears a historical responsibility by having chosen to play with the devil, and the princes who govern it could not ignore the fruits of this. Thus, *Le Figaro* of August 29, 2015 headlined, something unthinkable before the Manif pour tous: "The Church and the National Front, to end a false debate." *Le Figaro* docently explains that "two realities have changed in thirty years: the National Front itself on the one hand, the Catholic world on the other." I am not very convinced of the change in the FN, but I readily agree with the change in the Church. The invitation of Marion Maréchal Le Pen by Mgr Rey, the "ecologist" bishop of Fréjus-Toulon, and by Falk van Gaver's Observatoire sociopolitique du diocèse de Fréjus-Toulon, is only the submerged face of an iceberg that threatens the Church. On the one hand, the new battalions of the Church, those who vomit May 68, mobilize on themes that bring them closer to the extreme right, on the

---

150. en.novopress.info/194834/first-meetings-at-the-crossroads-horloge-interview-henry-lesquen/

other hand, the FN has not stopped giving pledges to the Church these last years, even going so far as to reject the fundamentalist Catholics who characterized its ranks, while not condemning the street prayers of these same Cathos. We can see how a fringe of the Church, under the pretext of opposing the street prayers of Muslims, takes advantage of this to reoccupy the public space. Vatican Radio ("the voice of the Pope and the Church in dialogue with the world") justified this cordial hand extended to Marion Maréchal Le Pen by recalling that she is a Catholic and by giving the floor to Father Guitton, responsible for the Socio-political Observatory of the diocese of Fréjus-Toulon: "Father Guitton insists on the more general meaning of this summer university: to reach out to all Catholics invested in politics, so that all can contribute, in their own way and according to their own responsibility, to the common good."[151] This invitation certainly offended some believers and even some faithful, but Vincent Neymon, the director of communications for the French episcopate, approves of the change in the Church's position toward the FN: "The reasons that led to the blacklisting of the FN fifteen years ago are no longer valid today. The party is changing, more diverse people are following it. The openly xenophobic theses of the FN are no longer as explicit. Marion Maréchal Le Pen brings together people who it is better to invite. I find this interesting, even if it is a trap. We are no longer at the time when we could stop at principles. All circles are affected, including Catholics. All the more reason to enter the debate."[152]

The National Front had strongly welcomed the election of the new "progressive" pope. Already through the voice of Jean-Marie Le Pen: "The National Front welcomes the election of Pope Francis, who has foiled the often mediocre calculations of the prognosticators, assimilating the conclave to the political cooking they usually do their honey. He is not surprised that he is already being slandered, as were all his predecessors since Pius XII. He does not doubt that he will be able to resist the unbearable and arrogant pressures of those who, under the pretext of "progress", are asking him to abandon Christian morality and the tradition of the Catholic Church. Then, through the voice of Bruno Gollnisch, former MEP, eternal rival of Marine Le Pen, who declared on May 1st, 2014 (so in

---

151. http://fr.radiovaticana.va/news/2015/08/26/le_front_national_rep%C3%A9sent%C3%A9_dans_un_d%C3%A9bat_%C3%A0_la_sainte-baume/1167655
152.   http://www.lemonde.fr/politique/article/2015/08/26/l-eglise-ne-tourne-plus-le-dos-au-fn_4737102_823448.html.

---

full knowledge of the facts since Francis has been Pope for a year at that time): "Pope Francis has held today a rich and elevated speech before the European parliamentarians gathered in session in Strasbourg. He exposed the causes of the disaffection of a growing part of the people towards the European Union. He recalled that human rights, which are invoked here at every moment, cannot be the expression of an individualistic and hedonistic claim, but that they derive from the nature and spiritual destiny of man. He spoke out against what his predecessor John Paul II called "the culture of death", and reaffirmed the need to respect human life from its origin to its natural end. For him, true ecology can only be understood as respect for Creation. He also recalled the importance of the family as the basic unit of society, the protection of the weak and the remedy for the tragedy of loneliness. He rightly stigmatized the devastating effects of a purely materialistic globalized economy.

The "de-demonization" of the FN will necessarily pass through the "Church". Thus, Eugénie Bastié, editor-in-chief of the ecologist-catholic magazine *Limite*, conducted an interview in the columns of Le *Figaro* with Mgr Rey. The green bishop (sic) defends himself from wanting to de-demonize the FN by inviting Marion Maréchal Le Pen, but adds: "We must create a dialogue, a debate, from which the FN is not excluded [...]. I admit that this is an innovative position compared to a form of oukase which consisted in putting the Lepenist party at a distance. There are indeed a certain number of Catholics who vote FN, it is a reality. These people can feel marginalized. Our objective is to create a dialogue of reason, a reflection with them. Eugénie Bastié recalls that "the editorialist and political editor of Le Figaro, Guillaume Tabard, attended the contested round table of the Sainte-Baume, organized by the diocese of Frejus-Toulon, where Marion Maréchal Le Pen spoke. For him, the cordon sanitaire erected by some Catholics around the National Front is not only anachronistic, but has no justification.

Marion Maréchal Le Pen seized the opportunity and explained in *Famille chrétienne* that the present situation is similar to that of the Terror: "Catholics were victims of Christianophobia during the French Revolution. After a period of calm, this phenomenon is returning. I observe a manifest form of aggressiveness towards them. This pushes the new generation to act. These young Catholics, who often belong to wealthy backgrounds, are aware that they belong to the elite of tomorrow. They want to give themselves the means to form themselves and to act [...].

I am part of this 'anti-May 68' generation. We can't say it better: it's really a matter of a Church and a right-wing with a vengeance that intend to put an end to what would have been only historical parentheses. This (extreme) Catholic right rejects 1981, 1944 (and the CNR program), 1936, 1917, 1848, 1793, 1789 and, for the more lucid, the humanism of the Enlightenment. The time has come not only to de-demonize the FN to make it a party like any other, but to seek convergence and build a common front. Thus Gilles Lebreton, FN deputy in the European Parliament and special adviser to Marine Le Pen on higher education issues, intends to point out the similarities between the Church and his party: "Like the Church, the FN defends the model of the traditional family constituted by the union of a man and a woman. This is why, against the PS and a large part of Les Républicains [ex-UMP], it protested against Marriage for All. Like the Church, the FN defends the dignity of the human person. This is why, against the procrastination of the PS and Les Républicains, it firmly refuses the legalization of surrogate motherhood (GPA), which transforms the child and the human body into merchandise. Like the Church, the FN defends Christians when they need help. This is why it has mobilized, more clearly than the PS and the Republicans, to call on international society to protect the Christians of the East against the persecution of Islamic terrorists. In reality, what these bishops reproach the FN with is its firm position on immigration. But this is forgetting what Pope Francis himself said in the European Parliament: the European peoples have the right to defend their identity. Moreover, the FN is in favor of a policy of cooperation with emigration states, in order to help them settle their nationals at home."[153]

The marriage between the Church and the FN would therefore no longer be unnatural... since it intends to do its "May 68 in reverse" and since it has launched its troops against gay marriage and against the fight against sexist clichés. This obscene marriage is naturally facilitated by the right-wing (if not the extreme right-wing) of the French electorate, and particularly of Christians. This new model is theorized under the name of "identity-based Catholicism", which relies on the development of other "communitarianisms", fundamentalism and fundamentalism as a lever. Paradoxically, the main resistance to this rapprochement comes today from a part of the FN, symbolized by Florian Philippot (vice-president of the FN, but formerly close to the sovereignism of Jean-Pierre Chevènement),

---

153. http://gilleslebreton.eu/2015/08/28/leglise-normalise-ses-relations-avec-le-front-national/

who displays his statism, his anti-immigration and secularist positions. I will not choose between the plague and the cholera, Marion Maréchal Le Pen or Florian Philippot.

An anti-capitalist pope?

The ecologist-cathos would have us believe that the Pope would have espoused alter-globalization theses and would have become an opponent of the capitalist system. Indeed, he never ceases to denounce "the money that governs instead of serving", "the new idolatry of money", "the economy of exclusion and waste", etc. That's all it took for some editorialists to play at being afraid. The magazine *Le Pèlerin* headlined "Is the Pope anti-capitalist?", the newspaper *La Croix* added: "This Pope who wants to change the economic system", *Le Monde diplomatique* added: "An anti-capitalist discourse from the South: the Pope against the devil's dung". The website Là-bas si j'y suis is amused: "Pope Francis is the NPA, the new anti-capitalist pope". The pontiff indeed confuses those who have forgotten that there are several ways of being anti-capitalist. Opus Dei's critique of consumer society is to degrowth what the National Front's alterglobalism is to the ecology of the poor. Do we have to be ignorant to no longer recognize reactionary anticapitalism? The Church's anti-capitalism is a mere figure of speech that calls for the moralization of capitalists and capitalism...

The international theological journal *Concilium, which is* close to liberation theologies, devoted an issue to the links between economy and religion, arguing that the Church has always defended and still defends capitalism. Francis certainly holds radical, alterglobalist and capitalist speeches, but he entrusts the Vatican bank (IOR) to the multinational Promontory Financial Group, one of the main actors of globalized capitalism. Do we need to remind the ecologist-cathos of the extreme wealth of the Vatican and that an important part of it comes from Mussolini as a token of his gratitude[154] ?

I recognize that sometimes appearances are misleading, as when the Front National speaks of equal rights for users of public services: "Every time a sector is transferred from the public to the private sector, it results in a regression of equality and an explosion of costs. I am therefore in

---

154. http://www.europe1.fr/international/la-richesse-fasciste-du-vatican-1389009

favor of a public service for transportation, education, health, banks and the elderly. And I am also in favor of state intervention in strategic sectors: energy, communications, telecommunications and media. I am also thinking about a tax revolution that would restore the balance between capital and labor."[155]

Who can believe that the conception of public service and equality is the same for a supporter of national preference and for the left? Candidate Chirac did the social fracture trick in 2002... As for Christine Boutin, doesn't she say she is ready to make the revolution (sic)? Pope Francis is much more serious and sincere when he presents himself as a critic of "really existing capitalism" but his anti-capitalism has nothing in common with that of the historical lefts and political ecology. "Some still defend," he writes, "theories of 'favorable relapse,' which assume that every economic growth, fostered by the free market, succeeds in itself in producing greater equity and social inclusion in the world. This view, which has never been borne out by the facts, expresses a crude and naive confidence in the goodness of those who hold economic power and in the sacralized mechanisms of the dominant economic system" [...]. "At the same time, the excluded continue to wait. In order to be able to sustain a lifestyle that excludes others, or to be able to get excited about this selfish ideal, a globalization of indifference has developed" [...]. "Today, everything enters into the game of competitiveness and the law of the strongest, where the powerful eat the weakest. As a consequence of this situation, large masses of people are excluded and marginalized: without work, without prospects, without ways out. The human being is seen as a consumer good, which can be used and then thrown away... The excluded are not "exploited", but "waste", "leftovers".[156]

Pope Francis' emulators, such as Patrice de Plunkett, who is not very sympathetic to the left and even less so to socialism, have an even more virulent anti-capitalist discourse: "It is a question of putting the economy back to its rightful place: investment at the service of the enterprise, the enterprise returning to a human dimension, and man subordinating economic activity to civilized ends. In other words, a total change of economic paradigm! Sobriety, proximity. Less goods, more links... *Small is beautiful*, as the Catholic economist Ernst Friedrich Schumacher said. But this paradigm shift requires the abolition of liberalism, in the

---

155. Interview with Marine Le Pen, *Causeur*, January 2011.
156. Encyclical *Laudato si'*.

interest of the human condition. Whatever the "conservative liberals" (an oxymoron) may argue in order to drown the fish, liberalism is a de-civilizing power: it consists in removing political counterweights in order to free the economy. But after having "liberated" the economic from the political, liberalism "liberates" finance from the economic and we arrive at the era of the cyclone, free money and madness: a permanent and uncontrollable tornado, capable of ravaging everything."[157]

Pope Francis has even had to correct the record by explaining in the daily *La Stampa* that he is not a Marxist (in the sense of anti-capitalist) despite his criticism of current capitalism. What the Pope condemns is unbridled, ultraliberal and globalized capitalism. This anti-capitalist rhetoric is not revolutionary but conservative in the literal sense. This position of Rome is not new, since the Catholic Church has always preferred the paternalist and industrial capitalism of the past to globalized and financial capitalism.

Francis is not anti-capitalist but close to Wilhelm Röpke and to ordo-liberalism[158]. Wilhelm Röpke (1899-1966), author of the famous book *Beyond Supply and Demand*, whose first French edition was prefaced by Jacques Rueff, is, along with Walter Eucken, the father of the German "social market economy"; with Hayek, he co-founded the Mont Pelerin Society in 1947 (which launched the world conservative revolution). Wilhelm Röpke was hostile to socialism and Keynesianism but also to National Socialism, despite all the attempts of the Nazi regime to win him over. His economic thinking was based on the pre-eminence of the family and on the principle of subsidiarity. He placed two quotations from Edmund Burke (1729-1797), one of the great counter-revolutionary thinkers in the sense of 1789, at the beginning of his major work. Wilhelm Röpke was a close friend and inspiration of the Jesuit Oswald von Nell-Breuning (1890-1991), a German theologian, the true author of the encyclical *Quadragesimo anno* (1931), considered by many scholars as an excellent synthesis of social doctrine and ordoliberalism. The objective is to build a "just social order" that achieves the Common Good in the

---

157. http://osp.frejustoulon.fr/plunkett-lecologie-integrale-ouvre-un-boulevard-a-la-nou-velle-evangelisation/

158. See Jean-Michel Ycre, "Les sources catholiques de l'ordolibéralisme allemand : Röpke et la pensée catholique sociale allemande", in *L'ordolibéralisme allemand. Aux sources de l'économie sociale de marché*, Patricia Commun (ed.), Université de Cergy-Pontoise, travaux et documents du Centre d'information et de recherche sur l'Allemagne contemporaine (CIRAC), 2003, pp. 163-172.

Vatican way. The Church therefore accepts the need for a strong state to create a legal framework that guarantees respect for private property and an end to abuse. This Church also calls for the fight against impoverishment by developing popular savings, for the rejection of consumerism through respect for the moral law, for the creation of participation in capital, beyond the principle of the "just wage," etc.

The fathers of ordoliberalism borrow from the Church the thesis that technical progress is not fundamentally a source of human progress. They explain that the real cause of the systemic crisis is anthropological with the "unbounded relativism" of values (sic). This idea of order, borrowed from Saint Augustine, serves to remind us that social order must be founded on the refusal of materialism and utilitarian philosophy, in short the market economy is a necessary but not sufficient condition for a free society, because there are, according to Alexander Rüstow (1885-1963), "infinitely more important things than the economy, such as the family, the community, the State, the spiritual, the ethical, the aesthetic, the cultural, in short, the human. The economy is only the material foundation. Its objective is to serve higher values[159]. Ordoliberalism proposes to build a so-called "natural" economic and social organization that can replace the artificial and arbitrary direction by the state, in order, on the one hand, to protect society from governments too inclined to listen to particular interests and, on the other hand, to reduce the welfare state in favor of traditional ties, such as those of the family and, more broadly, of "natural communities.

What Pope Francis denounces is not capitalism, but what specialists call "crony capitalism" (which others call "social-clientelism" and which North Americans call *"crony capitalism"*), which would be the fruit of the continuous extension of the intervention of the State in the economy and in the management of private matters, such as sexuality (by recognizing rights such as the right to abortion and contraception and by guaranteeing their exercise). Social inequalities would not be the consequence of capitalism, nor of "justly acquired property rights" but of privileges, which are first and foremost those granted to useless civil servants and unions. These same networks reproach Éric Zemmour for confusing liberalism, which he never ceases to attack, with this famous "capitalism of connivance" (sic) that even the supporters of pure capitalism, such as the think

---

159.   http://www.institut-thomas-more.org/actualite/merkel-ou-tsipras-vertus-et-reussites-de-lordoliberalisme-allemand-2.html

tank Institut des Libertés, blame for all the evils, in order to better clear capitalism of any responsibility. The solution would therefore be twofold: to reduce the State and to subject it to religious morality.

The Church is talking a lot today about the works of Sister Cécile Renouard, a religious of the Assumption, professor at ESSEC, and member of the Nicolas-Hulot Foundation think tank, and of the Jesuit Gaël Giraud, a priest and mathematician, chief economist at the French Development Agency (AFD), also a member of the Nicolas-Hulot Foundation think tank, author of *20 propositions pour réformer le capitalisme* (Flammarion, new ed. 2012), of *Le facteur 12. Pourquoi il faut plafonner les revenus* (with Cécile Renouard, Éd. Carnets Nord-Montparnasse, 2012), and *Illusion financière. Pourquoi les chrétiens ne peuvent se taire,* (Éd. de l'Atelier, 2012).

In the Assumptionist journal, Cécile Renouard explains that liberal capitalism can be preserved while correcting what caused the financial crisis: "It is true that the endless search for the indefinite increase of capital by its owners alone and the disjunction between the capital factor and the labor factor are two characteristics of capitalism which, if we push this logic to the limit, lead to disasters. But capitalism is also linked to the development of liberal principles which presuppose a consideration of the social dimension. Re-embedding the economy in the social dimension is the fundamental challenge. This is why in our book we propose a form of social market economy.[160] As for Gaël Giraud, "far from anti-capitalist incantations" (sic), he also seeks to sketch "the contours of a 'green', fair and pluralist capitalism".

The only serious challenge within the Church to its adherents of green capitalism... came not from the left-wing Catholics, who were totally silent, but from another Jesuit, Father Robert Sirico, author of the book *Defending the Free Market.* For him, the proponents of state reform of capitalism are making a serious mistake, because recourse to more state intervention would worsen the situation since the state itself is responsible for it through "crony capitalism. The church finally adopts Thatcher's slogan: "*There is no alternative*"... but capitalism.

---

160. http://www.vivrelafrance.fr/cecile-renouard_fr.html

The ecologist-cathos and the rescue of capitalism

The eco-cathos would like to convince us that the Church is attacking the Golden Calf. We can move forward in the reflection by looking at Edouard Tetreau's appeal to Pope Francis in the run-up to his last trip to the United States. This note, published at the end of 2014 in the journal *Culture et Foi* of the Pontifical Council for Culture, entitled "How the human species will survive the new economy of the 21st century, a plea for an initiative by Pope Francis in New York in September 2015"[161] has already made the rounds several times and is delighting eco-cathos. Its author, Édouard Tétreau, is a financial analyst, founder and director of Mediafin, and columnist for the business newspaper *Les Échos*. This right-wing Catholic economist has made a name for himself in business circles by launching a salutary appeal to shareholders in the face of the imminent crisis: "Take your *e-profits* before a possible *e-crash*" (sic) and on the left for having compared the National Front... to the left and in particular to the anti-capitalists: "The National Front confirms that it is not a far-right party, but a far-left party. It oozes hatred of the "rich"; distrust of anything resembling business, especially if it is large and prosperous; disgust with the free economy. He transpires, through every pore of his skin, to use Jean-Marie Le Pen's expression about "AIDS patients", the love of the most national and extreme socialism; the spirit of closure; the hatred of freedom." The daily *L'Humanité* of December 19, 2013 headlined "Édouard Tétreau is too, really too right-wing" and accused him of rewriting history to better convey the economic conceptions of liberal ideology. This right-wing Catholic economist heads the European Council on Foreign Relations (ECFR) in Paris, a think tank that campaigns for an integrated military defense with the financial support of several firms, including the George Soros Foundation.

Édouard Tétreau therefore invites Pope Francis to rally to the "preferential option for man" in the name of the fight against excessive financialization and the overly rapid digitalization of the economy. The enemy is not capitalism but the excess of liquidity in the economy that could provoke a new crisis and lead to revolutions. He therefore suggests organizing a conference similar to the Bretton-Woods conference (which in 1944 reconstructed the broad outlines of the international financial system)

---

161. http://www.edouardtetreau.com/wp-content/uploads/2014/12/PFNY_FR.pdf

and which would be led by the "great world religions" in order to draw up a "charter of good practices" that would make it possible to save capitalism. This initiative would make it possible to bypass states and official institutions, typically in the spirit of the detestable principle of Catholic subsidiarity. The big firms would agree among themselves on the new rules of the game. Edouard Tétreau is convinced that in order to legitimize such norms, "a moral authority is needed that can transcend financial, national and cultural interests" - in short, the Church should come to the rescue of a renewed capitalism. According to him, the Church's social doctrine should be the basis of this system, since it would put the "human person" at the center of the economy" (sic). This is probably why the same man describes as privileged the trade unionists who oppose Sunday work, who would not belong to the "real country"; this is why he dares to draw a parallel between EPO doping in cycling and the intoxication caused by the OP (compulsory levy) in society; This is why he calls for "throwing away the Labor Code", described as "a bad bible that prevents people who want to work from doing so" (sic); this is why he asks for the abolition of the prud'homale justice system and the joint management of social organizations; this is why he invites us not to pay a single cent of public money to those who already have a job and to give responsibility for vocational training to companies alone. Our zealot of the Pope is also a zealot of the hardest capitalism because "capitalism, like democracy, is the worst system except for all the others". Édouard Tétreau even defends obscene executive remuneration, which is a form of pollution, because, he says, "it is normal for corporate officers to be very well paid - sometimes not well enough - for companies that are the only sources of wealth in our societies in an open competitive world. Without them, who would finance our unemployed, our pensioners, our States?

The fathers of social Catholicism must be turning over in their graves, for had not the Church always believed that only work creates value and not capital? Édouard Tétreau explains that we must put an end to the "god of money that governs instead of serving" and that, to do this, we should bring together the North American "philanthropic system" (which would take the place of the social state) and the sharing economy (such as roommates or shared bicycles): "In the United States, the leading country in the new economy, the voice of conscience is called philanthropy. The *giveback*. Every year, 95% of American households give to charities, for a total of more than 300 billion dollars. This is the first way to defuse the trap into which the new economy is leading us, and to put people back at the center. The second path is European: the slow but steady emergence of the sharing economy. In Europe, perhaps more than elsewhere, there is an awareness of a world with limited human and natural resources. So, rather than adopting predatory and mercantilist attitudes, which abound in the rest of the world, we choose to share what is scarce, avoiding monetary transactions as much as possible. We share or exchange a car ride. A service at home. A home. Humanity takes back its rights; the local community too. The sharing economy - using a good rather than owning it - has a bright future ahead of it.

As Social Security celebrates its 70th anniversary, should we really go back to the generosity of the rich to satisfy the needs of the greatest number? The Church will never be done with lady bosses and directors of conscience!

When the Church praises capitalist economists

The so-called anti-capitalist and anti-globalization theses of Pope Francis can be judged differently by considering the economists honored by this same Church.

Every year the Pontifical Foundation Centesimus Annus-Pro Pontifice, which depends directly on the Secretariat of State (Vatican government), awards an Economy and Society prize that aims to promote the Church's social doctrine. The president of the Pontifical Foundation, Domingo Sugranyes Bickel, was keen to point out that the 2015 award was given, according to the indications of Pope Francis, to "give back all the social dignity it deserves to the depreciated word of solidarity". We can therefore consider that the winner is representative of Vatican thought and that, as a prolific author, he is also a good interpreter of Francis' thought. The Vatican has therefore promoted this year the Frenchman Pierre de Lauzun, for his book *Finance, un regard chrétien. From medieval banking to financial globalization*. The author is no stranger to the world, as he is the general delegate of the French Association of Financial Markets, which brings together stock market professionals, a former director of various banks and international financial organizations, including Goldman Sachs, and a former head of the French banking federation. He is also a regular columnist for the very right-wing Catholic magazine

193

Liberté politique. Pierre de Lauzun belongs to the elite of globalized financial capitalism. The association Attac France presents him in *Le livre noir des banques* as an influential evening visitor of Sarkozy's when he was in the Élysée Palace and as the editor of the bankers' arguments to defend their interests. The ecologist-catholic Pierre de Lauzun finds the encyclical *Laudato si'* to his liking: "A remarkable text, bearing essential messages. In particular the reminder of the major responsibility that we have in relation to the life which surrounds us and to the threatened balances of our planet, and thus the necessary personal and collective conversion" (sic). Pierre de Lauzun is not used to street demonstrations alongside the unemployed, the rightsless, the roofless, except for the Manif pour tous (against equal rights). His fear was not about the homo-phobic outbursts but about the weakening of the message in the name of political correctness: "Such a mobilization is a major novelty, in its scope and its methods. We haven't seen such a mobilization for thirty years or more. And above all novelty in its orientation against the current of the dominant political correctness. This is not easy in the media ecosystem we live in. I have already underlined in another article the hard constraints that this situation imposed on the public expression of the movement, starting with the demonstrations. There is always the risk of an excessive empire of political correctness - and an impoverishment of the message. But anyone with a minimal knowledge of the uses of political expression cannot fail to be struck by the extreme restraint and self-control that this movement has shown from the beginning."[162]

This financier, recognized by the Vatican for his work on the morality of the actors of the financial market in the light of the social doctrine of the Church, is therefore an authorized interpreter of Vatican thought. His blog, which reads "Blessed is the rich man who keeps himself without blemish and does not chase after gold" (Si. 31.8.), allows us to better understand this new economic order that would function in harmony with social realities and moral requirements, no longer as an end but as a means. Pierre de Lauzun calls for the development of the logic of gift and gratuity (which should please the director of the International Observatory of Free Public Services and Common Goods that I am!). However, we are not talking about the same thing when we talk about giving. Pierre de Lauzun calls for "giving in spite of the redistribution operated by taxes"... in other words, public services, common goods, social redistribution, "it

---

162. http://www.pierredelauzun.com/MANIF-POUR-TOUS-L-AVENIR.html

194

is not a real gift because it is forced (even if in principle it is voted and thus accepted)". The only real donation, in the end, would be the good old charity (that of the patronesses and Bill Gates)! Pierre de Lauzun then asks: "How much to give? His answer is inspired by the Christian Middle Ages (that period so dear to the Catholic Church): "It seems to us that Scripture and tradition (including the practice of the Church for centuries) give us just such a reference, which is the tithe. It is certainly not canonically obligatory; but it has been an essential basis for a very long time, and the Bible strongly proposes it. This would mean that it would be quite desirable, as a first indication, to give at least one-tenth of what one actually earns (net income, after taxes)." The objective being, however, to put an end to the false gift of taxation (since not only does Pierre de Lauzun consider that there is too much tax and that tax does not constitute a true giving mechanism), everyone will admit that tithing is still less redistributive than the ISF! To the question "To whom do we give?" Lauzun gives a staggering answer: "An appreciable portion must go to our Churches, which in France are not rich and live on donations." The Church before the poor, that was daring! The 1% of humanity that takes 50% of the cake can rest easy, the ecologist-catholic Pierre de Lauzun is not really a sharer: "High salaries are not to be condemned in themselves. But three points must be verified: that they are obtained legitimately (through economic processes that function correctly: commutative justice); the acceptance of a fair level of national solidarity (distributive justice); and finally that they are accompanied by a real accountability of the fortunes thus acquired for their long-term effect, with legal and financial liability in the event of bankruptcy: this notion of responsibility is at the same time part of the two concepts of justice. Lauzun also proposes to moralize capitalism: "The markets must be oriented in the direction of the common good, which means organized in the direction of a transparent participation of all those who wish it, without rent effect or capture (commutative justice); at the same time the organization of the financial markets must be reviewed, not to anaesthetize them but to orient them in a more transparent and long-term direction. On the other hand, investments must be oriented in a direction that is both responsible and demanding, over the long term: a truly socially responsible investment. These theses will probably appeal to right-wing degrowthists, since this pope of capitalist finance maintains that we must put an end to the idea that growth has the answer to everything: "Our political life is stagnating and becoming more sterile every day. The solution to all social dilemmas for the past forty years was growth. When there was less of it, it was the headlong rush into public debt, with all its risks. But now it doesn't work anymore: there will be little growth, and it will be spontaneously very uneven; as for credit, we have pulled too hard on the rope, it's over. We must therefore clearly change direction and propose something else to the French people. Questioning what a "Christian degrowth" could be, he makes the following argument, which is widely taken up by all those who confuse degrowth with austerity, degrowth with recession: "The belief in unlimited growth is recent [...] the immoderate thirst for everything has paradoxically become virtuous conduct. It exalts [...] the omnipotence of man, the refusal of any limit, of any pre-established rule [...], it organizes the liquidation of alternative beliefs and references, and in particular of everything that recognizes the lasting existence of violence, fault or evil, in a word, everything that admits our limits...". If Pierre de Lauzun does not want to be a supporter of degrowth, it is because he fears that it will not lead to less socialization and the State but to more socialization and the State. If Pierre de Lauzun is not a supporter of degrowth, it is because he sees that the majority of growth objectors who love the good life do not take into account "the only thing that counts, the individual and collective progress of our souls, the preparation for the true homeland, which is in the other world."

When big business talks about Francis

Pope Francis' equivocal remarks on capitalism have not been without debate in business circles and their think tanks. Of course, no one believes that Francis is anti-capitalist or even anti-globalization, in the sense that the left gives to these two notions, but the powerful are arguing about the nature of his support for capitalism! Indeed, we are witnessing a real game of fools: while the media are imposing the image of a pope who is supposedly "anti-capitalist" and "alterglobalist", he is receiving Christine Lagarde, director of the International Monetary Fund (IMF), and is not taking advantage of this opportunity to denounce this symbol of capitalism. He even called on major players in capitalism to modernize the Vatican. Liberal think tanks are therefore not mistaken and all consider Pope Francis as an ally of capitalism for those who want to read between the lines! Thus, on December 4, 2014, the Acton Institute (excuse the pun!) gave the highest of its annual awards, the Novak Award 2014, to a Finnish economist, Oskari Juurikkala, a specialist in pension reform (sic). The latter dedicated his reception speech, held before leading businessmen, to the theme: "A recognition of the market economy by Pope Francis". This economist, darling of the "entrepreneurial" Catholics, explained that "the Pope is anything but a Marxist" and even invited the followers of capitalism to draw inspiration from his theses in order to deepen the free market and definitively defeat the State. This pope, presented as a prophet of Christian poverty, would be the champion of the defense of private property and the "noble vocation" of entrepreneurs. The award was presented in Rome, a few steps from the Vatican, in the Pontifical University of the Holy Cross, which is run directly by Opus Dei. Juurikkala's thesis is that Bergoglio's message, with its emphasis on the poor, is not in contradiction with the market economy, but has a positive impact on it, because it helps to "purify and enrich it", in short, capitalism after Francis would be even more powerful. Juurikkala's speech was, of course, counterbalanced at the ceremony by that of Carlo Lottieri, a philosopher of law and member of the Bruno-Leoni Institute, a think tank that also happens to be clearly liberal. Lottieri, who teaches at the Faculty of Theology in Lugano, persists in seeing Francis not as a friend but as an adversary of economic freedoms, particularly because of the "Peronist" experience he assimilated in Argentina, an experience that "never really ended and was disastrous on the whole. The real debate is not whether Francis is a capitalist or an anti-capitalist, but whether he is a capitalist or still a supporter of the old corporatist system!

I admit that I feel closer to Carlo Lottieri's thesis. Pope Francis seems to me more honestly anti-capitalist than a liar. His anti-capitalism, however, has nothing in common with that of the left. He does not look to tomorrow but to yesterday and even to the day before yesterday. We can only be surprised at the profusion of theses that emphasize today that Christian Europe was not capitalist. The pontifical knight, commander of the Order of the Holy Sepulchre of Jerusalem but nevertheless an ecologist-catholic activist, Patrice de Plunkett, is not the last to claim that "the Middle Ages were not a 'precapitalism' that waited to be 'surpassed' - in a 'progressive' way - by the appearance, in the seventeenth century, of capitalism, which was supposed to be the 'true mode of production'. This is what liberalism and its derivative, Marxism, had said; this is what our society believes,

197

which is their outcome. This is what even some pseudo-Thomists believe. But it is false.

The stakes are high: it is a matter of defending the idea that the "Middle Ages was a civilization without capitalism" and not a semi-civilization "lacking capitalism". The values, the vital springs of the Middle Ages are other than the capitalist conception of existence. They are foreign to it! Thus, the capitalism of the 21st century cannot pose as a synthesis of History, despite the fantasy of liberals and Marxists... Present-day capitalism is not the crowning achievement of a global and inexorable process that has animated History from its origins to the present day. Capitalism is only an episode in the future of humanity. Humans had lived without it: they will live again without it.

I admit to agreeing with Patrice de Plunkett's analysis, but this agreement hides an even stronger disagreement, because what would be the outcome of this necessary exit from capitalism, would it be a return to the past towards an unequal society or the passage towards an egalitarian society?

The "anti-capitalist" society Tradition Family Property

The anti-capitalism of the Catholic Church, including that of its traditionalist currents today within or outside the Church of Rome, is perfectly illustrated by the sinister Society for the Defense of Tradition Family Property (TFP).

This extreme right-wing movement was founded in the service of counter-revolution. TFP is above all anti-communist and anti-materialist, as its dogmas prove, but also its political struggles, especially in South America. TFP is no longer in the odor of sanctity but some bishops continue to express their admiration for its founder Plinio Corrêa de Oliveira (1908-1995) and to organize masses for the repose of his soul, including in Rome[163]. TFP is also a laboratory of ideas that feeds the extreme right of God.

Roberto de Mattei, president of the Lepanto Foundation of Rome (which claims to defend the principles and institutions of Christian civilization), professor at the very Catholic European University of Rome, has written

---

163. https://www.youtube.com/watch?v=PB56B9YxhyQ

a book entitled *Le croisé du xxᵉ siècle, Plinio Corrêa de Oliveira* (Éd. l'Âge d'Homme, 1997) with a preface by Cardinal Alfons Maria Stickler (1910-2007), who was in charge of the Vatican's secret archives for a long time and was elevated to the dignity of Prince of the Church by John Paul II, despite (or because of?) his extreme positions.

The great reference of TFP is St. Margaret Mary Alacoque, who is experiencing a return to favor with Francis, who never ceases to call the faithful to remember this great saint. This love is not recent, since Cardinal Bergoglio, still Archbishop of Buenos Aires and Primate of Argentina, wished to have the relics of Saint Margaret Mary Alacoque venerated, which necessitated their transfer from Paray-le-Monial in Argentina (October 2004). Margaret Mary Alacoque (1647-1690) is not just any saint... I mean that not just any Christian chooses her as a reference. Margaret Mary Alacoque is famous for the apparition of June 17, 1689, in which God asked King Louis XIV to consecrate France to the Sacred Heart and to represent it on the standards of the kingdom, which he refrained from doing. According to the worshippers of Margaret Mary Alacoque, the consequence was that the Third Estate proclaimed itself the National Assembly a century later, to the day (June 17, 1789), thus creating a break with the France of Clovis. Since then, the Sacred Heart has been the emblem of the counter-revolutionary movements that rejected 1789 and the separation of the temporal and the spiritual. TFP did not suffer too much from the death of its founder. Its "anti-capitalism" and "anti-consumerism" are as virulent as ever. TFP's Vice President John Horvat II's book, *Back to Order: From a Frenzied Society to an Organic and Christian Society, has* already sold over 30,000 copies: "It is a clear indictment of our mad rush to get more and more stuff, no matter what the cost to society, to families, and to ourselves.... This book is also very helpful to anyone who sees the problems inherent in a culture whose only values seem to be 'more' and 'right now.'"

TFP is therefore anti-capitalist, but of a rather particular anti-capitalism. First of all, because TFP denounces only macro-capitalism and above all state intervention: "Macro-capitalism, which absorbs the individual wealth of a crowd of people into Moloch enterprises, is an evil. State capitalism is an even worse evil, absorbing the wealth of all into the hands of the state super-Moloch." Secondly, because this anti-capitalism is above all a way of combating what Tocqueville called "the tendency to equalize conditions thanks to democracy": the Catholic ideal would be that of a fraternal society because it is harmoniously unequal (sic) because, as a section of its site proclaims, "inequalities are just and necessary". Finally, because this anti-capitalism in the TFP style is put at the service of a preferential option for the traditional elites.

I had the opportunity to reproduce in *The Return of the Devil* excerpts from the very cordial correspondence between the boss of the New World Right, Paul Weynich (1942-2008) and the TFP and also between the North American TFP and President Ronald Reagan. The TFP, which fought agrarian reform projects throughout South America, which fought all liberation theologies, which contributed for three years to the campaigns that led to the Pinochet coup in Chile, has always been at the forefront of the crusade against anti-cult associations[164].

TFP is well known to the general public in France through its association Avenir de la culture, which initiated protest movements against plays such as *Corpus Christi* and *Golgotha picnic*, and through its petitions. His latest major appeal, launched jointly with Cardinal Burke, one of the most reactionary Roman cardinals, appointed, in 2012, by Benedict XVI prefect of the Supreme Tribunal of the Apostolic Signatura (the highest jurisdiction of the Vatican) and appointed, in 2014, by Francis, patron of the very powerful Order of Malta (some wanted to see it as a placard). This appeal, entitled "Supplication to His Holiness Pope Francis on the future of the family" has already collected 470,000 signatures; it denounces "a gradual and systematic evolution of morals opposed to the natural and divine law" [...] since the 1968 revolution" and "the aberrant ideology of gender". TFP is, of course, denounced by the French episcopate for its extremism, but among the signatories are former U.S. Senator Rick Santorum, Chilean Cardinal Jorge Medina Estévez, Archbishop Aldo di Cillo Pagotto of Brazil, Archbishop Robert F. Vassa, North American archbishop, but also the Frenchmen Bertrand Antony, president of AGRIF (General Alliance against Racism and for the Respect of French and Christian Identity), Guillaume de Thieulloy, director of Riposte Catholique, the traditionalist abbot Guillaume de Tanoüarn, member of the Institute of the Good Shepherd, director of the Saint Paul Center, etc.

The TFPs lead numerous campaigns against "public blasphemy", for the extension of Marian devotion, for the "defense of the traditional family", against left-wing Catholicism, against the socialist cultural revolution. With them, the Church can continue to inflict the expression "legal concubinage" on those who are "content" to go before the mayor...

---

164. Paul Ariès, *Le retour du diable*, Villeurbanne, Golias, 1997.

The fault of the materialists?

The ecologist-cathos explain that the ecological crisis would be the consequence of materialism, that is to say fundamentally of the retreat of the (good) religious thought. According to them, only a religious conversion, only an insurrection of consciences, only a renewal of spirituality, could save the planet. Any progress of the critical spirit, any progress of rationalism, any progress of philosophical materialism and atheism would bring the world closer to its end.

This discourse is not only stupid because it confuses a philosophical posture, that of materialism, with a way of life that is ecologically unsustainable, but it is also dangerous because it prevents us from seeing that environmental collapse is precisely the consequence of a new religiosity, that of capitalism! Not only is capitalism a religion, but this religion is in line with the dogmas of Roman Catholicism, and not only with those of Protestantism. If this thesis is correct, any religious progress would bring us closer to the end of the world. The fault would therefore not be with the materialists but with the spiritualists!

I had argued this iconoclastic thesis in the Catholic magazine *Cahiers de l'atelier* and in the magazine *Relations* published by the Jesuits of Quebec. Whether one takes the point of view of the anti or the pro-capitalists, the mechanisms of the market economy are very similar to the representation that one might have of a religion, with its rites, its temples, its laws, etc.

Paul Lafargue, Marx's son-in-law, well known for his famous *Right to Laziness*, stated, as early as 1886, in a small text entitled *The Religion of Capital*, the content of the new Tables of the Law, symbol of the alliance between capital and its ruthless god. We will quote only one extract:

"1° Meditate on the words of capital, your god; 2° I am a man-eating god; I sit in the workshops and consume the wage earners. I transubstantiate in divine capital the puny life of the worker. I am the infinite mystery: my eternal substance is only perishable flesh; my omnipotence only human weakness.

The capitalist system has its high priests (economists and advertisers), its cathedrals (the stock market and hypermarkets), its new missals (financial magazines), its objects of worship (the shelf, the shopping cart), its new temporality (the sales) its miracles (the lottery, technology), its pilgrimages (Disneyland), its creed (growth, sustainable development), its heretics (the growth objectors), its exorcisms (the drugs that cure "buying fever") its excommunications (banking prohibitions, the little people of the undocumented, unemployed, homeless, without a future) its acts of grace (ethical and fair trade) its ecstasies (the "experiential capitalism" described by Gilles Lipovetsky), its mystery of the Incarnation (the happiness present in every product), its sects (its tribes as sung by Michel Maffesoli), its infallibility (the great economists endowed with Nobel Prizes), etc.

Capitalism is a true economy of salvation since it organizes the means to liberate from evil. This salvation is given as a paradise which is found, at the same time, here below and in an afterlife, since happiness is never reached.

This anti-capitalist polemical register is undoubtedly politically effective, to the point that activists have created the Church of the Most Holy Consumption[165], but is it scientifically "accurate"? However, one does not ask the myth to be exact but to "lie true", that is to say, to allow a glimpse of even a small part of the truth. So, is the Catholic religion an agent of the devil's dung of which the pope speaks?

Catholic religion, capitalist religion, same fight!

In the wake of Max Weber's work, it was long thought that only the Protestant ethic had an intimate link with the spirit of capitalism. This thesis is contested by certain specialists with regard to Islam. Maxime Rodinson shows that, neither in theory nor in practice, Islam has been an obstacle to the development of capitalism. The Koran and the *sunna* ("custom") accept private property and wage-earning, and in the prohibition of *ribâ* ("loan with interest"), it is more the excess than the profit itself that is at issue. Many economists and theologians also consider Roman Catholicism to be the true religion of capitalism, as it is the religion closest to its six major theologies.

Michael Novak is thus a central figure in the Catholic intelligentsia: he is considered the co-author of John Paul II's encyclical *Centesimus annus*. An American Catholic philosopher specializing in social doctrine, close to Ronald Reagan, he was appointed United States representative to the UN Commission on Human Rights, and later ambassador to the OSCE. Today he is a professor of ethics at the American Enterprise Institute, a

---

165. http://www.consomme.org/

think tank close to the American business community. He received the prestigious Templeton Prize[166] in 1994 for his work on the social teaching of the Church. He is a member of the board of directors of Ave Maria Mutual Funds, a pension fund linked to the anti-abortion lobby. Michael Novak, who justifies Francis' encyclical as an attack on "crony capitalism," has for years offered a full-throated defense of "democratic capitalism" (as he calls it) based on the six most fundamental theological doctrines of Roman Catholicism[167].

Consumption realizes the Trinity by producing a human community without undermining individuality. It allows to be, at the same time, one and multiple, since men are united as one while preserving their personal freedom of intelligence and choice (gift of the Creator). Consummation also realizes the Incarnation since it is without illusion about man. It recognizes him as he is with his weaknesses and irrationalities. It knows that the world will never be a paradise. It also realizes the principle of competition (which would be pegged to the very heart of the Gospels) since the Christian recognizes freedom (and therefore choice) and sees human life as a constant struggle: not only are the stakes real but there is much to lose and much to gain. Consumption respects original sin since it admits that human freedom is capable of both the best and the worst. It knows that it produces benefits as well as inhibitions. It does not claim perfection but realism. Consumption respects the separation of kingdoms because it is open to all (not only to Christians) but is based on laws other than those of religion. Consumption would finally ensure the principle of charity (of love) since it allows to draw things out of nothingness as the improvement of the standard of living attests it. This great Catholic intellectual, adviser to the popes, is therefore convinced that the values of the market economy (from production to consumption) are those that are closest to Christianity. Consumption as well as production constitute a service to the divine.

The Catholic Church is actually at least co-responsible for the rise of the unbridled capitalism we know and that Pope Francis denounces. Long before Adam Smith, a group of Spanish clerics in the 15th and 16th centuries, known as the School of Salamanca, laid the foundations of capita-

---

166. The existence of this foundation has been explained *above* ("Les écolos-cathos au service du néocréationnisme").
167. Michael Novak, *Une éthique économique, les valeurs de l'économie de marché*, Paris, Cerf-Institut La Boétie, 1987.

---

lism and were arguably libertarians well before their time, since they affirmed not only the efficiency of capitalism but also its moral character. Libertarians are not mistaken in claiming this heritage loud and clear. In his *History of Economic Analysis* (published in 1954), Joseph Schumpeter (1883-1950) had already recognized the debt of liberal economists to these Dominicans and Jesuits, who were nourished by the thought of Thomas Aquinas. Some specialists even suspect, as Pierre Desroches recalls in *Le Québécois libre*, that Carl Menger (1840-1921), the founder of the Austrian school, was directly influenced by these Catholic thinkers, especially since Spain and Austria were then united under the same crown. Murray Rothbard, the father of anarcho-capitalism (libertarianism), even called these Spanish scholastics "proto-Austrians".

This ultraliberal thinking certainly receded within the Church in the twentieth century (because of the necessary compromises with the then dominant social thought) but it was always maintained in certain Catholic universities (Jesuits in particular), notably Fordham (New York) and Georgetown (Washington). Pierre Desroches quotes not only the Jesuit James Sadowsky of Fordham, but also his colleague John Toohey who taught at Georgetown University. He adds that it is also symptomatic that "the basic philosophical work most cited by American libertarian intellectuals is *A History of Philosophy* by Jesuit Frederick Copleston. The works of another Jesuit, Henry Babcock Veatch, as well as that of the English Catholic historian Lord John Acton (1834-1902) would also be crucial to the development of contemporary libertarian philosophy. One of the main actors of this movement was the economist Murray Rothbard, an agnostic Jew. It was because of his appreciation of the contributions of certain Jesuit moralists that Rothbard was expelled from Ayn Rand's inner circle in 1958. In fact, Rothbard's admiration for the Catholic liberal tradition - he considered it more favorable to the free market than the Protestant tradition in his history of economic thought - would have led some of those close to him to believe that he had converted to Catholicism. So today you find a minority of Catholics who firmly believe that the free market is not only the most efficient form of organization, but also the most moral."[168]

How then to take seriously the new evangelical preferential option for the poor and the encyclical *Laudato si'* of Jesuit Francis?

---

168. http://www.quebecoislibre.org/981219-3.htm. In *Satanisme et Vampyrisme. Le livre noir* (Golias, 2005) long passages to expose the thought of Murray Rothbard and especially that of Ayn Rand.

Conclusion
The evil Roman Curia versus the gentle pope?

History is already written for all those who chose to believe in Francis. This good pope would have been badly surrounded and prevented from acting by a bad Roman Curia. I am not unaware of the conflicts within the Vatican, the resignation of Benedict XVI or the premature death of John Paul [1] are there to remind us of their sometimes extreme violence. But Francis is more of a wild duck than a child of God! His whole biography proves that he has always been on the side of the powerful against the humble, during his youth corrupted by the Argentinean Iron Guard, during the dictatorship with his friendship for certain military leaders, during his incessant fight against the true theologies of liberation. Francis was elected by a council of old reactionaries for these feats of arms! How could one think that he was suddenly touched by revolutionary grace? How could this bishop, known for his doctrinal intransigence and authoritarianism, become the one through whom the Catholic Church would finally come to the people and the common people? Bishop Bergoglio was appointed pope to try to save a Church totally corrupted by financial, economic, political, institutional, sexual scandals. Even if Pope Francis were to do all he could to change the Church for the better, he could only rely on the armada left to him by his predecessors. That is why he relies on very right-wing movements such as Communion and Liberation, Opus Dei and on ultra-reactionary occult movements such as the Knights of Columbus.

It could not also go against the direction of the tide that today pushes to the front of the Church and into the streets minorities of the extreme right and the far right, who bring back with them a whole past that we thought was definitively over. This new identity-based Church is that of the Manif pour tous and its successors, that is to say, of the mobilizations against equal marriage rights and against the fight against sexism.

This new identity-based Church, which is celebrating its "May 68 in reverse", is breaking down the barriers between the Christian people and the extreme right in France, including the FN. The Church is not more right-wing than the rest of the population because of its demography, as young practicing Catholics are even more right-wing than their elders[169]. The more one practices, the more one attends the Church and its teaching, the more one votes to the right: 79% of practicing Catholics voted for Sarkozy in 2012 versus 48.36% for the total vote. These Catholics also say that they are more afraid of life, of the future, of foreigners... 60% of them believe that there are too many foreigners in France against 37% of atheists, 37% of practicing Catholics against 21% of those who declare themselves without religion believe that there are "races less gifted than others"! These practicing Catholics are also the most unkind to the unemployed, who are always suspected of being lazy bastards, "welfare recipients", etc. The Polish priest Krzysztof Charamsa, who has just *come out* by declaring that there are many homosexuals in the Church and especially homophobic homosexuals, has just forgotten to specify that they also have a (very) right-wing heart and that the agitation around the so-called gay lobby within the Church is above all a smoke curtain hiding the real issues.

The Church, especially its social currents, says it is sorry about these developments, but it does not ask itself what has led it to be on the side of the rich historically! I confess my concern: in the same way that John Paul II prevented the Soviet regime from being succeeded by a true socialism with a human face, as Gorbachev wished, Francis will be the pope who risks burying, along with the true theologies of liberation, the experiences of Amerindian socialism, and the projects of planetary ecosocialism. What is certain is that the Church of Francis is likely to be even more anti-social. Thus Jérôme Vignon, president of the Social Weeks, noting with regret the gap between the militant (social) Church and the community of Christians, wonders whether it is not necessary to consider that the social doctrine of the Church has aged and that it is necessary to

---

169. http://religion.blog.lemonde.fr/2012/05/07/79-des-catholiques-pratiquants-ont-vote-pour-nicolas-sarkozy/; Jean-Luc Richard, "Les catholiques, l'immigration étrangère et les tentations racistes en France. Quelques apports d'enquêtes d'opinion et de données macro-sociales," in *Migrations Sociétés*, vol. 24, no. 139, January-February 2012, pp. 253-266.

reflect on adapting it to make it more in phase with the times, I would add with this ordoliberalism which is wreaking havoc.

I am certainly not unaware that the Church is crisscrossed by the class struggle between its summit and its base, and therefore also by conflicts over the definition of the "good life". This is what gives hope and prevents us from claiming that the Church is merely an opium of the people. In 1993, the theologian Eugen Drewermann published a brilliant analysis of the conflicts between the various strata of the Church, which is still valid. A Christian minority acting alongside the popular movements will always exist. For the past, let us think of the Christian socialists around Philippe Buchez (1796-1865). For the present, let us think of the Quebec Jesuits of the magazine *Relations* who have rallied, for example, on the occasion of the preparation of the COP 21, to the *Manifesto for a global momentum*[170]. In this text, there is no reminder of "natural" and divine laws of which the Church is the only authorized interpreter, no condemnation of equal rights in marriage, no confusion between PMA, GPA and GMOs, no call to decrease and multiply, no ban on so-called non-natural contraception and abortion, no defense of lucrative private property and social inequalities, no condemnation of rationality and the scientific spirit in the name of a Christian science, no social doctrine opposed to the class struggle, but a commitment alongside those who fight to "change the system, not the climate", for a solidarity-based, post-oil, post-carbon and post-capitalist economy. Who can believe that Francis could be the pope of this new Church of the 21st century?

Francis is not a left-wing pope, but he knows that he must contain the right-wing movement of the Church so as not to cut it off from the people. To do this, he is giving pledges to a Catholic left that unfortunately no longer exists, at the risk of upsetting the right-wing currents. As a result, Pope Francis will finally lose on both counts! Already, the number of faithful present at General Audiences and Angeluses has dropped from more than six million in 2013 to just over three million in 2015, according to official, but very discreet, figures from the prefecture of the Papal Household, while the media say this is the most popular pope. This decrease in the number of faithful can be explained in part, but only in part, by Francis' attitude towards the most conservative movements that now boycott his General Audiences and Angeluses. The pope is said to

---

170. http://www.ledevoir.com/environnement/actualites-sur-l-environnement/436476/manifeste-pour-un-elan-global

have entered into open conflict with Archbishop Bagnasco, cardinal and archbishop of Genoa and president of the Italian Episcopal Conference... who is mobilizing the Catholic right-wing movements to organize *Family Days* against the Cirinna law granting marriage to same-sex couples, in the manner of the Manif pour tous in France and Spain... Pope Francis is certainly hostile to this law, but he thinks that direct confrontation is a bad thing because it will contribute even more to cutting the Church off from the real country. That is why in 2010 he forbade Argentine Catholics to gather in front of the Buenos Aires Parliament in order to prevent the vote of the law. The halving of public participation in the Vatican's General Audiences is, however, primarily the consequence of the double talk of a pope who seeks to reconcile opposites while remaining deeply reactionary. The people of the faithful are also voting with their feet as they slowly drift away from the Church.

Appendix

Ecology and Christianity, liberation theologies or the return of the Catholic right?[171]

We are launching a solemn appeal to Christians and atheists against the threat posed by the Christian right against political ecology and the degrowth movement. This operation has several faces, including that of the Indignant Christians (sic) whose name echoes the call for indignation launched by traditionalist circles in the field of the arts. Patrice de Plunkett, former editor-in-chief of the *Figaro Magazine, who has* been converted to a "neither right nor left" posture, but is still a "papist", is the main pivot of this operation. Associated with him are figures such as Vincent Cheynet (editor of *La Décroissance*) and Jacques de Guillebon (editor of the traditionalist bulletin *La Nef*). As Christians and atheists, we rise up against this bad blow to ecology. We cannot suggest that environmental collapse is the consequence of materialism or that the solution is the misnamed social doctrine of the Church, the Vatican's armed wing against socialism in the name of regulated liberalism, since 1891. This confusion is not only stupid but self-serving. It is stupid because it forgets that capitalism is the child of Christianity. The work of Colin Campbell, following that of Max Weber, makes it possible to understand how the process of formation of the productivist society originated in the seventeenth century with the

---

171. Text by Christian Terras, director of *Golias,* a critical Catholic journal, and Paul Ariès, director of Le *Sarkophage,* editor-in-chief of the journal *Les Zindigné(e)s,* published in the newspaper *L'Humanité* on Wednesday, March 21, 2012.

appearance of the consumer alongside the entrepreneur. While producti-vism comes from the Calvinist rigorist branch, consumerism derives from the pietistic sentimentalist branch. This confusion is self-serving because it aims at making the ecological question a new field of evangelization of the people. The question does not however oppose materialism and spiri-tuality but several materialisms between them like various spiritualities between them: there are thus two ways of crossing the Christian religion and the political ecology either by going on the side of the "theologies of the liberation" and thus of the socialist *buen vivir*, or by returning to a rigorist, fundamentalist, in short, clerical conception of the religion. In the first case, the result is a preferential option for the poor and an alliance with the left, and in the other case, Vatican orthodoxy and the Christian right. It is no coincidence that South America, which was the cradle of liberation theologies (in the 20th century), is also the cradle of this socia-lism of *Buen Vivir* (in the 21st century). If it fails to embrace the liberation theologians involved in the emancipation movements, such as Leonardo Boff, Frei Betto, Hugo Assmann, Dom Hélder Câmara, this "catholic right", objector to growth, will end up resembling the lady bosses of the 19th century who taught the good people how to do without everything they lacked. We, Christian activists and atheists, are therefore on the side of liberation theologies when they argue that the rejection of capitalism is not only the rejection of deregulated liberalism, but the rejection of an unjust class system, the rejection of a "structural sin"; we, Christian and atheist activists, are on the side of liberation theologies when they endow ecology with a class content, when they affirm a "preferential option for the poor" which is not only a way to love or to love the poor but to struggle with them, when they advocate solidarity with the struggles of self-eman-cipation of peoples; we, Christian activists and atheists, are on the side of liberation theologies to say that the enemy is not atheism but idolatry (wealth, national identity, the mystique of the State, sexual essentialism, the defense of "Western Christian civilization"); we, Christian activists and atheists, are on the side of liberation theologies to affirm the primacy of the anthropological element over the ecclesiological element, of the critical element over the dogmatic element; We, Christian and atheist activists, are on the side of liberation theologies to say that the idea of socialism cannot be judged by the practices of "real socialism" any more than Christianity can be identified with the Holy Inquisition; we, Christian activists and atheists, are on the side of liberation theologies to denounce the link between the imperial style of power in the Church, the hierarchical authority, the tradition of intolerance and dogmatism, the myth of papal infallibility and the patterns of thought and action that lead to the destruction of humanity and the planet; We, Christian and atheist activists, are on the side of liberation theologies to say that the oppression/liberation paradigm applies as much to the dominated classes as to the Earth; we are on the side of liberation theologies to say that a total separation of Church and State, if it supposes that there are no Christian parties, also means that there are no Christian social movements, even if they are in the ecological field, because the peak of oil, the crisis of biodiversity are the same for all. We, Christian and atheist militants, are on the side of liberation theologies to say our refusal of the return to political Catholicism (under the cover of a dangerous and hypocritical "neither right nor left") and to say our refusal of any message which, under the pretext of denouncing ultra-liberalism and socialism ("socialism is an enemy, so is liberalism" - France Jeunesse Civitas website), would intend to impose a model in conformity with the laws of God... We warn the Christian people as we warn the social movements who let themselves be misled by false pretenses. For as Father Guillaume de Tanoüarn (Fraternity of Saint Pius X) says: "Anti-liberalism is also a very old theme of what we would call the most intransigent 'Christian right." So don't count on us to reject moral, philosophical and religious freedom, don't count on us to turn the fight against the cult of growth and unlimiteditism into a new "holy war" against atheism and philosophical materialism, don't count on us to trivialize the Christian right under the pretext of a sacred union to save the planet and humanity. We, Christian and atheist militants, affirm that the only laws that count for the city are the secular laws made by men in conscience.

Table of contents

From the same author 7

Foreword The (unsexy) underside of the Church 9

Francis, the best of the worst 11

The *reconquista* 13

Part I: Will Francis save the Church? 15

A Marxist pope? 18

A green pope? 22

Neither God, nor Caesar, nor tribune! 24

All with Francis? 26

Why did Bishop Bergoglio become pope? 28

Bergoglio's hidden youth 32

The Church of Francis against "21st century socialism" 37

Why is Bergoglio called Francis? 43

What preferential option for the poor? 49

The preferential option for the poor, seen from the left 52

The preferential option for the poor, seen from the right 53

The preferential option for the poor with Opus Dei 55

From the preferential option for the poor to the privileged love
of the rich 57

Francis a reforming pope? 58

Francis' close guard: a quarteron of *monsignori* 61

The Pope's networks 66

Pope Francis and Communion and Liberation 66

Pope Francis and the Legionaries of Christ 69

Pope Francis and Opus Dei 71

Pope Francis and the Knights of Columbus 74

Massimo Introvigne, the protector of the Church 78

Faced with sectarian aberrations 78

Francis and the "gay lobby" 79

When the Church plays the victim 84

... to justify his aggressiveness 85

Why is Pope Francis reading the novel *The Master of the Earth*? 87

Pope Francis (really) believes in the devil 90

Could the good Pope Francis canonize a genocidal priest? 94

How the Knights of Columbus are found at work 97

Can the good Pope Francis beatify an anti-Semitic priest? 98

Part Two: Will Francis save the planet? **103**

The hidden face of the encyclical *Laudato si'* 106

"Christian science" versus science 109

The ecologist-cathos at the service of neocreationism? 112

The ecologist-cathos against the freedom of thought 117

The ecologist-cathos, soldier-monks of austerity 123

The ecologist-cathos instrumentalize anthropology 127

Ecological Catholics in the service of a pessimistic anthropology ... 132

The eco-cathos against emancipation 134

Healing the couple to heal the planet 136

The eco-cathos against women's rights 142

The ecologist-cathos, soldier-monks of the social doctrine
of the Church 148

The ecologist-cathos, soldier-monks of private property 151

The Common Good versus the Commons 154

The ecologist-cathos, soldier-monks of the principle of subsidiarity . 158

Against technicist hybris or against atheism? 161

The ecologist-cathos against political ecology 168

The ecologist-cathos and the "neither right nor left",
therefore right-wing 170

The ecologist-catholic networks at work 172

The ecologist-cathos and the National Front 181

An anti-capitalist pope? 186

The ecologist-cathos and the rescue of capitalism 191

When the Church praises capitalist economists 193

When big business talks about François 196

The "anti-capitalist" society Tradition Family Property 198

The fault of the materialists? 201

Catholic religion, capitalist religion, same fight! 202

Conclusion The evil Roman Curia versus the gentle pope? 205

Appendix 209

Ecology and Christianity, liberation theologies or the return
of the Catholic right? 209

Best sellers Max Milo Editions

Hitler's banker, Jean-François Bouchard

Confessions of a forger, Éric Piedoie Le Tiec

The Koran and the flesh, Ludovic-Mohamed Zahed

Governing by fake news, Jacques Baud

Governing by chaos, Collectif

A political history of food, Paul Ariès

Mad in U.S.A.: The ravages of the "American model",
Michel Desmurget

Mondial soccer club geopolitics, Kévin Veyssière

Putin: Game master?, Jacques Braud

Treatise on the three impostors: Moses, Jesus, Muhammad,
The Spirit of Spinoza

TV Lobotomy, Michel Desmurget